The Magician

AND THE

Cardsharp

The Magician
AND THE
Cardsharp

The Search for America's
Greatest Sleight-of-Hand Artist

KARL JOHNSON

A Holt Paperback
HENRY HOLT AND COMPANY   NEW YORK

Holt Paperbacks
Henry Holt and Company, LLC
Publishers since 1866
175 Fifth Avenue
New York, New York 10010
www.henryholt.com

A Holt Paperback® and ® are registered trademarks
of Henry Holt and Company, LLC.

Library of Congress Cataloging-in-Publication Data

Johnson, Karl, 1959-
The magician and the cardsharp : the search for America's greatest
sleight-of-hand artist / Karl Johnson.
    p. cm.
Includes index.
ISBN-13: 978-0-8050-8059-9
ISBN-10: 0-8050-8059-7
1. Vernon, Dai, 1894- 2. Magicians United States Biography.
3. Villasenor, Amador. I. Title.
GV1545.V47J64 2005
793.8'092 dc22
[B]   2005040447

Henry Holt books are available for special
promotions and premiums. For details contact:
Director, Special Markets.

Originally published in hardcover in 2005 by Henry Holt and Company
First Holt Paperbacks Edition 2006

*Frontispiece by William Woodfield,
courtesy of* Genii *magazine*

Designed by Paula Russell Szafranski

Printed in the United States of America
3 5 7 9 10 8 6 4

THIS BOOK IS DEDICATED,
WITH MY LOVE AND MY LIFE,
TO MIRA

His magic is performed with complete naturalness, its artistry that of the art that conceals art. The consummate skill and technique is there but it is never displayed; it is, on the contrary, so carefully hidden that the performer is applauded not for his nimble-fingered dexterity but because he has, with the effortless ease of a real magician, exhibited a feat of what must be real magic.

—*Jean Hugard and Frederick Braue,*
Expert Card Technique, *Third Edition*

CONTENTS

Contents

THE MAGICIAN

AND THE

CARDSHARP

1

PERFECT

To Dai Vernon, Amador Villasenor was a lucky draw, like turning up three aces in the last hand on a losing night. To the cops in Wichita, who had searched for him for three long years, Villasenor was a gambler, a cardsharp, a thief, and a killer.

Though perhaps not a first-degree murderer. Villasenor swore he had acted in self-defense, and the police and his jailers believed what he had to say. The distinction was a technicality, maybe, but his freedom depended on it. Villasenor had, after all, taken a man's life. He had confessed to shooting one Benito Leija and leaving him to meet his maker in the grit of a Wichita alleyway back in the red-hot summer of 1929. He said he had even watched as Leija—like himself, a young Mexican in his twenties, a gambler well accustomed to the feel of cards and dice—had staggered off the sidewalk outside Manuel Garcia's poolroom in Wichita's North End, contemplating his speedily approaching end. Villasenor had jumped in his car on that July evening and bolted out of the city as Leija pitched forward from his knees into a pool of his own blood.

Vernon, who had just come to Wichita, knew little of what had landed Villasenor in the city's Sedgwick County Jail, where he was meeting him on a wet winter night during the first gloomy week of February 1932. The crime had happened long before Vernon arrived in Wichita and it didn't really interest him. To Vernon, Villasenor's predicament was a scrape like a million others, a "gambling mix-up," he called it. Vernon certainly wasn't one to make a hobby of murder. That was not his line.

What roused Vernon on this chilly evening was the possibility he might learn something from Villasenor he could use in his magic. Vernon was a magician, an artist. Magic was his obsession. It was what he cared about more than anything else. For three decades, Vernon, now thirty-seven, had been consumed by magic. At times, it possessed him. It was what he puzzled over, theorized about, dreamed of.

Magic would keep Vernon up for days at a time with no thought of food or rest. Magic softened these hard times of the Depression. Magic made his dull days cutting silhouettes in a department store in this wheat-and-oil town passable. He was a world away from the ritzy Park Avenue soirees where he had once been the featured attraction, but magic made even that bearable. It was what allowed Vernon to walk blithely into a jail to shake hands with a killer. Vernon would smile and follow the devil himself if it meant he could bring back something, a sleight, a ruse, a line of patter, that he could use in his art.

In the Twenties magic had offered audiences a cocktail of glamour and glitz, elegance and escape, to chase away the humdrum workaday world. To most of the great illusionists of that golden era, bigger was better. Magic, to those veterans of the slam-bang vaudeville tours, meant stage spectacles on a grand scale. The tuxedoed, ministerial Howard Thurston, then considered the most popular magician in the world, offered up his portentous Wonder Show of the Universe with ever-more-elaborate levitations and disappearances, including the "Vanishing

Whippet Automobile," packed with seven gorgeous young beauties. Horace Goldin, known as the Whirlwind Illusionist, jammed so many effects into his dizzying act that he had stopped speaking on stage altogether lest he slow down the pace. "Silence is Goldin," a British competitor had quipped. But to Dai Vernon, spectacle had little to do with magic. To Vernon, the magic was not in the size of the stage or the number of tricks on the bill or the box-office receipts.

Vernon had first started popping up at New York's fabled magic shops around the end of World War I. He was from Canada, dashing and cultured, and he handled cards with a gentle grace, coaxing such startling effects from them that even the most experienced magicians were flummoxed. In short order, he was ushered into the hallowed back rooms where only the most elite practitioners of the ancient art were allowed to gather.

Quickly, quietly, he had begun to steer his art in a new direction. He was as different from an old-style illusionist as an Impressionist was from a sign painter. Rather than larger and faster, he preferred to make magic that seemed more casual, and thus more natural. And as he became more well-known, a small group of nimble-fingered sleight-of-hand artists, who came to be dubbed the Inner Circle, gathered around him. They were a quiet band of artistic assassins killing off the old Victorian ways of magic. Vernon was the Lenin to the rest of these revolutionaries. He became magic's Picasso, its Hemingway, its Duke Ellington.

Vernon had little interest in the old stage ruses. He believed that sleight of hand and psychological subtlety far surpassed the hidden mirrors and wires used by conventional illusionists. To him, the proper stage for real magic was not the expanse of the vaudeville boards, but the unadorned human hand, held out just before his spectators' eyes. And the best props were not floating women or disappearing automobiles, but bits of string, colorful silks, cups and balls, coins and cards. Always cards.

Cards were Vernon's first love. They were the choice instrument for his audacious style of magic. He moved away from the pick-a-card tricks that always started the same way, preferring instead to have people merely think of a card without touching the deck. Then he would look

them in the eye and tell them the exact card they were thinking of. He re-
placed the dull Victorian patter with sharp, modern tales peppered with
slang. With a rakish grin, the smoke of his cigarette curling up around
his dark eyes, Vernon would deftly maneuver the cards with his long, el-
egant fingers, improvising with them the way a jazz musician might with
his cornet, beginning an effect without knowing exactly where he was go-
ing to take it.

The Wichita jail was an imposing building that held a small
town's worth of prisoners, over eight hundred, from murderers
down to bad-check writers. Since the Depression had tightened
its grip and winter had settled, a new class of prisoner had begun
to appear—hobos, drunks, and other down-and-outers looking
for a hot meal and a warm, dry place to stay the night. Vernon's
friend Faucett Ross, a fellow magician who had gotten the tip
about a gambler in the lockup who was a whiz with a pack of
cards, went in with him. After Ross gave the inmates some
smiles by doing a few tricks, the guards went down to the cell
block to fetch Amador Villasenor.

No wave of a wand or abracadabra could make the Depression disap-
pear. By the Thirties, magicians were hard-pressed to keep themselves
from vanishing. Audiences were smaller now and with the advent of the
"talkies" it was much harder to captivate them. For just a quarter, there
was the roaring King Kong astride the Empire State Building, his paw
wrapped around the scrumptious Fay Wray. How could magicians com-
pete with movies? Back in the heyday of vaudeville, the great magician
T. Nelson Downs had dazzled thousands around the world with his
"Miser's Dream," pulling a seemingly endless supply of coins out of the
air. But now in the Depression, audiences were longing for "Pennies
From Heaven." Downs was retired and friends were sending him postage
stamps in their letters to be sure he could afford to write back. After the
stock market crash, even Vernon's lucrative engagements for the Astors,
the Vanderbilts, and the Schwabs at their swanky parties and Long Is-

land country clubs began to disappear. With few prospects, he and his wife, Jeanne, with their young son, Ted, in tow, had left Manhattan and hit the road.

Vernon became an artist in exile, aimlessly making his way across the country. He supported his family by cutting silhouette portraits, an improbably reliable profession despite the times. In the summer of 1931, the Vernons were in Virginia Beach when they decided they might as well head west. After reading in the newspaper about the gambling resort of Reno, they decided to work their way across the country to Nevada to see what all the fuss was about. By the middle of July, having braved the parched countryside of Kansas and Oklahoma, they rolled into Colorado Springs.

After the Dust Bowl, Colorado Springs was a delightful oasis in the Rockies. It was cool and instantly restorative. Vernon was thrilled to find master magician Paul Fox working a little carnival there, and he and Fox struck up a fast friendship. Vernon set up his silhouette stand at Manitou, the posh resort at the foot of Pike's Peak. At summer's end, the Vernons moved on, not to Reno, but to Denver now. There they met up with Faucett Ross, who invited them to come to live near him in Wichita. Ross had told Vernon he could cut silhouettes at the exclusive George Innes Department Store, the city's finest.

"Show these fellows a couple of those things you were doing with the cards," the guard told Villasenor when they brought him up from the cell block. Villasenor was younger than Vernon, about twenty-nine. He had a broad, roughly framed face and thick, black hair. Soft-spoken, with hesitant English, he seemed eager to please the jailers with this demonstration. He was an experienced sharp with several sleights in his repertoire, moves to "get the money," as the gamblers said. He began by showing the magicians a slick one he had worked up to beat the game of monte, not the well-known three-card short con of riverboat and fairground fame, but a card game popular among the Mexican workers who had been brought up north to labor in Wichita's slaughterhouses and train yards. Vernon watched intently. He could see that Villasenor was a professional, but he could also tell that the Mexican was no great virtuoso. His card handling was workmanlike, good for fooling these jail guards maybe, or drunken marks at a roadhouse, but he was not a genuine sleight-of-hand artist. After demonstrating his monte move, Villasenor showed off a couple of other sleights—a slip and a shift. Then, he moved on to his false deals. Vernon saw everything coming.

From the time he was a boy, when, by accident, he discovered how his father had accomplished the first true magic trick he ever saw, Vernon had been steeped in secrets. Magicians live with secrets, naturally, but few of them ever come to fully understand their deepest intricacies. Vernon did. Early on, he came to see that the secret behind the trick wasn't the only ingredient needed to make great magic. But a secret was often the starting point. So as he became obsessed with magic, he also became obsessed with secrets. When Vernon was still in knickers, rambling around Ottawa on his bicycle, he developed a drive to track down those who held the secrets to his art. If he heard a rumor about some boy who could make a coin disappear, Vernon would jump on his bicycle and ride for miles until he found him. If he saw con men at the racetrack, he would skulk around for hours, deflecting their threats, until he discovered just what they were up to. His life became a quest for secrets.

The deepest secrets in magic, he discovered, were usually found in the skillful, fearless hands of those Vernon called the gamblers—the cardsharps, the broad tossers, the dice mechanics who could subvert any game they played without the slightest hesitation. Vernon came to see them as the greatest magicians of them all. He had found some of the cardsharps' secrets in a mysterious book called The Expert at the Card Table, *a bold volume he took as his bible but which most other magicians shied away from, dismissing it as indecipherable. Still other secrets he learned in person after tracking down gamblers. Magicians had been borrowing sleights from card cheats for hundreds of years, but Vernon had an unprecedented knack for prying the cherished tricks of the trade out of these closed men. He was tenacious, and he could handle people as well as he handled cards. He laced his tricks with devastating moves taken from the card table—false shuffles, palms, card switches, and many more. Other magicians couldn't follow them. They came to hold Vernon in awe.*

Of all the gamblers Vernon learned from, he was probably most enamored of the false dealers. They were the elite among the cardsharps. The second dealers, called Number Two men in gambling slang, could smoothly slide the second card off the deck and make it look exactly like they were taking the top card. The bottom dealers—subway dealers, they were called—could do the same with the bottom card. These sleights required years of practice to master, and they could be devastating in a card game. Vernon sought these men out diligently. Their techniques were rare in magic, and invaluable, allowing him to do tricks that even other accomplished card magicians thought were impossibilities.

Still, there was one master among these false dealers, with one great secret, that had always eluded Vernon. It had eluded everyone. Even among the most gifted of the cardsharps, this virtuoso remained just a rumor, a fairy tale. Vernon had heard the tales over the years, of a cardsharp who could pick up a deck that had been fairly cut according to the rules of play, and deal out any card from it that he wanted. With a single deal from the center of the deck, this cardsharp could make all the rules and the very laws of chance itself vanish. Just like a magician.

The faint murmurs about the center dealer, who supposedly lived somewhere in the Midwest, swirled into myth. From time to time, Vernon heard new reports of this unparalleled master, but in the end he had always dismissed the vague tales as hokum. He came to agree with those who considered such a feat beyond reach, and removed the center deal from his list of obsessions—until he got to the county jail in Wichita.

"You've been a gambler all your life haven't you?" Vernon asked Villasenor as their visit wound down. After the Mexican had finished showing what he could do, they had started to chat. Sure, Villasenor agreed, he had been gambling pretty much all his life. "Well," Vernon continued, "have you ever witnessed anything unusual . . . ? You've played cards all your life, have you ever seen anything you don't understand?"

Villasenor's English may have been a little shaky, but he didn't hesitate now as he answered the magician. "In Kansas City," he replied immediately, a surge of excitement in his voice, "I see a fella. He deals cards from the center of the pack. . . ."

Suddenly, the magician was no longer just looking to liven up a stormy night. Ross was stunned to see how Villasenor's words electrified Vernon. Indeed, the way the Mexican announced this news, so boldly, made Vernon think it could be the truth. He began firing questions, asking Villasenor again and again how the man's deal had looked. "Perfect," the gambler answered every time. *Perfect.* It was a word Vernon always shunned. Yet Villasenor threw it down confidently, as he would a winning hand or a pair of loaded dice. *Perfect.*

The end of his session with Villasenor marked the start of Vernon's search for this secret that had been beyond his imagining, a secret held by a man he would come to consider the greatest sleight-of-hand artist of them all. For decades, he would tell other magicians about it, a story many of them would dismiss as a tall tale. It all began in a Wichita jail, Vernon would say.

But the story of his great quest didn't begin on that wet, raw night in Wichita. It started much earlier, in Canada, where a small boy came upon some playing cards strewn along the railroad tracks. He would pick them up and use them to create his first tricks, devilish tricks like no one had ever seen before.

2

CARDS ON THE TRACKS

Dai Vernon the man would chase after the secrets of cards all his life. But for David Verner the boy, growing up in the Canadian capital of Ottawa at the opening of the twentieth century, cards seemed to chase after him. They appeared everywhere, blowing down the street like dry leaves or dropping at his feet like whirligigs from the maple trees on a spring day.

Like most boys, David and his buddies liked to play along the railroad tracks, catching sight of the great trains as they roared off into the big, unknown world beyond their hometown. These trains sometimes left intriguing flotsam in their wake. The sharp-eyed David began to discover cards, even entire decks, scattered willy-nilly along the tracks.

David didn't know it right away, but the cards he happened upon were a by-product of one of the more audacious ploys of the teams of crooked gamblers who "played the rattlers"—worked the trains—at the turn of the century. The rails were the common form of long-distance travel in those days, and card playing was a popular diversion to help make the hours pass.

Passengers frequently gathered to organize impromptu games in the club or dining cars, and lone travelers especially would often be invited in to round out a short-handed bridge game, which would then be conveniently shifted over to poker at some point. They made easy targets, fat pigeons, for the roaming mobs of cardsharps who specialized in the notorious "cold-deck" switch.

The scam was simple but bold. The sharps would purposely pick seats by a window that was easy to lift open. Then, as the mark settled in comfortably, the group would play for a bit, chatting amiably and enjoying what seemed to be an agreeably sporting diversion to while away the long train ride. At some point, one of the sharps would begin to puff aggressively on a cigar and proceed to spill ash all over the table, the cards, and the money. As the chorus of complaints from the other gamblers, who were actually his cohorts, grew louder, another member of the team would suddenly gather the cards to scoop up the offending ash and throw it out the window.

Unbeknownst to their victim, the cards would sail out the window, too. When the cheater who had just brushed the ash off the table placed the cards back down, he would actually switch in a different deck, which was stacked to deal certain winning, and losing, hands. This new deck was known in the argot as a "cold deck" or "cooler," because it was supposedly cooler to the touch than the one the players had been handling. Although the move was as direct as a two-by-four between the eyes, the sucker usually never knew what hit him. The distraction of the house-keeping charade, or some similar ruse, served as efficient cover, or "shade," as the sharps called it.

These cards on the tracks inspired young David Verner to craft one of his first magical wonders. He would mark up a handful of his own cards—smudging one with dirt, tearing the corner off another—so that he could read them without having to turn them over. Then he would scatter a few facedown on the ground along the route he typically took home from school with his friends. If they passed by later that day or the next day and no one noticed the cards, David would keep quiet. If one of his friends did happen to see one of the cards, he would never connect it to David. The boys were accustomed now to seeing cards lying around where they weren't expected.

"Hey, you're a magician," one of his pals would call out, pointing. "Tell me what that card is!" David played out the effect for all it was worth, hemming and hawing, hesitating. "I can't do miracles . . . wait a minute . . ." Then he'd name the card. The trick worked perfectly. He floored his little school chums. Cardsharps inspired David's magic from the very beginning.

Dai Vernon called himself "born to deceive" and undoubtedly he was, in the same sense that Nijinsky was born to dance or Bix Beiderbecke was born to blow his horn. But clearly he was also shaped by the city where he was born David Frederick Wingfield Verner in June 1894. As it turned out, Ottawa was not a bad place at all for this precocious, preternaturally perceptive boy to begin to forge himself into the most influential magician of the twentieth century.

The city was a bustling national capital with a lively cultural scene when David was growing up there as a child in the comfortable middle class. Still, as the new century dawned, Ottawa seemed to cling tightly to Queen Victoria's skirts, even as her long reign finally came to an end in 1901, when David was five. If a woman smoked, it was a truly shocking event, and if her ankle was so much as glimpsed while getting on a streetcar, the resulting scandal could ruin her. "Legs" were referred to as "limbs" because the very word *legs* was considered just too provocative. Much to his eventual amusement, David's mother, Helen, was thoroughly immersed in these stuffy ways of thinking. Of Scottish background, she was stern, religious, and looked on with distress as her son's interest and skills in magic developed. She considered performers crass, beneath them. They were by nature immoral people. She wanted David and his two brothers, Napier and Arthur, to play only with children from the "right" families.

David's father's attitude was more relaxed. James Verner, an official with the Canadian Department of Agriculture, was by all accounts an easygoing, fun-loving man who apparently had a bit of the trickster in him, too. He first sparked David's interest in magic by demonstrating simple yet vexing tricks. It all began with a card trick, of course, the day David's father showed him a pack of Lord Fauntleroy "patience" cards (the British name for solitaire). "Pick out an ace, a red ace," his father directed him. "Now put it in the center of the pack." After David pushed the card into the middle of the deck, his father instructed him to blow on the deck. "Harder," his father commanded. Then he turned the pack over and there was David's ace, now on the bottom of the deck.

His first magic, and it was right under his nose. "Dad, do that again!" David cried. He begged to see the simple trick over and over again, and then he implored his father to tell him how it was done. But David's father held out for quite a while before he showed him the secret. And he went on to perform other tricks for his son, some of them much more elaborate than the trick with the red ace.

Once, on his birthday, his father announced that he was going to show him something he would really like. He led David over to the big dining-room table—a great oval wooden piece with heavy leaves—took off the tablecloth, and told the birthday boy to go fetch an eggcup and his colored chalk. Then they sat down and his father made three chalk marks on the table: one red, one green, and one yellow.

David's father pointed at the marks and told him to choose one. After he did, his father covered the mark with the eggcup and then brought his hand down on the cup. When he held up his hand, David could now see a trace of chalk on it. The color had gone, magically, right through the cup.

David was amazed, mystified, stumped, delighted—the wonderful emotional brew that good magic can cook up. He immediately demanded a repeat performance. But this time he challenged his father. He was already dissecting the trick. "Can you do it with the green this time?" he asked. His father obliged, placing the cup over the green mark now, and then bringing his hand down over it. When he held it up, David could see it was now smudged with green. David pointed to another mark, and his father went through the routine once more.

Just as with the card trick, David's father didn't reveal his methods too quickly. David discovered this secret on his own. A few days later when he was playing with some toy trains under the dining-room table with his brother Napier, he happened to look up at the underside of the table. He spotted something— three colored chalk marks. He was staring at the secret to the birthday trick. David, his young mind racing, began to understand that his father had made the corresponding marks under the table before he ever did the routine with the eggcup. It was so simple. David duly reported to his father that he had figured out how the trick was done. But he had learned a valuable lesson for magic. While the secret behind the trick could be uncomplicated, if the presentation was direct and engaging the effect could still have thrilling results. David's mania to get to the bottom of magical methods was sparking to life.

David began what he called his "attack" on magic when he was about six. He had an early obsession with tricks with string and decided that he was going to master 52 of them, the same number as cards in a deck. When he first began experimenting with cards, he was forced to start with a miniature deck, called Volunteers, because the regulation poker-size cards were much too wide for him to handle. He used to look at his hand and wonder when it would be big enough to palm the adult cards.

David also demonstrated at an unusually early age that he had an immense appetite for practice. He struggled, but he developed a drive to conquer the most difficult techniques. He emulated the great musicians who would practice all day, and he could easily lose himself for nine, ten hours at a time. In this way he would take on, with relish, the toughest sleights. He thrilled to the challenge. In 1906, when he was just twelve, he started in on the second deal, long considered to be one of the most difficult of the gambling-based card moves to master. Later, he added the bottom deal, another supremely difficult sleight from the gaming tables. When he was still learning to read, he began his first attempts at what magicians call the pass, still another hand-cramping sleight. The pass is an invisible cut of the entire deck, and in the early twentieth century was the leading method to bring a spectator's chosen card to the top of the deck. David's parents, seeing how studious and diligent he was, thought he would make a fine engineer one day.

While he was exceptionally bright, David's passion for practice often landed him in trouble in school. Striving to master a trick or sleight, he just could not put it aside and so he would practice at his desk. His favorite class for this little scam was geography because the large atlas they used provided a good screen for him to hide behind. Inevitably, his teacher would discover what he was doing and report him to his mother, who would get upset. But David wasn't worried much about his mother's reaction. What bothered him the most was that the teacher typically confiscated whatever little magic props he had been fiddling with behind the atlas. She would steadfastly refuse to return them until the term was over.

Whenever he could scrape together enough money David would send away for still more effects and magical literature from the leading supply houses of the day: Roterberg's in Chicago and the esteemed British shops Gamage's and Davenport's. He also tore through the boys' magazines, *Chums* and *The Boys Own Paper*, for any articles or ads that even hinted at magic. His parents got *The Strand Magazine*, which sometimes featured spreads on gambling and cheating. David waited excitedly every month for the new issue to arrive. One day, in the new YMCA reading room in Ottawa, he discovered a copy of the influential magic magazine *Mahatma*. He read every word.

He also began devouring whatever books on magic he could get his hands on. He started with the "legerdemain" section in the family encyclopedia, trying to work out the few sleights that were mentioned there, usually with only the sparsest of descriptions. Then he moved to the vast cornucopia available to him in Ottawa's Carnegie Library. David loved to read and was methodical and comprehensive in his approach to subjects. If he was interested in baseball (he was a gifted natural athlete), he needed to read up on which wood was used to make the bat. With tennis, he did research into how they strung the racket with gut. He applied the same focused study to magic books, although there weren't many readily available in those days. The handful that were became classics: *Sleight of Hand* by Edwin Sachs, *Our Magic* by Nevil Maskelyne and David Devant, and *Modern Magic, Later Magic,* and *More Magic,* the works of the prolific British lawyer Angelo John Lewis, who wrote under the name Professor Hoffmann.

But no book had as great an effect on the budding magical genius as a slim, mysterious volume known as *The Expert at the Card Table*. The book, apparently written by someone using the pseudonym S. W. Erdnase, first appeared in 1902, when David was eight. *The Expert at the Card Table,* or simply "Erdnase," as it is often called, did what no magic book had ever done. It presented detailed, comprehensive, and clearly illustrated descriptions of most of the major sleights employed not only by the cardsharp but by the magician, too. It also contained highly original handlings that had evidently been devised by the author, whose identity has never been satisfactorily confirmed in the more than one hundred years since the book was published (amazingly, it has never gone out of print in that time). Accounts vary as to just how old David was when he first managed to lay his hands on a copy of *The Expert at the Card Table*. Fittingly, given the elusive nature of its author, the history of the book is cloaked in uncertainty. In those days in Canada, copyrights were, oddly, administered by the Department of Agriculture, the very department where his father worked. It's possible David may have seen *The Expert* when it was first passed through his father's office. But despite listing a Canadian copyright after the title page, there is no solid evidence it was ever submitted there. (The book, which was printed in Chicago, did have a valid U.S. copyright.) It's much more likely that David first acquired *The Expert at the Card Table* after 1905, when it appeared in paperback with a bright, bold king of hearts design on the cover. He would have been eleven. Whatever his exact age, he was still in his formative years as an artist. The book would have a thunderous influence on him and, through him, on magic in the twentieth century.

David lost himself to *The Expert at the Card Table*. He carried the book everywhere, to school, even to church. Once, he sat in the pew toying with cards on his lap with his father's hat covering his hands. The rector looked down and noticed. Also tucked under the hat was his copy of Erdnase. Eventually, David tore the fraying cover off the book, the better for folding so that he could fit it easily in his pocket.

It was an extraordinary coming together, this meeting of David Verner, the child card prodigy who would go on to be the most influential card magician of all time, and the ghostly Erdnase, who looms over the art like some ancient, hidden god. It was as if someone had given Einstein the boy an anonymously produced treatise on the general theory of relativity or the eight-year-old Freud a tract on the interpretation of dreams and said,

"Okay, why not just start from here. Study this." It's quite a trick of history.

After discovering *The Expert at the Card Table*, young David Verner applied his unstinting practice ethic. As the difficult sleights started to work their way into his hands, into his muscle memory, the language of the book—Erdnase's voice—worked its way permanently into his head. Erdnase's voice in fact entered David's consciousness so completely that, over time, it started to merge with his own. He reached the point where he could quote *The Expert* word for word. He memorized it like Scripture.

Erdnase's voice rises commandingly off the pages of his classic. It's authoritative and dominating, but never stodgy. His is a highly literate voice, worldly, assured, sardonic, dismissive of the past, a modern voice. Erdnase sometimes uses the omniscient tone of the first-person plural—the all-knowing, Victorian "we"—and sometimes adopts the remove of the third-person singular. The style is fluent, literate, and peppered with educated phrases and stylish words: *ad libitum, simon-pure, congé, twinkling.*

The book moves fluidly over a range of subjects. Erdnase offers instructions and thoughts, from the importance of a specific section of an individual finger for successfully executing a sleight, all the way to humankind's primal urge to gamble or entertain. To Erdnase, those subjects are not disparate at all. They're expressly, intimately linked because they're all crucial to one who works with cards for a living, whether in a game at the card table or entertaining with tricks in the drawing room. "The finished card expert considers nothing too trivial that in any way contributes to his success," Erdnase declares. He certainly applied that standard to the book. Even the illustrations, drawings by Chicago artist Marshall D. Smith, were groundbreaking for their clarity.

What did David learn when he applied himself to dissecting *The Expert at the Card Table?* He discovered a vast array of sleights and tricks, what would be for him an inexhaustible fountainhead of material. For all its hardnosed philosophical musings, *The Expert at the Card Table* is first and foremost a detailed instructional manual. Magic had never seen one so thorough and exacting, and it has seen only a small handful of that caliber since. David, in his exacting way, first studied the technical terms outlined by Erdnase in the introduction. He instinctively saw the logic to how Erdnase had organized the masterpiece. It made sense to David, even as a child, to get a thorough grounding first.

Erdnase's bank of terms—stock, in-jog, out-jog, throw, blind, run cut, and so on—expanded on the earlier works about card handling. His definitions are succinct, clear, and complete. "To crimp," he writes, is "to bend one or a number of cards, so that they may be distinguished or located." A "jog" is "a card protruding a little from any part of the deck, about quarter of an inch, to fix the location of any particular card or cards." These and the other terms laid out at the beginning of *The Expert* became the basis for the technical vocabulary of modern card magic. Later, David would begin to develop his own variations of the sleights detailed in Erdnase's book.

The book also offered David something else that was new to him: the idea of thought behind action, philosophy behind technique. Erdnase's book is imbued with the unapologetic notion that there is an artistic approach to card handling, even if it is in the service of the crime of card cheating. Indeed, Erdnase continually refers to the entire endeavor, cardsharping and card magic, as "art." His handlings all stress efficiency, practicality, and elegance, and he recommends certain methods because they are "artistic" and disdains others because they are "inartistic." Erdnase could sound like a scold on that score. The full subtitle of his great work read *A Treatise on the Science and Art of Manipulating Cards.* Those were two powerful words, *art* and *science.* David got the message early on.

But of everything Erdnase imparted to David Verner, perhaps the most powerful element was yet another obsession, one rooted in a simple yet potent rule of card-table play. Erdnase stresses in *The Expert* that he is offering moves appropriate for the cheater who works alone, what he dubs the "player without an ally" and what cheaters later called "single-o." It's one of the reasons the book has been so useful for card magicians, who mostly work alone. (Conversely, the vast majority of cardsharps work in teams.)

The "player without an ally," Erdnase states, faces huge problems and risks at the card table. None is more daunting than a sequence that is as much a part of poker as the cards themselves. "The greatest obstacle in the path of the lone player is the cut," Erdnase states with finality. "Were it not for this formality his deal would mean the money." The "formality" of the cut, Erdnase makes plain, is quite effective when it comes to combating many of the classic solo cheating techniques of his day (Erdnase is somewhat coy about revealing just how much cheating he may have done himself). Erdnase shows in *The Expert* that he was obsessed with the cut. It was an obsession that David caught, and it helps explain his manic drive to find the center deal.

"Trust everybody," went one version of the old saying, "but always cut the cards." Other versions had it, "Put your faith in Providence . . ." or "Trust in God . . ." or even more directly, and probably more to the point for wayward gamblers, "Trust your mother. . . ." In poker, by far the most important of the card games for the men Dai Vernon would spend his life chasing, this dictum surely resonated. Anybody who spent time around a card table in the early twentieth century knew that the cut was one of the inviolable rules of proper card play.

In the days of Erdnase and the young Vernon, it was still common for the deck to be passed after each hand to the next player on the left, who would then deal the new round. Thus, each player got a regular turn to deal, to hold the deck and distribute the cards. For Erdnase's "player without an ally," it meant that the means to chicanery were placed regularly in his hands during the game.

But the cut served as a highly effective defensive measure against this potential. Each new dealer would shuffle the deck thoroughly, apparently mixing the cards. The rules of poker then required that the dealer place the pack facedown on the table directly in front of the player to his right, the previous dealer. That player was required to cut the top half of the deck to the table. Then the dealer placed the bottom half on the top half, known as "carrying the cut," gather up the deck, and begin dealing. The whole sequence was to be performed deliberately and out in the open for all to see. Naturally, the other players watched it closely. It was a solemn moment, almost a ritual.

Since the glory days of the dandy riverboat sharps, who worked the packet boats on the Mississippi and Red rivers in the second half of the nineteenth century, the player doing the cutting was known as "the pone" (apparently derived from the Latin verb *ponere*, to place.) The term was included in the rule books—*Foster's Hoyle* and so forth—well into the next century, but most card players of the era had probably never heard the word. The other key position at the poker table, besides the dealer himself, was called "the age," who sat to the dealer's left. The age always opened the betting that began with the new hand. The dealer, the pone, and the age changed constantly throughout the game. That tradition, of course, helped encourage the development of all the classic modern techniques of the cardsharps.

Cheaters worked overtime to come up with ways to get around the cut. Suppose a crooked dealer could, through a difficult series of false shuffles, "run up," or "stack," a desired hand or hands. Perhaps he could keep the cards he wanted on the bottom of the deck, where he could then deal them surreptitiously. (Erdnase in fact considered the bottom deal the "greatest single accomplishment" of the cardsharp.) But he would still have to present that deck to the pone for the cut. "Though he may run up a hand however cleverly," Erdnase writes, "the cut sends him to sea again." For the cardsharp, the cut was the ever-present hurdle, "the beté noir of his existence," as Erdnase puts it.

A cheater might get lucky, Erdnase points out, and encounter "a player who is careless enough to occasionally say, 'Run them'—i.e., he waives the cut." Ever mindful of odds, "professional players always calculate on such a possibility, and will continue to stock on every deal to some extent with that chance in view." But it's an unlikely scenario in fast company. So, in *The Expert*, Erdnase turns his attention to other possible routes around the cut. He reviews several—false cuts, palms, and some others. Realist that he is, he ruthlessly assesses their strengths and weaknesses. None is strong enough for him to endorse wholeheartedly.

Erdnase includes still another method, one with which he was clearly obsessed. The "shift" is one of the oldest moves in what Erdnase calls "the whole calendar" of card sleights. It apparently originated among cheaters hundreds of years ago, probably during the sixteenth century, and has evolved since then into one of the bedrock moves of card magic, where it is known as the "pass." Its standing in magic was certainly based on its being a direct and versatile sleight. But it also retained a certain aura because it's tremendously difficult to execute well. Some card magicians who have mastered it want to show it off like a quick-draw artist.

The shift certainly makes great theoretical sense: while carrying the cut, the cheater uses sleight of hand to shift the two halves back to their original order, all in an invisible blink. But as Erdnase makes clear, the shift really moved into the repertoire of the magician chiefly because it was so much more suited to his "environments." "A half turn of the body, or a slight swing of the hands, or the use of 'patter' until a favorable moment occurs, enables him to cover the action perfectly," Erdnase writes of the conjurer looking to execute a pass.

But for the cheater who desires to shift the deck in a card game, it's a parched landscape indeed. "This artifice is erroneously supposed to be indispensable to the professional player," Erdnase writes, echoing one of the great misconceptions of modern card magicians. "But the truth is it is little used, and adopted only as a last resort." The reasons are obvious to anyone who has ever played cards seriously. "The hands may not be withdrawn from the table for an instant," Erdnase warns, "and any unusual swing or turn will not be tolerated." Not only that, "a still greater handicap arises from the fact that the object of a shift is well known, and especially the exact moment to expect it, immediately after the cut." Erdnase was pessimistic. "The shift has yet to be invented," he declared, "that can be executed by a movement appearing as coincident card-table routine."

It wasn't for lack of trying. Erdnase clearly labored mightily to come up with a shift that would work under the sharp eyes of the other players in a money game. He offers seven different versions of the venerable sleight, each different from the preceding one. Some were his own highly original creations. But he parks most of them in the magic section of his book, where he knows they ultimately belong because they just don't fit "as coincident card-table routine." The sharp's shortfall was the magician's boon.

If Erdnase was obsessed with the cut and the shift, well then so was David Verner. It was at the root of his later drive to discover a center deal. If a sharp could deal the card he needed out of the middle of the pack, he wouldn't have to give the cut another thought. He would banish Erdnase's bête noire once and for all. It would be the ultimate crooked move. It would be magic.

Somehow, Erdnase himself managed to vanish more thoroughly than any of David's cards or coins ever could. Erdnase seemed to leave no trace of himself, other than his book. No one seemed to know who he was when *The Expert at the Card Table* came out, and over the decades his identity became an ever-deepening mystery. Yet, just as fully as Erdnase the man seemed to recede into the shadows of magic history, his book—his sole book, as far as anyone has been able to determine—only became more prominent.

Because the U.S. copyright on *The Expert at the Card Table* was never renewed, the book entered the public domain. Thousands of copies have been printed during the century after it first appeared. Its standing evolved ever upward as it came to be considered the fundamental text, the standard classic, on handling cards for magic. And this ranking was due, in large measure, to the absolute devotion and relentless proselytizing of Dai Vernon, Erdnase's most prominent protégé and the greatest student of the book. It was as if Erdnase had made some devilish bargain to erase his own identity in order to guarantee the immortality of his masterwork. The switch seemed as clean, as complete as when Vernon changed one card for another in the deck, a move he first perfected by studying *The Expert at the Card Table*. Erdnase's vanishing act stood with the greatest tricks in the history of magic.

No magician can learn solely from books, no matter how monumental. An apprentice needs to see how the masters do it. David Verner was no different. As he developed, he began to learn from others who shared his interests. His "sessions," as magicians call them, ran the gamut. He met with other boys who were just starting out and he sought out the top names of his art. Some sessions were planned. Others were chance encounters.

One unexpected lesson came in the Canadian north woods when David was about ten and his father took him on a fishing trip. They would fish for rainbow trout all day and then bring their catch back to the lodge, where it would be cooked for their dinner. Then they would sit on the veranda, take in the night air, and chat with the other sportsmen.

One night, one of the other guests suddenly pulled out a pack of cards and started doing some tricks. They were uncomplicated, direct, and extremely powerful, and David noticed that the man's technique was flawless. He asked David to pick a card and then he produced it with the best pass the boy had yet seen. It was clean, clearly superior to what David had seen or imagined in his young life, and it somehow ignited his ambitions. He was suddenly filled with an overwhelming sense of the value of such a polished move — a single, beautifully executed sleight. He wished, as a child will, that he could barter for it. He would be willing, he thought, to trade all the tricks he knew just to do that one trick with the pass.

But it wasn't just the sleight that captured young David Verner's imagination. It was the man himself. He, too, was somehow different. David sensed it, and he was taken with him. Yet he was puzzled, too. When he asked his father about him, he answered forcefully that the man was a gambler. David's father gave the word some weight, some emphasis. It seemed to have some hidden meaning. He didn't say that the man was a magician. It was the first time David was aware of a difference, and it became an important distinction in his mind. From then on, whenever he heard about a gambler he would make a point of trying to see what he could do. Gamblers just seemed to be so much better at the skills that David was looking to acquire.

In 1904, at the Carnegie Library in Ottawa, David had still another unplanned meeting that helped steer him along his remarkable path in magic. He had been spending a lot of extra time in the library and on this day was particularly engrossed in an article in *Scientific American* by Hereward Carrington, the era's leading investigator of psychic phenomena. When David happened to look up, he noticed a man watching him while he read. Over the next several days, every time he returned to the library, he saw the man keeping an eye on him. Finally, the man approached and spoke up.

The man said he could see that David was "very much interested" in an article on magic he was poring over. David agreed readily, declaring that magic was his "hobby." Do you know any tricks? the man wanted to know. Sure, David said, and proceeded to pull out his miniature deck, which he always carried with him to practice his pass. He demonstrated the sleight for the man, who then took the cards from him. "You have to do it this way," he told him as he executed the move flawlessly. He instructed David to keep the pack perfectly squared, a crucial detail, before attempting the pass, and he added several other helpful pointers. David saw right away that the advice improved his handling. He asked the man if he knew any other tricks.

They spent the rest of the day at the library, the man demonstrating moves and thrilling David with stories about the fascinating characters in the world of magic. David was filled with a sense of love for the art and for the first time got a strong feeling that this is what he wanted to do with his life. Later, he liked to fantasize that the man, whom he never saw again, was actually Erdnase, his unknown mentor.

Sometimes, David would head to the racetrack to see what he could pick up. Ottawa's track had a lively scene, and David would wander into the fairgrounds to watch the various scam artists plying their trade. These were still the horse-and-buggy days, and the hustlers would ride in, park on the midway, and hitch up their horses. Then they would climb up on their carriages to conduct their little shows. Sometimes they sold fake watches or cheap goods, and sometimes they turned quick short cons. The track was British in style, and young David got an up-close look at many of the hustles prevalent in England at the turn of the century. Horse racing, "the sport of kings," was a much-favored diversion of the rich in those days. The wealthy spectators made natural suckers for the grifters.

Two common scams David observed were "thimble-rigging" and the "purse swindle." Thimble-rigging was a British version of the venerable three-shell game played with three large thimbles and a real pea. The game was actually much more difficult to put over than the three-shell game, requiring exquisitely developed sleights to present effectively. The vexing "purse swindle" was a common play popular in the markets of London. A hustler would draw a crowd with a spiel about an impossible bargain for a small leather purse he was selling. He would make the deal even more tempting by openly placing a coin in the purse, offering to sell both for some absurdly low price.

Naturally, the huckster switched the coin at the last second, employing a sleight called the "purse palm." When the buyer moved off and opened the purse, she found not a coin but a brass slug advertising the leather maker or some other business. These purses always sold well at the racetrack, as the swindlers were taking advantage of people's innate desire for an impossible deal. (Dai Vernon would later incorporate the purse palm into a classic coin routine he created called "Spellbound.")

But David saw more than just sleights at the racetrack. He was adding to his store of artistic theory. Watching the hustlers, he saw how good they were, how utterly natural their movements looked. Their deceptions were direct and seamless, just like the man's shift at the fishing lodge. A swindler on the fairgrounds might do only one move, but he did it casually and imperceptibly while a crowd of people surrounded him and watched him closely. David saw that these cheaters had no choice but absolute mastery. If they made a mistake, it could mean bodily harm.

Naturally, these swindlers weren't too interested in giving lessons to some pesky kid. Sometimes David would crawl up on one of the wheels of the carriage to get a closer look. If they noticed him hanging around, they'd angrily chase him off. "Get down, boy!" they'd shout. "Get down! Get away from here! We don't deal with boys!" But David was undeterred. He saw a lot at the racetrack.

David learned about his art in a more traditional venue, too. His apprenticeship wasn't limited to racetracks and lodges deep in the woods. As Canada's burgeoning capital city, Ottawa was a prime stop on the vaudeville circuit and the city was studded with rollicking venues: the Bennett Theater, the Russell Theater, the Family Theater, and the king of the vaudeville theaters, B. F. Keith's. The Keith chain eventually grew so large that it took over most of the other theaters. It was in these great old houses that David Verner first saw some of the giants of modern magic, including T. Nelson Downs, Nate Leipzig, J. Warren Keane, and Louis Jerome McCord, who performed under the stage name Silent Mora.

David wasn't content with just sitting in his seat and then going home. He would work his way backstage and sit patiently until he got a chance to talk with the performers. He made a point of being scrupulously polite and complimentary, never brash, and wound up starting friendships that, in some cases, would last for decades.

Keane and Leipzig, both of whom he saw at the Bennett, were especially important early influences. Keane, pronounced "keen," lived up to his name, as Vernon later liked to put it. He was sharp, worldly, and cultured, and billed himself as "The After-Dinner Entertainer" and "The Society Entertainer." Keane generally avoided fraternizing with other magicians and never followed the pack, preferring instead to craft his own effects, which stumped audiences and conjurers alike. His card work depended heavily on psychology and closely observing people, their natures and reactions. One trick in particular impressed David.

It was a direct effect, simply presented, David's favorite kind. Keane spread the pack facedown and removed a single card, leaving it, too, facedown. Then he asked David to name a card. When he named the ace of clubs, a lifelong favorite, Keane slowly turned over the card he had segregated from the others. It was the ace.

Keane gazed intently at David. "I know this interests you," he said. David was flabbergasted. "I don't know why it shouldn't," he said, gulping, "it's the greatest thing I've ever seen." Keane, who liked David and felt he was serious about magic, decided to tell him how he did the trick. "This is very hard to explain," Keane warned him, "and even harder because you are a young boy, but I'll try to make it as simple as I can."

Keane went on to detail how he had duped David by letting him see the ace without letting him register that he had seen it. "The principle lies in engaging your attention," he explained, "your undivided attention. You are concentrating on one vein of thought and your mind is on this one track." He then led him into the deception. "If you are conscious that you have seen it, this thing won't work," he told David. "You must *subconsciously* see that card. Now if I can hold your attention beyond this point by continuing the conversation, the trick has a larger possibility of success. I suddenly say, 'Name any card in the pack,' and you will name the card that registered on your subconscious mind."

Here was psychology employed directly as a tool of art— David's art. It was tantalizing, complex, and it made for an unorthodox, and staggering, card trick. It was also full of obvious risks. How could you be absolutely sure that you had influenced someone? Plainly, you couldn't. Keane's approach required confidence, experience, and the rawest of nerve, a cardsharp's nerve.

It required an escape strategy, too, what magicians call "outs." But David saw that, as chancy as the method was, the effect was well worth the risk. It was, far and away, the best trick he had seen yet. It seemed to be true magic.

Keane's work galvanized David. He began reading William James and other works on psychology, and these studies opened up still more paths. He began to see the extraordinary potential behind blending sleight of hand with powerful, and tricky, subtleties. He was learning the elements of advanced deception.

If David was deeply intrigued by Keane, he fell flat in love with Leipzig, the consummate master of sleight of hand whose handlings and performances were always elegant and restrained. But what really set Leipzig apart, and prompted David to look up to him, was that he was a true gentleman. He was born Nathan Leipziger, a Swedish Jew who had come to the United States as a teenager and matured as a performer during the late-nineteenth-century flowering of vaudeville and sleight of hand. Leipzig's magic was shown to best effect close up, at society parties and club dinners, where his startling card and coin work could be seen easily. But when he was booked on the Keith vaudeville tour, he really made his international reputation by showing what an effective showman he was.

"I learned from actors' presentation," Leipzig once wrote, stressing the importance of stage presence, voice, and audience management. In fact, his stage card work was based almost exclusively on one exquisite move, called the side slip, which he helped to perfect. "Without proper presentation the best sleight of hand is nothing but a juggling feat," he declared. Leipzig was famed for putting card tricks over in big halls. Typically, he would invite a randomly selected committee of spectators up onstage, and then he would perform for them. Their reactions would impart the magic to the house beyond, spreading the delight to the entire audience. He passed on to David what he considered the ultimate secret: "The audience must like you."

An advertisement in the newspaper first opened David's eyes to the great Max Malini. The ad was for an upcoming show at the Rideau Club, an exclusive Ottawa men's club where David's father was a member. It showed a picture of a short, chubby man in an overcoat and promised loudly that he would perform "miracles" using "borrowed articles" and "no trick apparatus of any kind."

"Dad, you have to take me to see this Malini," David announced to his father, who turned him down flat. There were no children allowed at the club, he told his son. But on the night of the show, David sneaked in, trying to find the best perch from which to watch Malini surreptitiously. David ended up skulking just outside a pair of sliding doors that led from the lobby to the performance area. The doors weren't completely closed. His view was obstructed, but he was still able to catch glimpses of Malini.

The brash little magician was the "last of the mountebanks." His billing swore "Honest to Goodness, I Only Cheat a Little," and promised that "You'll Wonder When I'm Coming—You'll Wonder More When I'm Gone." Both claims were the truth. He was an improbable figure who would have an outsized influence on David and other modern close-up magicians who came of age in the early 1900s.

Malini was a tiny fellow. His hands were so small they couldn't cover a standard playing card. He had to have his gloves made in a small woman's size. Although he mangled the English language in his thick, guttural eastern European accent, he nevertheless found great fame wandering the world, entertaining royalty and the wealthy. Malini once lunged at Senator Mark Hanna in Congress in 1902, loudly ripping a button off his jacket with his teeth. Then, just as quickly, he restored it. At a royal command performance in England, he addressed the Princess of Wales as "Mrs. Wales," as in "Mrs. Wales, take a leetle peek at a card, please."

Most magicians of the era had mastered the cigarette vanish.

Malini would go them one better by taking a borrowed cigarette—-he preferred if it was an exotic, hard-to-find brand—tearing it to shreds, mixing the tobacco into a clump, and then vanishing the clump from between his fingers. Just as abruptly, he would magically produce the restored cigarette and return it to its owner. Malini could sit at a bar and make a mug of beer appear under his hat. In an incident that became famous in magic, he did a similar trick at a restaurant in New York, this time lifting a fine Parisian hat he had borrowed from a woman at his table to reveal a large block of ice.

Malini's approach was to prepare his seemingly impromptu miracles long in advance. And he was a master at waiting until just the right moment to execute a sleight or perform a trick. He collected straws from the bars of hotels around the world so that when he returned he could perform a captivating, and apparently casual, little trick in which he would tear and then restore the wrapper. When he was in Washington, Malini would routinely visit the exclusive tailor shops and have them sew playing cards into the jacket linings of various dignitaries' suits. Days, weeks, even years later he might run into the official at a reception. "What a physique you have!" he would exclaim as he patted the target of his deception. If he felt that the card was still in place, he would turn another spectacular effect. His audiences would, indeed, wonder about him when he was gone.

Eventually, David was accomplished enough that he, too, took to the stage. It wasn't exactly vaudeville, but he did have a live, attentive audience the day he provided the magic portion of the program for a school variety show. His parents attended. David performed some fairly sophisticated effects, not the routine beginner's fare typical of such shows. One trick involved firing a borrowed watch out of a rigged blunderbuss and another required him to borrow a hat from an audience member. He displayed the hat, showing that it was empty, and then he even turned down the sweatband inside to show there was nothing hidden under it. After his little show, David, glowing with pride, joined his parents. He found his mother in tears, practically sobbing.

"I was so ashamed of you," she scolded her son. Why? he wanted to know. The show had gone off so well. It was the hat, she explained. The hat? David's mother told him that the way he displayed the hat was in extremely bad taste. When he fiddled with the band inside, she told him, he was implying that there were "some crawling things in there." Beyond that bizarre leap of logic, she was also upset with the whole air of his performance. "I was also ashamed at how beastly professional you were," she announced, which also struck David as absurd. The other children had performed their segments "politely and sweetly . . . as children should be," she explained. David's professional airs she found grotesque. "People might well think I adopted you from a circus," she said.

David was more amused than disturbed by his mother's reaction. He loved her, but he saw that she just didn't understand his approach to magic, which was studious and diligent. Her attitudes seemed to him to be from a distant time and place. Besides, he didn't need to be a circus child to get the kind of schooling that interested him. Comfortable, genteel, Victorian Ottawa had turned out to be a pretty good burg after all for an aspiring magician. It had given him a sound grounding in the deceptive arts.

Ottawa had even given him a new, more magical sounding, first name. When David Verner, an excellent athlete, won a local diving contest, an Ottawa newspaper mistakenly spelled his first name "Dai." When his friends asked him about it, he told them he didn't know what it meant. But the name stuck and when he eventually found out that Dai was a Welsh nickname for David, he let it stand for good. (As an adult, he had all kinds of quips about the name Dai. He would say that his name was David but that he had taken out the "VD." And when people asked him whether it was pronounced "Day" or "Die," he would answer "eee-ther or eye-ther.")

David's parents still held out hope that their oldest son would become an engineer, or, failing that, perhaps a traditional artist. He was talented at drawing and painting, skills that ran in the family. But to them, a career in entertainment was out of the question. When he reached high school age, they decided to send him to Ashbury College in Ottawa, which was not a college in the American sense but a prep school that had opened a few years before, in 1891. The British founder, George Penrose Woollcombe, who had immigrated to Canada, was an Oxford University graduate who named the school after his home back in England. Ashbury was as thoroughly steeped in the classical British prep school tradition as an Earl Grey tea bag, which pleased David's mother immensely. She thought the British schools were much more upstanding and correct than the English-French schools of Canada.

But David's strongest memory of his time at Ashbury was of more Victorian absurdity. He threw himself into athletics at the school, and loved baseball, but Woollcombe didn't allow the game because he felt it led to bad language and rough behavior. Ashbury offered cricket instead, which David found to be agonizingly slow and boring. It was a ridiculous game to him.

After Ashbury, David's father secured him a place at Canada's prestigious Royal Military College in Kingston, Ontario. The college was modeled on the famed Sandhurst in England. It was supposed to turn out finished, disciplined military men with professional skills to boot. The RMC had a top-notch engineering program, which made it attractive to David's father. As at Ashbury, David excelled in sports, but the real highlight of his RMC stint was the time he happened to find a stray card lying on the floor of the locker room after a football game. Cards were still following him around.

David picked up the card as he headed into the open showers and began absentmindedly fiddling with it, palming it, passing it from hand to hand and wondering how long it could hold up under the stream of hot water. Just then the commandant of the college strolled in and began greeting members of the team. When he got to David, whom he knew to be an amateur magician, he greeted him with a bellow. "Let me see you produce a card now!" It was a joke, a locker room throwaway, but David answered by reaching down between his legs and apparently bringing out a soggy card. The commandant nearly fainted.

At first, David coasted at the Royal Military College, casually enduring the hellish first year when the raw recruits were shaped up. In the winter, they were marched out to Lake Ontario, where two large holes had been cut in the ice. They were ordered to dive in one hole and swim under the ice to the other. Those who balked were summarily pushed into the Arctic-like water. David didn't have to be pushed. He went right in and came right out again. It was nothing to him.

But his nonchalance, and physical hardiness, didn't mean he was warming to the idea of military life. Nor did it mean he was starting to accept his father's plan that he become an engineer. He wanted to be an artist. The Royal Military College, to David's thinking, was just something to be endured until the third year. The third-year students were the kings of the campus. They could command the recruits at will. But David's third year never came. The First World War did instead. He left the college and went into the armed services.

David began his military career with a commission in the artillery. He found the training stimulating in its way. (Incredibly, he would apply what he had learned in artillery training to magic.

He adapted what he knew about velocity and big-gun recoil to devise a unique sleight that enabled him to vanish an apple-sized ball while seeming to pass it from hand to hand.) Like a lot of young men of his generation, he wanted to go overseas to see some action. But instead of shipping out, he was assigned to military headquarters staff. Because of his drafting skills, he was given office work and soon found himself deskbound. He agonized when his younger brother Napier, a private in the infantry, was sent to Europe and ended up in the fearsome combat at Verdun.

David wore the uniform, but he wasn't fighting. He wasn't going anywhere. He sat at a drafting table, thinking about his brother, thinking about the war, and thinking about New York City. That's where he really longed to be. Somehow, since he was a child, he had been fascinated with the idea of New York. Between Ashbury and the Royal Military College, on a trip alone, he had gotten a fleeting taste of the city. Now he wanted the whole plate. It had struck him how New York was on the cusp, the new overtaking the old. There were electric lights next to gas jets, new subway trains shooting along just under the horse-drawn streetcars. But New York was no Victorian town. It was throwing off the past like an old woman's shawl.

In 1917, when David was twenty-three, his father, his first tutor in magic, died. His mother decided to move to Toronto with his other brother, Arthur, who was only a child of seven. David, after transferring to the Royal Canadian Air Force, finagled a six-week leave and headed down to New York, to Manhattan. Soon, people were stopping him on Broadway and asking him how many German soldiers he had taken care of. They could see that his uniform was not American and assumed he must have come from "over there." He decided to switch to civilian clothes to avoid any confusion or embarrassment. That was one trick he wasn't going to play.

David kept extending his leave. He wasn't going to go back.

He couldn't. Like other great artists at the dawn of what was about to become a great, modern variety show, he knew that New York was where he should be. It was inevitable. Ottawa had turned out to be a wonderful place to plant the seeds of magic, a fertile field in the spring. But New York was magic itself.

3

PLEASANT HILL

Thousands of miles from Manhattan, where David Verner was taking off his uniform, another aspiring card artist was worrying about whether he was going to have to put one on. It was early November 1918, and the war in Europe had already been grinding and raging for four years. The United States had swaggered into the fight a good year and a half earlier, boasting it could make the world safe for democracy. Yet in the farming town of Pleasant Hill, Missouri, Allen Kennedy still had his eye on the draft lists. He was waiting to move up.

It had been five months since Allen, along with his brother James and thirty-four other Cass County boys who had turned twenty-one in June, had registered with the selective service board. Like the soldiers they itched to be, they had dutifully taken their physicals, filled out their questionnaires, been classified, then ordered to be ready for transport to one of the regional camps. Pleasant Hill recruits were being shipped to Camp Funston or Fort Riley over in Kansas, where they got their basic training. Once in fighting trim, they would hop another troop transport for shipping out from one of the coasts. From there, it was on to the "battle lines in France to help dash off the Fritzies," as the *Pleasant Hill Times* put it.

But Allen's call-up had been slow in coming through. August, which could drag so lazily in Pleasant Hill, brought instead a wave of tribulations that seemed to spring from the pages of the Bible. First, a crunching drought had parched the fields without mercy. Then, clouds of grasshoppers had descended on the county, flaying whatever corn had managed to survive the dry weather. Farmers, like Allen's father, John, had to fear not only for their crops, which were fast withering under this assault from nature, but for their livestock, too. The desiccated corn couldn't be used for feed and the animals were in danger of starving. And because of the war and the rush to enlist, there weren't enough able-bodied men to help with whatever work could still be done. Schoolboys were being given wartime leaves from class to go work in the fields.

Generous rains at the beginning of September may have soothed the drought worries, but they couldn't allay the fears that were beginning to shroud the town. The oompah-pahs and give-the-Kaiser-hell speeches had made for some rousing send-offs down at the Missouri Pacific depot. But these hurrahs were muted by the news in early October that one of Pleasant Hill's sons had lost his life the month before on the battlefield in France. It was the town's first casualty, one of the first boys who had rushed to enlist back in the summer of 1917. Then, another young man from Pleasant Hill fell in the Argonne. They were out there, battling and dying. All Allen Kennedy and the boys on the August list were doing was waiting.

And then it turned out that death wasn't just a telegram wending its way from France to Missouri. It was strolling right through the peaceful streets of Pleasant Hill. At the end of September, a local man succumbed to typhoid, setting off a scare that would fade only with the panic ignited by the arrival of the Spanish flu epidemic. To fight that onslaught, the Pleasant Hill Board of Education ordered all the schools in town to be closed indefinitely. Then the mayor issued a decree banning all public assembly, wiping out the annual street fair in October, which usually drew crowds in the thousands. No Wild West shows or carnivals, either. Those were summarily canceled, too.

By November, the wave of influenza had crashed with such ferocity that the sexton of the Pleasant Hill Cemetery announced that the pace of deaths was overwhelming the available burial space. Old graves—forgotten graves, they were called—would have to be dug up to make room for the new ones. The funeral parlor was up to four ceremonies a day. This was not exactly the boom that the town fathers were looking to tout in Pleasant Hill. For the last fifteen years or so, the town had been laboring successfully to transform itself from just another Missouri backwater. The railroads had been steadily continuing their expansion, and the town was now a main switch point for two lines, the Missouri Pacific and the Rock Island. And there had been talk of Pleasant Hill becoming the county seat. But now there was only sadness and worry as Allen Kennedy and the other new enlistees continued their wait for news of their departure. They couldn't do much to fight influenza. But they could still get in their licks against the Hun.

Finally, on Friday, November 8, 1918, the announcement came down from the Cass County military board that the young men were heading into action. Kennedy and nineteen others from the August and September lists were ordered to ship out. The group included boys from other towns in the area, Harrisonville and Strasburg and Garden City and Lone Tree. They were scheduled to leave the following Wednesday, November 13, for Kelly Field in Texas, not far from San Antonio. No more killing time, spoiling for a fight that never seemed to come.

Sure, there was already some vague talk that Germany might be getting ready to wave the white flag. The announcement of the boys' call-up in the newspaper was even followed by a small, attention-grabbing item: "Germany Has Quit War?" the headline asked, followed by a short report on a rumor that the enemy might, indeed, be ready to surrender. But Provost Marshal General Crowder was still calling for more than 18,000 new enlistees. And another major mobilization was planned for the end of November. Even if the war was winding down, the military still needed soldiers. Didn't they?

But the "Mo Pac" train never left town that following Wednesday with Allen Kennedy or any of the other would-be soldiers. Instead, the trains in Pleasant Hill stayed in the yards to celebrate the end of the war. At a little after three in the morning on Monday, November 11, word reached Pleasant Hill that the armistice had been signed after all. It was still the middle of the night and the streets were empty except for the trainmen, the night watchman, and the other assorted nighthawks who flitted through downtown. But the engineers in the Missouri Pacific yards did their best to wake everyone up. They took to their engines and for the next three hours or so, until daybreak, piped their whistles in unison to celebrate the stupendous news.

As word spread quickly that the train blasts were not heralding a fire or some other catastrophe, that it was the end of the awful war, the townsfolk of Pleasant Hill rushed downtown to join the cacophony. They rang the fire bell. They blew off guns of all types; so many people fired shotguns into the air that the authorities had to order the stores not to sell any more shells unless they first removed the shot. They honked the horns of the few automobiles in town, which were then joined by others streaming in from the surrounding farms. They banged pots and pans. The "angelus," the church bells, pealed. Someone even fired off a small cannon, just an exultant noisemaker now, nothing like the fearsome artillery in Europe. Relief and joy built to a deafening crescendo. Pleasant Hill's celebration of the end of the Great War could be heard for many miles.

Although enlistees had been told to "hold themselves in readiness," the orders to keep the training camps running were quickly rescinded. "The sudden cessation of the war through the signing of the armistice," the *Pleasant Hill Times* announced, "has resulted in an order holding up entrainment of further draft contingents. . . . The probability is . . . that not only are all future drafts permanently cancelled, but that men lately sent to camp will soon be ordered home." Allen Kennedy and the others weren't going anywhere after all. They wouldn't be seeing the front, wouldn't be trading the burn of the drought for the scorch of mustard gas, the hungry hum of the grasshoppers for the buzz of machine guns.

The only trenches they would be digging now would be the familiar ones, the neat, shallow ones left by their plows. How close they had come. Just three days before the end of the war, Allen Kennedy had finally gotten his orders. Three days. And then he had missed out. Three days out of a miserable, four-year war. What were the odds on that? Allen Kennedy sure had some kind of luck.

But what luck was it, exactly? Was it good or bad? Had he been saved or just stuck? Now he faced the same question that so many of the young men in Pleasant Hill did as the war came to an end. What was he going to do with himself? For some in town, of course, there was no real choice. They were going to do whatever their fathers had done, get behind a plow horse, or help run the grocery store. Others might look beyond the boundaries of Pleasant Hill and take up work with one of the rail lines stitched across the map of the Midwest. Some might even head up to Kansas City for a position with one of the many businesses busting out all over that booming Cow Town.

Allen's choices were a bit starker, though not run of the mill. He was still living with his parents on their tenant plot out on the Bill Allen farm northwest of town. He knew farming, and that was one choice. He had been doing it since he was a boy, working alongside his father and brothers. But the soil was not where his ambitions lay. He had other talents, natural skills he was much more eager to cultivate than crops. Instead of throwing feed to the chickens, he thought about throwing dice. Instead of plowing, he wanted to give shuffling a try. Now that he wasn't going to be a soldier, he could go back to being a farmer. Or he could become a gambler. Either was a natural choice in Pleasant Hill.

It was true that Allen's ties to the farm, where he had been born, were strong. But they were not really his ties. They were his parents'. He looked more to town now. If he wanted to develop what he was coming to see as unique abilities—his skills at mastering complicated moves with cards and dice—he couldn't continue farming for a living. The danger to hands ruled it out. Farmers in Cass County were constantly losing fingers and hands to saws, wires, sledges, and dropped shotguns. A gambler couldn't take that risk. He had to keep his hands in tiptop shape. He had to pamper them.

For the farmers of western Missouri who were not so squeamish about their hands, the bounty, if not the profit, could be staggering. In Pleasant Hill, crops seemed to just climb right out of the coffee-colored ground. On some days, if the weather were right, a field newly planted in the morning seemed to show some growth by later that afternoon. The stalls at the street fair downtown fairly burst each October with the finest examples of Cass County's agricultural plenty. Just that January before the Armistice, local farmer Sam Poindexter had shipped a full rail car of corn, 86,370 pounds, to Iowa. He set the record for the largest corn shipment out of the town till then. Many farmers also raised cattle, hens, and hogs, which commanded increasingly good prices from the slaughterhouses up in Kansas City.

The Bill Allen farm, where Kennedy's parents lived, was one of the biggest spreads in the area. It had been established, like so many in Missouri, in the second half of the nineteenth century by pioneers from Kentucky. Many of these families had brought their slaves along with them, and after the Civil War ended, the ostensibly freed slaves often just stayed on. They lived in tiny, clustered shacks and worked right alongside the poor white tenant farmers who also gravitated to these large farms. Some of the Kentucky farmers, and others from Tennessee, didn't make the exodus to Missouri until after the Civil War.

Allen's mother, Hattie Belle Scott, was born in Kentucky in 1865 and had come up to Cass County with "her people," as they called relatives in those parts, when she was sixteen. There she met and married Allen's father, John Ed Kennedy. His people had also migrated from Kentucky, though earlier than Hattie's, sometime in the 1850s. John had been born near Pleasant Hill. He and Hattie married in 1884 and then promptly began to have children. Eventually, there would be seven in all, four boys and three girls. It meant more mouths to feed, but also more hands to work the farm. Allen was born in June 1897.

Allen apparently got both his proper name and his nickname from the owner of the land, Bill Allen. He was said to promise $10 to the parents of any baby born on his farm if they named it after him. Perhaps John and Hattie hoped for a daily double on their middle son. They named him Allen but also called him Bill. (His real middle name was Bryan.) Like the other Kennedy children, Allen started school in the St. Elmo District. But by the time he was eight, in 1905, he was listed as "removed" from the rolls along with his brother Mallory, who was five years older, and his sister Una, who was eight years older. They were probably needed to work on the farm.

The farmers of Pleasant Hill certainly didn't have to wait for the Great Depression to know hard times. Farming in rural Missouri in the early part of the century was one of the hardest lives imaginable. Yet many couldn't imagine any other. The tests were relentless. "The long drought has hurt many of the tillers of the soil," the *Pleasant Hill Local* reported in 1911 during one especially tenacious dry spell. "But there seems to be little disposition to fuss about it." If it wasn't the cruelties of the weather it was the ravages of disease. Tuberculosis, the "white plague," was still rampant when Allen was growing up. One estimate in 1911, when he was fourteen, put the number of deaths in Missouri for the year at 8,000. Although being out in the countryside, away from downtown, might offer a measure of protection from typhoid and influenza epidemics, other diseases hovered constantly. Tetanus was an ever-present threat on a farm, where the chances of getting cut were high. The corresponding odds of getting to a doctor in time for the "lockjaw shot" were perilously low. Usually, an injured farmer had to hitch his plow horse to a buggy and trundle, bleeding all the way, into town.

It wasn't just the farmers, but their animals, too, who lived in constant danger from these unchecked diseases. Hog cholera was a particular fright. There were pests, like grasshoppers, and predators. Pleasant Hill held an annual wolf drive to combat lupine marauders, which could strip out a herd or maul their fowl. The drive was a daylong, madcap affair, with frantic teams of armed men tearing around the countryside gunning for any wolf that dared show its head. The newspapers, somewhat ambitiously, called the hunters "Nimrods."

The wolf drive didn't deter human predators, though. Chicken thieves, a constant irritant, were usually locally based. But the bunco men more commonly hailed from Kansas City and points beyond. They would swarm in to sell bad seed for "imported wheat" and other illusory crops and to cheat these already poor farmers on the price of their produce and their livestock. The whole idea of putting one's faith in the Board of Trade was considered gambling for high stakes.

They knew all about gambling in town. "If you want your boy to be a gambler there is no better place for him to receive a thorough and complete education . . . than right here in Pleasant Hill," declared the *Cass County Republican* in an exposé headlined "The Art of Gambling" in 1922. "It is conceded that the Pleasant Hill instructors are experts and well equipped to deliver the goods." The *Republican,* a short-lived GOP paper that tried to challenge the dominant *Pleasant Hill Times* and the Democratic powers that be, moralized in a way that the *Times* never would. It was undoubtedly one of the reasons it didn't survive. Pleasant Hill never seemed to take to moralizing.

"Just go downtown some night and see how many men and boys you can find loafing on the streets from ten o'clock on up to daylight," the paper fumed in its ungrammatical, stream-of-consciousness front-page editorial. "See how many congregate in the restaurants and about the depot, watch their movements, notice how many trips they make up and down certain stairways on First Street follow their forms to and from the railroad yards and in and out of Certain business concerns that Keep late or all night hours and after a few nights spent as 'lookouts' we believe you will reach the same conclusion we have reached and that you will know that the boy who continually comes home late of nights has at least been exposed to one of the worst maladies (gambling influences) that ever invested any town or community."

The two games most popular in western Missouri as Allen Kennedy came of age were poker and craps. The historical origins of both, perhaps fittingly, are somewhat sketchy. It seems likely that they descended from games imported into the United States. Poker may have evolved from a French card game and craps was probably a somewhat simplified offshoot of the British dice game Hazard. Both had been popular in New Orleans in the early nineteenth century. They then spread out across the territories faster than dried seedlings on a westward wind, and may have found the most fertile ground of all when they alighted in Missouri farm country. Cards and dice just seemed to take root in Cass County as deeply as all the other prized crops. The ever-stricter laws passed by the Missouri state legislature did little to curb them.

The Pleasant Hill ladies had their lunchtime bridge. The town fathers had their friendly pitch matches on Friday nights. But for the all-night "men and boys" who kept the *Republican* fulminating, poker was the game. Poker was, in the words of one newspaper, "baseball's indoor rival." It had almost completely outrun the venerable game of faro to become what another paper, the *Cass County Leader,* called "the great American game, famous around the world as the Yank's favorite indoor sport." (Faro, which had ruled the West, required a more elaborate house setup to run effectively and profitably. And it was known to be a thoroughly crooked game, with most houses doing the bulk of the cheating rather than roving cheaters.) Draw and stud poker were both popular, but for serious gamblers, five-card stud emerged as the favorite.

"Notice how many trips they make up and down certain stairways," the *Republican* had warned, and it was true. Card games were commonplace along First Street, the main thoroughfare of the Pleasant Hill business district. Many of the businesses along First Street had offices or apartments upstairs, and those often served as game rooms. The pool hall on First, the oldest continually operating poolroom in the state of Missouri (a status it retains today), was another popular gathering spot for the local sports. "Our own boys or your boys may be gambling," the *Republican* cried, continuing in its repetitive, emphatic way, "and when they are out late at night in Pleasant Hill they will be gambling unless they have strong enough will power to say NO."

Both Pleasant Hill and Harrisonville, the nearby county seat, developed into full-fledged poker centers. To the hardscrabbling farmers in the surrounding areas, Pleasant Hill was "the city." They visited regularly to shop, pick up supplies, deliver their goods, and visit with their neighbors. And nothing broke the grinding monotony of a week in the fields like a lively game of poker.

A nip of home brew or the local moonshine, "white mule whiskey," added to the conviviality. Both were strong, expertly crafted, and readily available. Homemade hooch, the "undertaker's delight," was established as a specialty in that part of Missouri long before the Eighteenth Amendment went into effect in 1920.

Pleasant Hill had managed for years to steer its way between wet and dry, but in 1907 it came under the intense focus of the Women's Christian Temperance Union and the Anti-Saloon League. By mid-1908 all three saloons in town had lost their licenses. The day after its license was lifted, the owners of the Swarthout Saloon posted a sign in their window advising, "Smile, damn you, smile." Still, by 1916 one minister was thundering that Pleasant Hill was the "wettest" of the dry towns in the area.

The "cackle" of dice, as the gamblers called it, could also be heard everywhere in Pleasant Hill. Indeed, the "little ivory cubes" were so associated with that region of the country that in gambling slang they were sometimes known as "Missouri marbles." In some ways they seemed to be even better suited than cards to the unique pace of rural life in and around Pleasant Hill. For one thing, a pair of dice was like a portable gaming club, no bigger than sugar cubes. Crapshooters didn't need a room above First Street, or even so much as a table, to get some action going. An alleyway, the back wall of a shed, the rear corner of the poolroom, the train yard, a blanket at a farm sale—all worked for "rollin' the bones."

So did church pews, apparently. In one locally infamous case dating back to 1890, just a few years before David Verner was caught studying Erdnase in church in Ottawa, two boys were discovered shooting craps in the back of the First Baptist Church during evening services. "We have heard their names mentioned," the *Pleasant Hill Local* intoned, "but hoping this notice may meet their eyes and prove sufficient warning without exposure, we refrain from giving them now." (Many of the Pleasant Hill papers followed the practice of withholding the names of transgressors of the gambling laws well into the twentieth century. The justification was always, as one 1921 report put it, the "hope they will take the lesson to heart.")

"A continuation of present conditions will develop many professional and hardened criminals," the *Republican* warned in its 1922 editorial, "and may force some of them to face the bar of justice for some more serious crime, for gambling is just a stepping stone to other vices." The paper was technically correct, for gambling was surely associated with other criminal activity, most commonly bootlegging and prostitution. But it failed to make some crucial distinctions about what it called the "Art of Gambling." ("Some Higher Education in Pleasant Hill," read the subhead of the exposé.) So-called honest gamblers didn't consider gaming itself to be criminal, just cheating. And the cardsharps and dice mechanics considered gambling nothing but cheating. To them, that was the true "art" in gambling.

As straightforward and convenient as craps was, cheating at the game was similarly direct. There were some spectacularly difficult sleight-of-hand moves, especially controlled shots with fair dice, like the Whip Shot, known in the Midwest as the Pique Shot or Peekay Shot, or the Blanket Roll, or the Greek Shot. The more common approach to "slam-bang," as the dice mechanics called their special work, was to switch in doctored dice. Most Pleasant Hill crap games were played with what were called "candy store" or "drug store" dice, which, as the nickname makes clear, were picked up cheaply at a local store. It was easy to acquire a pair of crooked dice that matched these "cubes." Drake and Co., on McGee in downtown Kansas City, was one of the leading suppliers of such "gaffed," or doctored, dice.

The possibilities were varied. One was loaded dice. These were weighted in different ways so that they would not roll true, but would fall to show certain numbers much more often. If the dice were opaque, which many of the candy-store dice of the day were, the typical method was to drill a small hole in one of the dots, load the die with platinum, gold, or some type of metal amalgam, and then seal up the hole. This technique was called "plumbing the bones" or "plumbing the doctors." Usually, the loaded dice would be set to favor certain combinations. These were "percentage dice." "Passers" were set to favor winning bets. "Missouts" were loaded so that the 7 would come up more often. Sometimes cheaters would switch two different pairs of dice in at different times in a game. They would bet for winning or losing rolls depending on which were in play.

Other gaffed dice were called "shapes." In this version of the cheater's handiwork, the dice were doctored in a way so that they were no longer perfect cubes and would no longer roll true. From the standpoint of the sharp, some were stronger than others. For "flats," the cheater actually planed down the surface of one side, just a few thousands of an inch, to favor certain numbers coming up. Like loaded dice, shapes could be worked to serve as either missouts or passers. Other methods for manufacturing shapes included cutting the edges, beveling the surfaces of the dice to make them slightly convex or concave, and capping one of the surfaces of a die to make it roll a certain way more often.

Perhaps the most popular gaffed dice were "tops," short for "tops and bottoms," and also called "tees" or "tonys." Unlike loads or shapes, which could lose their action through wear, tops were foolproof. They were actually mis-spotted dice that could never roll certain combinations because they didn't have those numbers. Sometimes they were even called "mis-spots."

Whichever special dice were chosen, the cheaters still needed sleight of hand to make the dice do their dirty magic. A cheat had to "bust" the dice in at just the right time, and then "rip" them out of the game, too, so that the mark wouldn't "tumble," get suspicious or catch what was happening. This dice switching

could be developed to an exquisite level. In one particularly devastating switch, the dice mechanic would pick up the pair of
legitimate dice already in play, and with a simple, nonchalant
swing of the hand, roll them out again. In the instant before
the roll, he would switch in the doctored dice palmed in the
same hand and palm out the legitimate dice. Switches like this
were the highest expressions of the dice cheater's peculiar art.

A craps game could be as raucous as an Ottoman bazaar, especially as the game was played in the alleyways and livery stables
of Pleasant Hill. The pace of the game, what the dice men called
"the weight," seemed to be suited to cheating. There was the
shouting, the constant shifting of position by the players, the
blowing on the dice for good luck, the fans of cash gripped tightly
in the hand. (Indeed, an excellent move used the cover of the
bills to hide the switch.) But the margin of error was still excruci-
atingly fine. Cheaters always had to fear that even if they made
their switch perfectly, the fake dice could be noticed during play.
After all, if they wanted, the other players could handle and inspect the "bones" for themselves.

Dice even managed to bring the races together, routinely and
nonchalantly, into casual and unself-conscious social and commercial contact. By the Twenties, dice and crap shooting had already long been associated with African-Americans. As far back
as the eighteenth century, slaves were adapting the British game
of Hazard to their own style of play. Much of the rhyming patois
connected with dice—"Eighter from Decatur," "Nine-a from
Carolina," and so on—had apparently originated in the slang of
black gamblers. Still other dice slang was flat-out racist. Dice
were sometimes called "African dominoes," and one game was
dubbed "Abyssinian polo." Another was "Congo." Often, in the
South especially, craps was referred to bluntly as the "nigger
national sport."

In April 1921, the *Pleasant Hill Times* ran an item it had picked up from the *Cass County Leader* in nearby Harrisonville concerning some recent local arrests. "Constable Mose Mahaffey continues to work his dragnet in Pleasant Hill," the paper related. "On Friday afternoon of last week Mose suspicioned several of the Pleasant Hill inhabitants of flirting with the fickle Goddess of Chance." Apparently, Mahaffey had approached "a certain barn" with "a stealthy step" and when he spied through the window saw a scene of revivalist intensity. "There upon their knees, with bodies tense and eyes alert were gathered certain of Pleasant Hill's citizens, of various hues, calling upon the little cubes of ivory to favor them and imploring them with tears in their eyes to 'Little Joe' or 'Fever in the South.' "

Mahaffey arrested five local men. The paper made a point of noting the racial breakdown of the group as they were paraded before the local judge: white, black, black, black, white. "You will note," the paper duly instructed, "he had the colored part of the haul flanked by the white, making a good color scheme and a very neat array." The judge marked down their trials for the following month, "when he expects to hold a 'Crap Shooter's Convention,' " the paper reported.

Pleasant Hill's status as a railroad switch point for the great Missouri Pacific and Rock Island lines also contributed to its standing as a gambling center. In Pleasant Hill, card and dice mechanics didn't need to work the trains in search of suckers, as the cold-deckers in the trains whizzing through Ottawa did. They didn't have to worry about going out into the world, because the world came to them. Pleasant Hill, like many of the surrounding towns, had eagerly joined the furious competition at the turn of the century to win designation as a stop on the new lines being built by the railroad companies. And like other towns, it had had to make payoffs and sometimes steep concessions to the companies in order to lure them in. Both the "Mo Pac" and the Rock Island leased local lakes at one time in a bid to make Pleasant Hill a country resort destination. Pleasant Hill grew in direct proportion to the railroad's presence. The electrical system, the water system, even the local roads, all improved over the decade after the trains came to town.

By the Twenties, the rail lines had become Pleasant Hill's main arteries, continually pumping new blood in and out of the heart of the town. The town had a population of about 2,500, but hundreds more passed through at all times of the night and day. Train travelers often had lengthy waits while their engine was switched or until their connection came through. After the drought and the epidemics, the other big news in the fall of 1918 was the opening of Bert Gilmore's new twenty-four-hour restaurant on North Lake Street, which included a bold new feature: a ladies' room. "Something of this sort has been a prime need in this man's town for many moons," the *Times* observed approvingly. "For instance, on a recent night there were twenty-one women waiting between trains at the Missouri Pacific station. A place such as Gilmore's would have made very much of a hit in this instance."

Trains also meant train workers, crowds of them. And it wasn't just the engineers, conductors, porters, or the others who actually worked on the trains. There were also yard men, guards, switchmen, and the workers who handled the difficult job of maintaining the various stretches of track. These skilled, rough-and-ready "gandy dancers" often stayed in the area for weeks at a time, tending to a particular section of track and bunking at one of the town's several boardinghouses. Naturally, many of these workers were gambling men.

Pleasant Hill's downtown area was condensed, but it swarmed with people at all times of the night and day. And though the town appeared bucolic on the surface, it was far from sleepy. The overnight scene hopped. It couldn't compete with Kansas City just north, few cities could, but it was certainly a rural chip off that block. Gilmore's was far from alone on the graveyard shift. From 1910 and into the 1920s, Pleasant Hill easily sustained a handful of all-night establishments, on top of the regular places that operated during the day. The Beauchamp Café . . . Burton's Restaurant . . . Bastian Lunchcar . . . Bon-Ton Lunchroom . . . Japanese Garden—these eateries all took advantage of the steady stream of humanity moving through Pleasant Hill. Most of the druggists stayed open around the clock, too, because it was simply good business. Sometimes visitors wouldn't even start their shopping until midnight, so even grocery stores began staying open until one or two in the morning. For those who needed a room for the night, there were several hotels and boardinghouses available to accommodate them.

As the *Republican* had stated, with the bitter opposite of civic pride, "It is conceded that the Pleasant Hill instructors are experts and well equipped to deliver the goods." Allen Kennedy probably began to avail himself of these instructors sometime in his teens. Unlike magicians, cheaters don't start with books to learn. They go straight to other sharps for their specialized education. As Allen began this schooling, he discovered that he had a facility for the work.

As early as 1915, when he was eighteen, he even showed up in what seemed to be a harmless report in the *Pleasant Hill Register* about a big Halloween fest hosted by the Grange. The paper reported warmly that "the evening was spent in amusements and contests" and made a point of noting that Allen Kennedy and another young man had each won the "booby prizes." They came in last. But it may well have been a thrown game. The paper also noted that the winner of the first prize was Mrs. Beggs, the thirty-year-old wife of George Beggs, another farmer who lived just outside Pleasant Hill. The paper left out her maiden name, which happened to be Kennedy. She was Allen's older sister.

After he missed out on the call-up for the war in Europe, Allen decided to try a new line, as they might say in Pleasant Hill. As badly as David Verner wanted to get down to New York from Canada, Allen wanted to get off the farm. But he wasn't looking to end up in an office as a bank teller or clerk. He wasn't going to wait around to become what the hustlers called a "slave," a lifer stuck in a dead-end job with nothing to show for it but a skimpy pay envelope every week. He chose instead to become a thief. His first foray did indeed succeed in getting him off the farm. It took him clear out of Pleasant Hill altogether. Other than that, it was a complete failure.

The Missouri Pacific line typically parked boxcars loaded with merchandise in its Pleasant Hill yards. Some of the goods were for local trade, but much of it was slated for shipping out of town. Often the boxcars were left standing overnight until they could be coupled and routed to their final destination. The yards were largely unguarded and the boxcars attracted thieves as reliably as the hives dotting the orchards and groves of Cass County drew bees. Before long, Pleasant Hill found itself in a swarm.

"It is bad policy to feed sugar to children," the *Republican* chided once more in 1922, this time turning its ire on the chaotic situation in the train yards. "For once they get a taste of sweet things it's so hard to 'break away.' The interest alone on the losses charged up to the Pleasant Hill yards would pay two night watchmen the year round." As it stood, the city's lone night watchman, who was responsible for keeping order throughout the raucous downtown area every night, couldn't possibly keep up. Neither, apparently, could the rail companies' security details. Thieves helped themselves pretty freely and the only fallout from this unfettered larceny seemed to be an increase in both the workload of the insurance companies and the consternation of the *Republican*. As it did with most of the break-ins in Pleasant Hill, the

Republican constantly speculated, without offering any particular evidence, that the boxcar robberies were the product of what it dubbed "local 'talent.' "

In the late spring of 1920, when Allen was almost twenty-three, several boxcars filled with automotive accessories were emptied quietly one night in the Missouri Pacific yards. This heist was definitely the work of "local talent." And it was another local talent, the reliable Mose Mahaffey, who cracked the case almost a full year later. Mahaffey solved it because he had a sharp memory, and because of a seemingly inviolable rule of life in the town. At some point, everyone comes back to Pleasant Hill. They just can't stay away.

In 1920, Ona Courtney was still just a kid really, at eighteen almost five years younger than his friend Allen Kennedy. Like Allen, he too felt the urge, the pull, to do something other than farm, something with a little excitement, something a bit larcenous perhaps. Unlike Allen, he had already been stung for giving in to his urges. Courtney had been convicted of the high crime of chicken stealing. In the spring of 1920, he decided to improve on that fearsome record by joining some eight or nine other like-minded Pleasant Hill youths and focusing on those fat boxcars sitting so alluringly in the Mo Pac yard. One night, he and the rest of the crew cleaned them out.

This light-fingered gang wouldn't have qualified as successors to the James Gang. Within a couple of weeks, Mahaffey had rounded up most of them. Two other local youths disappeared not long after the heist. One was Courtney, a definite suspect. The other was Allen Kennedy. When Kennedy vanished from Pleasant Hill shortly after the boxcar heist, it apparently wasn't noticed at first. Besides the other skills he was honing, Allen seemed to have already developed a talent at avoiding attention. He was certainly handsome, in a rugged way, with dark hair and eyes and a wiry build. He was laconic, yet always polite, and seemed to stay just on the edge of the shadows. After the heist, he and Courtney left Pleasant Hill in a hurry and headed to Chicago. It was a smart play, as the grifters would say, because as they were running, a warrant was issued for Courtney back in Pleasant Hill.

Allen and Courtney stayed in Chicago for more than six months. The Windy City could make Kansas City look like Pleasant Hill in comparison. Thieving, bootlegging, cheating, cards, dice. Chicago offered opportunities in all of them, the chance to learn from the best in the Midwest. It was the world beyond. The two stayed on until one day Courtney got that urge that just seems to take hold of everyone from Pleasant Hill who finds himself far from his hometown.

"A few days ago a longing for his old friends and companions beset him," the *Cass County Leader*, a Harrisonville paper, reported of Courtney in its January 27, 1921, edition, "and leaving his new home in Chicago he returned to Pleasant Hill, arriving there Monday." Pleasant Hill was a small town, but it was still teeming, jammed and milling constantly with flocks of outsiders, train travelers, salesmen, and others just passing through. It wouldn't have been hard to hide there. But Courtney didn't even get a chance to try. As soon as he arrived, he ran into an old acquaintance.

"He had no more than looked over the town," the *Leader* reported, "when he was spied by Constable Mose Mahaffey. Mose, it appears, has a splendid memory." Mahaffey braced Courtney and made him stand for a search. The constable checked through his pockets for identification and then, as the *Leader* noted, "a smile of satisfaction lighted his erstwhile serious countenance as he read a warrant for Ona Courtney's arrest, for that is the name of the man he had found." Mahaffey placed Courtney under arrest and took him first before the Pleasant Hill justice of the peace, T. H. Cloud, who set bail at a whopping $1,000. When Courtney couldn't make it, Mahaffey took him over to the county lockup in Harrisonville.

George Chamberlin, the Cass County prosecuting attorney, expressed "disgust" after interrogating Courtney, the *Leader* reported, because "the prisoner admitted his guilt." "Mr. Chamberlin had hoped that the man would strenuously deny all knowledge of the crimes charged to him and that there would be a stiff trial," the paper explained. "You see Mr. Chamberlin has not been the prosecuting attorney of Cass County for a very long time and this would have been his first opportunity to display his powers as a defender of the law and order of the community." Still, Courtney's case was set down to be heard by circuit court judge Ewing Cockrell during the next session. It was a swell homecoming.

How did Allen Kennedy, Ona Courtney's good friend, partner in crime, and fellow lamster, react to his friend's predicament? Did he run again, moving farther east and away from the epicenter of their current troubles? Did he burrow still further into the mine-deep underworld of Chicago? Of course not. Shortly after Ona Courtney made his ill-fated return to his beloved hometown, Allen made his.

Courtney had returned to Pleasant Hill on a Tuesday, the twenty-fifth of January, only to be picked up immediately by Mahaffey and stored in the hoosegow over in Harrisonville. By the end of that very same week, Allen was also back in Pleasant Hill. And instead of staying out of sight or laying low on his parents' farm, he headed straight over to Harrisonville to the county jail to check on his friend. It was not a decision an experienced thief would have made. Within minutes, he had not only announced his presence back in the county, he had alerted the authorities of his ties with Courtney. As the two friends began to chat, the jailer, Sheriff Dell Dutro, made a point of sitting nearby to eavesdrop. Within just a few minutes, the two friends gave up enough to blow the whole game.

"By their talk the Sheriff judged that Kennedy knew all about the little 'party' or was a member of it," the *Cass County Democrat* reported. Now Dutro braced Kennedy. He took him aside and asked him flat-out if he, too, had been on that boxcar job the previous spring. Allen denied it. What heist? He didn't know a thing about it, he told Dutro. The sheriff pressed further and Kennedy "finally admitted his guilt," the *Leader* wrote. He was placed under arrest, "lagged" as the cheaters would say, and Dutro took him straightaway to the Harrisonville justice of the peace, Frank Bybee. Allen decided to plead guilty before Bybee, who disposed of the case almost as fast as a good dice mechanic could switch in a pair of tops. He took the guilty plea from Allen and then fined him $90, to be paid within ten days and guaranteed by his father. "Sheriff Dutro is to be congratulated upon the skill with which he handled this matter," the *Leader* crowed, employing an image with which Allen would surely have been familiar: "for although he is new at the game he goes after his work like an old hand at the game."

It was the first big job of Allen's new criminal career, and he had ended up right back where he started. But at least he knew that his luck, the luck that had kept him out of the war, was still good. It was better than Ona Courtney's, anyway. In March, Courtney drew a five-year stint in the state pen. The judge immediately paroled him but also ordered that he serve out the five-year parole stretch on Frank Taylor's work farm. If Courtney had been looking to get off the farm, he hadn't gotten too far.

Allen had no choice but to return to the farm and to his parents. They were not happy. They were stand-up people, what the cheaters called "square paper." They didn't need this whole mess and Allen's father certainly didn't need the $90 fine. He had already had a couple of strokes and was not well. It was the third stroke of "paralysis," as they called it then, that finally put Allen's father down for good. John Ed Kennedy died in late January 1922, a year almost to the day since his son had returned from Chicago to his hometown and his arrest. Allen and his brother Mallory, the unmarried sons, were on the farm when their father died.

When her husband died, Hattie Kennedy immediately petitioned the probate court not to make any moves against his estate. She had little and didn't want it threatened. Their holdings were worth less than $700, she swore to the court, the personal property consisting of four horses, three cows, four hogs, some farming implements, and ten U.S. War Savings Certificates from 1918 worth $46. By the time she sought this protection from the court, both Kennedy boys had already moved away. It was less than a month after their father died.

Allen went to live in downtown Pleasant Hill. By the end of 1922, he would be living just up from the First Street scene and its "business concerns that Keep late or all night hours downtown," as the *Republican* had put it. He would be hitched to an older woman and he would be working steadily. In his case, the *Republican* was actually wrong. Gambling had not led to more serious crime. It was the boxcar misadventure that had led Allen back to the "art of gambling." Allen clearly didn't want to go straight. He wasn't looking to be square paper. But now he was going to be smart and diligent. He was going to leave behind the chicken thieves and take up a deck of cards and a pair of dice in earnest. He was going to take care of his hands. He still wanted to be a thief. But now he was going to be an artist about it. And what an artist he became.

4

WITH IT

John Sprong was as obsessed with cards as Dai Vernon was. He worked as a doorman and then as a night watchman just so that he would have extra quiet time on the job when he could practice. And he used to tell Vernon that his idea of a dream vacation would be to go out to the country with a suitcase filled with nothing but decks of cards, sit under a tree, and just work on sleight of hand all day and all night.

Although he was twenty-seven years older than Vernon, Sprong and the younger magician had struck up a solid, if long-distance, friendship. Whenever Vernon was in Chicago, where Sprong lived, they would session. Vernon thought Sprong was extremely clever, and he admired Sprong's original versions of many sleights. Sprong also had a keen interest in gambling moves. He had studied *The Expert at the Card Table* closely and occasionally he even picked up tips and bits of information about cardsharps. Chicago was swarming with them. It was a regional capital of cheating, known in hustler patois as "the Village."

Once, in the early Twenties, Sprong even went over to see Frederick J. Drake, the Chicago publisher who was putting out the second edition of *The Expert*. He pestered Drake, trying hard to get him to reveal the true identity of S. W. Erdnase. Drake wouldn't tell him much, but he did reveal that the author's real name was E. S. Andrews, a simple reversal of S.W. Erdnase. (As basic an anagram as that was, many magicians had apparently missed it.) It was a clue of a sort, but despite his snooping, it didn't lead Sprong to the author of the book. Sprong would write to Vernon regularly, giving him reports on Erdnase and other news, and swapping tricks and moves. His sign-off to Vernon was always the same: "Yours for pure sleight of hand."

In the late Twenties, Vernon was in Asheville, North Carolina, when he received a letter from Sprong that he would remember for decades to come. Vernon would be able to recite it almost word for word from memory. "There's a rumor," Sprong announced in his letter, "that out West somewhere there's a man who can deal from the middle of the pack." Vernon knew Sprong was skilled enough to understand the importance of the sleight and to imagine how great the sharp who had mastered it must be. Sprong mentioned that he knew Vernon was constantly traveling around the country, cutting silhouettes and sessioning with gamblers.

"If you ever get out West and can trace down this gambler," Sprong continued, "I'm willing to pay $100 for any information at all." He wasn't expecting much, he stressed to Vernon, certainly not the details of the sleight. "Just get me any information about him." He repeated what it was worth to him: "I'd be willing to send $100." It was a generous proposal, especially for Sprong, who made his living at low-paying day jobs. He was not a professional performer. The mention of a payment was intended to emphasize how serious he was.

Sprong's offer of money made Vernon smile. But it didn't

make him believe that the center deal really existed. He answered Sprong's letter right away. Don't worry, he wrote to the older sleight-of-hand man. Save your money. "I'd be just as anxious to meet him as you would. You don't have to send me any $100."

When he first arrived in New York from Canada as the Great War was coming to a close, David Verner didn't have a definite plan or a strong vision of what would come next. He wasn't exactly aimless. But he was young, just twenty-three. He had some vague ideas of attending the Art Students League to study painting. And he had some definite ideas about staying in the city, enjoying it, and learning more about magic from some of the fabled names he knew through reading. He certainly couldn't see ten years ahead, when he would be married, with a young son, traveling around the country and receiving letters from top magicians with tips about mysterious card handlers.

David had tried to sell his New York adventure to his family by vowing that he planned to study art seriously, and perhaps become a society portrait painter. It was the consolation prize for the engineering career he had rejected. But it was really just a cover, a story to tell his mother about why he was staying on in New York. The Art Students League, on Fifty-seventh Street in Manhattan, should have been the perfect place for David Verner. It combined top-name teachers and rigorous instruction. Yet it had a relaxed culture, with a flexible curriculum and no set requirements.

But even that setup was too restrictive for David. Although he may have attended some classes sporadically, he never enrolled officially (the school has no record of him on file). He let himself be convinced, while talking with working artists, that art school would just stifle his creativity and originality anyway. He was, however, much more diligent when it came to the League's regular Friday night parties, which attracted a lively crowd of artists, writers, cartoonists, and society types. Those he tried never to miss.

David's schooling in New York City was to come from various institutions of an even less structured nature than the Art Students League. Soon after arriving, he began to make the rounds of the city's famous magic shops in Midtown. He started with Martinka's Palace of Magic on Broadway, where he was bitterly disappointed. He had been reading about Martinka's for years, since he was a boy, and had built it up in his mind. He expected it to actually look like a palace. Instead, it was a dark, dingy little place. There were just a handful of little tricks, standard items that were well-known, displayed in a dusty case. An old woman was behind the counter when David came in but when he tried to ask her something, she handed him a catalogue brusquely in answer. "If you want anything call me," she said as she wandered off to the back of the store.

He had much better luck over at Clyde Powers's magic shop on Forty-second Street. Powers's shop was newer, just a couple of years old, and much more modern-looking than Martinka's. The very first time he was there, David completely fooled the man behind the counter, a well-known magician named Paul Carlton, with some card tricks. When David approached the counter, he soured Carlton by offering to pay $20 for any trick that fooled him. Here's some arrogant rich kid, Carlton must have thought, but he couldn't fool him, and when David performed a few of his own card tricks, Carlton immediately ran to the back of the store to get Powers. "Young man, you must be pretty good if Paul Carlton says so," Powers announced as he greeted David. "He's one of the best magicians in New York."

Powers tried to fool David with a card trick of his own, one he said was so powerful he didn't show it to his regular customers. He told David to get that $20 ready. It was indeed a good trick, a fooler under normal circumstances. But David caught the method, which he immediately proceeded to detail for Powers. "My God," Powers exclaimed, "you mean to say you just analyzed that right now?" Powers was deeply impressed with the handsome young Canadian. They chatted amiably and Powers went out of his way to make David feel comfortable.

Powers pointed to the back of the store. "We don't have our customers back there, only professional magicians," he said of this inner sanctum. It was where the top magicians gathered, and where the deepest secrets of the art were discussed freely. "You can go back there whenever you like," he said, adding that David should make the shop "your home." David did, practically. He started coming in almost every afternoon, his attendance more faithful than at the parties at the Art Students League. It was in Powers's back room that David met still more of the era's leading magicians—Harry Kellar, Dr. James William Elliott, even the great Harry Houdini himself. He was thrilled when he got to know these giants of the art, and others he had long heard about, and long dreamed of meeting. But he wasn't intimidated. He knew now that he would be able to hold his own.

He was more uncertain about how he was going to make a living. After the military, David had no job and few prospects. Despite his skills and inventiveness, he was no professional magician. In fact, he didn't even consider performing magic professionally when first in New York. He looked at it as an avocation, an art to be pursued and courted. His performing ambitions at that point were still confined mostly to demonstrating tricks and moves for other devotees. He was content to savor his daily magic sessions at Powers's shop, trying out new material on the magicians he met there and absorbing and improving upon their secrets.

As he became more known around town, he struck up strong friendships with various characters in the magic community. One was Sam Margules, a warm, energetic man who worked primarily as a producer of magic shows. Margules had worked as an assistant with Horace Goldin, the "Whirlwind Illusionist" out in Coney Island. He was also close to Houdini, having almost a father-son relationship with the great escape artist. Margules had been something of a performer himself, specializing in a mind-reading act under the stage name Ramee Sami. He was both well liked and well connected, certainly a trick in itself. And he was truly a caring man, a guardian angel to wayward magicians, lending them money and lining up engagements. He made a point of taking David under his wing as he struggled to establish a life for himself in New York. The two would become close, as close as brothers for a time.

Margules not only took David into his home (where David marveled at his first tastes of Jewish home cooking), but he also got him his first real job in New York. The two men had met in Coney Island and now Margules assured David that work was plentiful there. "There are hundreds of jobs on Coney Island," he told him with finality. "I'll find you something."

To David, Coney Island was more than just a far-flung neighborhood or a weekend playground. It was a complete world unto itself, a magical world. If the Ottawa racetrack had been his elementary school in the ways of hucksters and con men, Coney Island was now his graduate program. But it gave him much more than just a continuing education in trickery or new insights into how cheaters worked and talked. It also gave him a new last name. It gave him a unique trade that would keep him afloat during the thin times. It even gave him a wife. David entered this world of Coney Island in rapture.

Coney Island after the Great War was much more than an amusement park. It was like an endlessly entertaining series of stage sets, each presented to the accompaniment of what was, for David, an intriguing musical chorus he heard only there. The tunes of the carousel blended with the calliope, which blended with the player piano. Then the rising and falling sounds of the barkers and the games joined in. Surf Avenue and the boardwalk, miles long in those days, were the main thoroughfares, where a million people might descend on any given weekend. There they filled every last square foot of beach and feasted on the first real American hot dogs, the quality of the franks steadily going up as a price war between Feltman's Ocean Pavilion and Nathan's drove the bill down to just a nickel.

Coney Island featured ferocious roller coasters, like "The Dragon Gorge" and "The Mile-High Sky Ride," and a stomach-wrenching parachute jump. The carnival-like Dreamland Circus Sideshow was a particular favorite of David's. It was where he first saw magician Al Flosso (born Albert Levinson), the "Coney Island Fakir" who worked several times a day doing the classic egg-bag routine—in which he caused an egg to vanish repeatedly from a small black bag—and pulling coins out of the air. Flosso would also become a close friend. Dreamland also offered classic carny sideshows like the bearded lady, sword swallowers, and a woman's talking head suspended on the tip of a sword. Over at the lavish, minareted Luna Park, the "Tower of Jewels" sparkled with so many blazing electric lights that it seemed to be trying to go chest to chest with the Great White Way over in Manhattan.

David soon found himself surrounded by the grifters and cheaters of Coney Island. For the first time in his life, he was right inside their scams. He wasn't being chased off wagon wheels at the racetrack in Ottawa anymore. The first job Margules secured for him was with a guy named Goldie, who ran many of the rigged games at Coney Island. Goldie put Vernon to work running a tag-dart game.

It seemed simple enough. A customer would throw a dart and try to hit a numbered ticket, a cardboard disk hanging on a board. If the dart penetrated the ticket, the customer would win a prize corresponding to the number. If the customer missed the ticket, he would be given the closest ticket. It seemed like a sure winner, just like all scams. The prizes ran the gamut from valuable items like watches and leather pocketbooks, even hunting knives with $20 bills stuck to them, to worthless junk. David quickly learned how to partially cover up the number on the ticket with his finger so it looked like a different number corresponding to a cheaper prize. It was easy to make an 18 look like a 10, or a 19 like an 11.

He learned other carny tricks, too. He saw how the guy who would guess a person's weight could, while seeming to steady the chair on the scale, push or pull on it to add or subtract pounds. At the glassblower's booth, customers would pick a card to win one of the handmade glass pieces. David saw how the operator would then switch their chosen card at the last second, just like a magician, for a blank card or one offering just a trinket. The bowling pin game was rigged, and the venerable milk-bottle toss could be magnetized so the bottles wouldn't always fall over. All the admission booths routinely shortchanged people. Even the shooting gallery, which was tough to rig, would provide only 17 or 18 pellets for the gun, when the sign promised 21 for a quarter. If, in the unlikely event the operators were caught, they would just act as though it was an isolated oversight.

David also learned how to pepper his speech with the patois of the Coney Island carny grifters. These words and phrases would liven up the patter accompanying his brilliant card tricks. The game, the con itself, was "the store" and the gimmick to the game was the "gaff." But as that word became more well-known, it was shortened simply to "G," as in, "What's the G of the joint?" A "grand" was $1,000 (which also became known as a "G") and a "C-note" was $100. Both those terms became commonplace, too. Even $5 had an alias. It was "a pound."

The most important phrase was "with it," which meant that a person was in on the scams. If a person were approached by a grifter trying to start something and said "with it" he would be left alone. David thought it was almost magical in that way, an incantation. But the tone was also important. Grifters were street psychologists, too, David saw. If a person used a haughty or hesitant tone when saying "with it" he might be taken for a slummer trying to be "half-smart." Then the con men would try twice as hard to trim him.

The distinctive New York accent convinced David Verner to change his last name, too. He had started using "Dave" and even his nickname "Dai" for his first name, but he found that New Yorkers had difficulty pronouncing Verner correctly. They said "oy" for "er," as in "Hoivey and Goity were sitting on the coib reading the *Woild*." Verner came out "Voynoy." It seemed like everyone talked like this all over the city. David became frustrated having to correct people constantly. He decided he wouldn't fight it. He was also aware of the popular dance duo Vernon and Irene Castle. So, he became Dave Vernon, and then Dai Vernon. Eventually, he even started to talk like something of a New Yorker himself, so much so that his mother, in horror, told him over the phone during one of his regular calls to Canada that she could hardly recognize his voice anymore. He sounded, she said, "so beastly American."

It wasn't all fun and games at Coney Island for Dave Vernon. He was now on the inside of the carny life. He was "with it." But he found the boy from Victorian Ottawa could still feel guilty about the cheating. Sometimes he would let customers win fair and square at the tag-dart game. He even learned firsthand what it was like to be taken himself. One rainy afternoon he was working the dart game when a man rushed in, announcing that he was waiting for his "old friend" Goldie and was out of cigarettes. "Could I borrow your coat to run across the street to buy some?" the man asked, eying Vernon's fine British raincoat. It was a beautiful coat, certainly expensive at $60, but Vernon passed it over to the man to borrow. Naturally, he disappeared. Vernon felt like a sap. A lot of these little ploys on the grift were cheap. They might be entertaining to learn about, but they were little more than common thievery. There was nothing skillful about running off with someone's coat. That approach was decidedly "inartistic," as Erdnase might put it.

Vernon decided not to stay in the games for long, after all. When he quit Goldie's dart game, he was faced once more with figuring out how to scratch out a living in Coney Island. He definitely wanted to stay in New York, but he wasn't all that keen on scuffling around in these cheap grifts. His greatest fear was the thought of having to return to provincial Canada to take up the deathly dull life of a clerk. He still hadn't seriously considered becoming a professional magician yet and now he saw that he didn't have it in him to become a full-fledged cheater.

His solution was to go to work as an artist, but not in magic or painting. To make money, he would not look ahead to the modern, but back to the quaint. Instead of cards or a brush, he picked up a pair of scissors and became a silhouette cutter. What seemed like a highly unlikely career choice, which would prove to be a lifeline for Vernon, was actually based on an experience he'd had as a boy on a summer vacation with his family in Old Orchard Beach, Maine. He had happened upon a silhouette cutter on the pier and then tried to imitate the man's work back at the Old Orchard House, where the family was staying. His father judged his beginner's silhouettes as more sophisticated than the portraits cut by the man on the pier.

Silhouette cutting originally caught Vernon's fancy because it seemed like an easy, enjoyable way to make some money. At Old Orchard Beach, David had been impressed most of all with the weight of an umbrella cover the man had hanging on his stand. He was using it as a bag, and David felt how heavy it had gotten with the quarters the man had collected that afternoon for cutting portraits. Silhouettes were already a fading art by the early twentieth century, redolent of the days of the hoop skirt and the quill pen. The so-called scissor artists had long been supplanted by photographers. Yet people were still intrigued when they came upon someone cutting shadow portraits. Often, they decided to plunk down the 50 cents or so to give it a try. It was like getting a new effect out of something that had been long forgotten. That was an approach that Vernon would use in his magic, too.

Vernon had recently met the zany Larry Grey, a fledgling British card magician who was also trying to scrape together a living in Coney Island, and the two teamed up to run a booth on Kensington Walk, which led down to Steeplechase Pier. Grey would sell magic tricks, fake decks, and cheap little props, and Vernon would cut silhouettes. He put together a stand, cut several ornate silhouettes to decorate it, and set up shop. The first night, he took in a whopping $18 cutting "silooties," as they called them in Coney Island.

There was only one other silhouette cutter on Coney Island, a man named Perry who had a booth at Luna Park. Even he had to admit that Vernon was, indeed, a natural with the scissors. The two "shadow artists" became friendly and Perry gave him a valuable tip on how to sell a portrait to an indecisive customer. "Never ask a person if they want it," he told Vernon, "say 'Just stand exactly as you are. . . . Hold your head up a little.' Cut the silhouette and hand it to them. Nine times out of ten they'll take it."

Vernon and Grey, who would come to be known as "The Dizzy Wizard," began rooming together. They lived for the nights of Coney Island, working until late and then having something to eat at three in the morning. Then they would sit up and talk magic until daylight was breaking. Grey was also skillful with a deck and was developing a loud, comic style, completely different from Vernon's, but entertaining, with commercial possibilities. The two roommates would sleep late, until a nearby bank bell tower clanged out "The Star Spangled Banner" at one o'clock. They would then leap out of bed and, because there wasn't much to do on Coney Island in the daytime, they'd spend the day on the beach, swimming and lolling. Only at sundown would they head over to open their booth.

Although the first time Vernon met the petite, ravishing Eugenia Hayes was at a country fair in New Canaan, Connecticut, she too was a veteran of the hectic Coney Island scene that Vernon loved so much. She was still a teenager, but she already worked as one of the two lookers in Goldin's classic "Sawing a Woman in Two" illusion. Because she was so shy, the audience didn't get to see much of young Miss Hayes. She played only the lower half of the artfully vivisected woman, so all they ever glimpsed were her feet.

When they first met and chatted at the Connecticut fair, Vernon was instantly impressed because she knew that the word *silhouette* came from Etienne de Silhouette, a minister in the French government under Louis XIV. She had long had show business ambitions of her own, and had been trying to break into musicals before she landed the job in Goldin's act. She was a Brooklyn girl who lived in Sheepshead Bay, just next to Coney Island. (There was even a vague legend in her family that a king of England had once deeded Coney Island to her ancestors. Supposedly, it had then been stolen away by corrupt New York politicians.) Jeanne, as she was called, was a little less than five feet tall, weighed about 85 pounds, had dark blond hair and big eyes with lashes Vernon swore were an inch and a half long. He swooned when they first talked, and soon after that he decided he wanted her to be his wife. They were married in Manhattan, at the Little Church Around the Corner, in 1924, some three months before Vernon turned thirty.

The Twenties marked Dai Vernon's great creative surge, his emergence as a revolutionary force in his chosen art. It was the period when he blended dexterity, psychology, and improvisation into his close-up magic and crafted many of his most enduring tricks and techniques. There's an old saw in magic that if only the spectators could actually see the incredible sleights behind the tricks, they'd be even more impressed. That really is magic, they'd say. The truth behind the maxim is only sharpened when the spectators are other magicians, who presumably should know what's going on even if they can't see it. To other magicians, even to other acknowledged masters of the art, Dai Vernon was a little like a character in a blues song, someone who might have sold his soul to the devil himself in exchange for his unearthly skills.

The opening years of the twentieth century had seen a flowering of sorts in sleight of hand, a rebirth of interest in that branch of magic. But the trend had taken a turn toward the fad. The wrong type of sleights, in Vernon's estimation, had become popular. So-called flourishes and card manipulation, flashy, obvious moves such as one-handed fans and back palms, which were designed to play well on a stage, became all the rage. They were meant to declare, openly, how skillful the magician was. In his classic 1909 book *The Art of Magic,* T. Nelson Downs, who knew something about putting sleights over on stage, was already deriding (with the help of his ghostwriter John Northern Hilliard) how that style of magic had "degenerated into a mere juggling performance."

Downs, Leipzig, Malini, and a few others, despite their stage successes, had helped, through their influence on other magicians, move the art back toward the intimate level where they thought the true miracles belonged. But it was Dai Vernon who really pushed close-up magic into the modern era. He was like Ernest Hemingway in that regard. Hemingway certainly didn't invent writing. He didn't even invent naturalism or realism. But he refined his art, and brought to it an electrifying new sensibility, style, and language that was so startling in its time that it seemed it must be new. Vernon did the same thing with magic in the Twenties. But instead of words on a page, he used gambler's sleights, psychology, and improvisational nerve with a deck of cards. And he did it, at first at least, without performing much for the general public.

Vernon wasn't alone, of course, but he was the main catalyst. A group of like-minded sleight-of-hand artists began to gather around him, elite practitioners of a style of wicked and uninflected close-up tricks that Vernon felt best fulfilled the potential of magic as an art. The city was the epicenter and they became known as the New York Card Men, the so-called Inner Circle. Their association with one another was based in friendship as well, but they were really conducting an unending session.

Leipzig was one member of this Inner Circle. So was Al Baker, a comic magician and longtime veteran of the Chautauqua circuit. They were the seasoned professionals of the group. Others were Dr. Jacob Daley, a noted plastic surgeon and amateur magician with soft hands who worked closely with Vernon to develop his techniques for improvising his way through card tricks. Arthur Finley (or Findley, as it was sometimes spelled), also an amateur magician, was a commercial artist by trade and a startlingly clever inventor of several influential moves and ruses with cards. Sam Horowitz was another member of the gang, a quirky professional who performed under the stage names Leo Hartz and Mohammed Bey. They were mavericks and innovators all.

But as great as these other magicians were (and their tricks are still performed by magicians today), Vernon was the ringleader. He became the hottest soloist in the band, the Babe Ruth in the Murderers Row. Nobody could quite match his sense of invention and sheer skill. They also couldn't match his mania. In an obsessive art, he was the most obsessed. Stories quickly sprung up about just how single-minded Dai Vernon could be when it came to cards.

Time meant nothing to him when he was working on a sleight or a trick. At night, he could spend hours with nothing but a deck, working through the wee hours, never leaving his spot at the table. In the morning, the only change, it would seem, was the new cigarette burning away at the corner of his mouth. That would be fresh. Dr. Daley would say that cards should be held gently, like flowers, and Vernon really did hold them as if they were living things. When he went to see the latest Ziegfield extravaganza "Rio Rita" with magician Fred Keating, rather than relaxing and getting an eyeful of the hordes of scantily clad dancers, Vernon spent the whole show bugging Keating about some card move he had just demonstrated for Vernon at dinner before the show.

Perhaps the most enduring tale of Vernon's obsession with cards followed the birth of his first son, Ted, in 1926. On the night Jeanne was at the hospital, Vernon was at home with Larry Grey. He was, of course, working on yet another new card effect. He had divided the deck into two random piles and was instructing Grey to select a card from one of them. The phone rang, interrupting his instructions to Grey. Vernon answered and then listened for a moment to the news of the birth of his son. When he hung up the phone, he immediately turned back to Grey and, without skipping a beat, went back to instructing him on how to continue with the trick. Vernon always insisted this anecdote was a tall tale, a "legend" that was related to great effect by the comic magician Judson Cole, a noted joker. But the story was always told in great detail and magicians all over town believed it. By then, they could easily picture Vernon behaving that way.

Except for Leipzig and Baker, the members of the Inner Circle were largely unknown to the general public. But other magicians were starting to hear about them through an influential column penned by Max Holden in *The Sphinx* magic magazine. Holden, a magician who by the end of the Twenties would open his own chain of magic shops, called the column "Trouping Around in Magic." The twist was that he would give only detailed descriptions of the effects. He didn't describe the methods used because he wasn't privy to them. Vernon's name began to appear regularly, often associated with the effects that, without any explanation of the methods, sounded impossible. Indeed, they sounded like real magic.

Holden's columns were followed with great excitement by magicians around the country. They spread Vernon's influence in the art before he had even become a professional performer. Some of the more diligent magicians in the hinterland would apply themselves to coming up with their own methods of achieving a Vernon effect they'd read about. Without really being aware of it, the New York Card Men were now helping to spark creativity in magicians they had never met. The aura of the Inner Circle widened.

Within the magic community in New York City, their underground celebrity grew to even absurd dimensions. One day when he was buying some socks at Macy's, Horowitz changed a half-dollar into a quarter for a stunned sales clerk. News of what he had done spread quickly around town and many of the amateur magicians started to claim the incident as their own. Vernon laughed when they didn't even bother to change the setting of the story to Gimbel's instead of Macy's or the item being purchased to a tie instead of socks.

Once, when he was sessioning with Horowitz and Finley after a magic-society meeting, Vernon played a joke on some magicians who were eavesdropping on them, trying to pick up their secrets. Vernon made a big show of demonstrating a move that was purposely useless. He simply made it up on the spot. He made sure the other magicians were watching as he began whispering, leaning in conspiratorially to his two friends. He slid a card slowly halfway into the deck, rotated it completely, and then pushed it in. Soon after, it seemed like all the amateur card magicians in New York were imitating this move without the slightest idea that it actually meant nothing. To them, if it came from Vernon, it had to be important.

Some of Vernon's most original, most enduring tricks came during this creative era. Many were improvements on or influenced by existing tricks. The great Leipzig had a pet effect called the "Slow Motion Coin Vanish." As he went into the trick, he would announce that it wasn't necessary for the "quickness of the hand to deceive the eye," and then gently, leisurely, vanish a coin from his fingertips. Vernon thought the same effect could work with a card. It was common to vanish a card onstage, but it was much tougher to do it close-up, using just sleight of hand. Vernon would take it between his fingers, and it would seem to slowly melt away. Then, just as slowly and gently, he would bring it back to his fingertips. Vernon would smile, as if he were relieved at the card's return.

In the devastating, and risky, "Five Card Mental Force," Vernon distilled the concept of the think-a-card trick to its essence. Such effects, in which a spectator merely thought of a card rather than picking one out of the deck, had grown in popularity. But most were based on rough ruses or lengthy, complicated shuffling or dealing sequences. (Some were also based on the premise that, if presented correctly, the spectator would be left with the impression later that he or she had thought of a card, when what the person had actually done was look at one in the deck and then thought of it.) But Vernon wanted to strip down the effect so that it really appeared that he, too, was thinking of the card the spectator was thinking of. It was Keane's approach taken to the extreme.

Vernon kept applying stricter conditions for himself when trying to devise a new version (it was not for nothing that they called them card "problems" or "experiments" in those days) until he came up with his masterpiece. Essentially, it involved talking a person into choosing one particular card out of five he'd casually placed on the table. There was no sleight of hand at all, just pure psychology. "You don't draw a card, you merely think of one" became his motto.

The Jazz Age was in full rollick when Vernon developed his improvisational approach to card tricks: beginning a trick without knowing exactly what the ending was going to be or how he was going to get there. In a sense, he would let the effect take him and his spectators for a ride. This was pure jazz, swirled with a measure of Erdnase, of course. Vernon's new approach allowed him to assess the setting, the demeanor of his audience, the lay of the cards, and coincidence. He was able to produce ever more out-of-reach effects, tricks that came one time only and then were gone. The next time around he might go in a completely different direction.

Here, indeed, was a jazz soloist, with cards as his horn, who would start to blow, building up steam as the notes reeled out in unexpected, surprising directions. Here, too, was modern art. "I don't feel the same way twice," said the great, haunted cornetist Bix Beiderbecke, another prodigy from a far-off town who loved to run through the New York night, chasing his muse. "It's one of the things I like about jazz, kid. I don't know what's going to happen. Do you?" Vernon didn't always know, either. But he knew that whatever did happen, it would be magic.

He didn't always want to know what was going to happen with the cards. It was more exciting for him, fresh and never boring. This new approach ran counter to the vast majority of magic tricks, which by their very nature had to be carefully planned, even scripted. But it didn't mean Vernon totally winged it. He actually worked quite hard at practicing this seemingly casual artistic attitude, devising scenarios on which to improvise. As he pursued this study, he and "Doc" Daley would sit for hours testing each other, measuring how the other would improvise a given situation to a magical conclusion.

Sometimes, more than one "out" would present itself, and the magician had to decide which was the more powerful. The process spurred ever more creative tricks, tricks that form the bedrock of the modern canon. But this approach, too, was tough to write up. When Vernon finally did include it in one of his card books a few decades later, the only title he could think of was "The Trick That Cannot Be Explained." Essentially, it's an attitude, he concluded. As for method, well, there were "52 methods"—as many as there were cards in the deck.

It was getting to be almost routine for Vernon to fool the top magicians of the day with his innovative techniques. They had come to expect it, and many thrilled to it. He was using gambling sleights they didn't know, and when he used sleights or principles they knew he did it with a whole new slant they couldn't pick up on. Occasionally, magicians would ask him where they could learn to do what he did. More often than not, he gladly responded by directing them to *The Expert at the Card Table*. They would recoil, protesting that the book was too difficult, too much like "geometry" to get anything out of it. Vernon's secret text continued to hide in plain sight.

One magician who didn't relish being fooled, by Vernon or anyone else, was Harry Houdini. Vernon's chance to try came one day in 1922 at the Great Northern Hotel in Chicago. He made the most of it.

To the general public, Houdini, then forty-eight, was the most famous magician in the world. To magicians, though, he was primarily an escape artist. They looked at it as an entirely different line. He did do stage magic shows, with elaborate illusions, but it was the escapes that had brought him worldwide renown. To Vernon, these escapes were not magic. There was little mystery, he felt, in wriggling around in a straitjacket. Houdini was also a relentless publicity hound, a trait that set Vernon's teeth on edge. "Don't mind what they say," he told Vernon, "get it in the paper by hook or by crook." He was absolutely relentless. If Houdini happened to ride by a fire or some incident on the street, he would rush over to the officer on the scene and announce his presence, all in the hope of seeing his name show up in the paper the next day.

Still, Houdini had that unparalleled name, which gave him stupendous standing with the public. And he had been the president of the Society of American Magicians. He still considered himself a magician at heart, and a great arbiter of talent and secrets. He had posed a standing challenge to magicians: Show me a trick three times in a row and I'll be able to tell you how you did it.

Vernon showed him a card trick, a simple effect, seven times and Houdini couldn't get it. He didn't come close. Worse, for the explosive Houdini, Vernon did it in front of other magicians. He had Houdini pick a card, mark it clearly with his initials "HH" and then slip it back into the deck. In a snap, there it was right back on top. (This was Vernon's version of a trick dubbed "The Ambitious Card," for a card always striving to rise to the top.) Vernon repeated the trick once, and then again. It didn't matter where he put Houdini's card, it always ended back on top. He even slipped it . . . slowly . . . and . . . obviously . . . right under the top card. Vernon showed it right there, second from the top, and then, there it was right back on top again. Everyone could see the "HH" still clearly marked on the card. It was Houdini's card, all right.

"You gotta have two cards alike," Houdini finally declared. He was a small man, but he was athletic, chesty, and he always puffed himself up. He spoke in pronouncements framed with finality. It was the third go-round of the trick and this was Houdini's verdict: a duplicate card. "With your initials, Harry?" Vernon answered casually. He had been most careful to get Houdini to initial that card. Houdini tried again.

"You use a thumb writer!" he practically yelled at Vernon now, referring to the little device magicians would clip to their thumb tip in order to write secretly during a trick. "How could I use a thumb writer when it's in ink?" Vernon countered. All the magicians knew that thumb writers, also called nail writers, only wrote in pencil. They waited now to see how Houdini would get out of that one. "They make them in ink now!" he finally blustered with authority. None of the magicians had ever heard of an ink thumb writer. The great Houdini was clearly floundering.

"Harry, you're fooled!" cried Sam Margules, who had been watching closely. "Three times!" Margules yelled now. "Three times!" Houdini started to boil. "Do it again!" he barked at Vernon. "Do it again!" Vernon obliged happily, running through the trick a fourth time, one more than Houdini's self-imposed limit. "Once more!" Houdini commanded still again. He was breaking his own rule here, demolishing it, but Vernon didn't care. He could do this trick a hundred times if Houdini liked. There was the card, the "HH" obvious to anyone watching, and yet there it was right back on top once more. Vernon did it again, and still again, seven times in all for Houdini, more than twice the number of times called for in his challenge.

Of course, Houdini never admitted he had been fooled. But Vernon knew, and because of the other magicians in attendance, the word spread. That particular trick became known in magic as "The Trick That Fooled Houdini." Vernon even received a note from no less an authority than Harry's wife, Bess, confirming that Houdini had stayed up half the night after seeing Vernon's trick trying to figure out how he had done it. (Bess Houdini became, through a happy chance meeting with the Vernons in Atlantic City a few years later, the godmother to Ted Vernon, who almost a year after his birth still hadn't been christened.) "Although he never made the admission," she wrote to Vernon, "he certainly made the admission to me . . . he won't give up until he solves it." He never did.

Vernon was certainly pleased he fooled Houdini, but he wasn't so impressed with himself. After all, to Vernon, Houdini was strictly a butcher when it came to card handling. He couldn't even shuffle a deck without making a total mess of it. Early in his career, he had featured some stage manipulation with cards, springing them from hand to hand and spreading them in a neat ribbon along his arm. But that had been the extent of it. A child could fool Houdini, in Vernon's opinion.

Houdini could certainly act like a child, too, throwing vicious, Vesuvian temper tantrums. A couple of years later, after a meeting of the Society of American Magicians at the Hotel McAlpin in New York, a group of magicians and their wives repaired to the nearby Riggs Restaurant on Thirty-third Street between Broadway and Fifth Avenue. Vernon was there, as were the two Sams, Horowitz and Margules, and the two Als, Baker and Flosso. A few friends, non-magicians, joined them at their table. Houdini, who was president of the society once again, swaggered into the cavernous Riggs and joined them at their table for dinner.

A deck of cards was sitting on the table, and Houdini picked it up and did a few tricks. The magicians couldn't help noticing right away that every time Houdini palmed a card, he "flashed," or inadvertently let the card be seen. It was obvious, and the laymen caught it, too, but the magicians didn't say anything. Later, once the magicians were alone, Margules piped up, "Harry, why don't you let Dai show you how to palm a card?" Vernon had perfected a simple and elegant palming technique called "topping the deck" (named after another early cheating move), which was becoming the preferred method among magicians. That's all Houdini had to hear. He went berserk.

"You sonofabitch!" he shouted at Margules. "You're gonna

tell me how to palm?!" Houdini was shaking with rage, losing control. It looked to the magicians, as he turned his wrathful attention to them, too, that he might even rush Margules, who thought he had made an innocent suggestion. Vernon's palming technique was the hot new method, an underground secret, and magicians usually delight in being in on what they call the "real work." Not Houdini. "You're a buncha amateurs, ya see!" he yelled at the group. "You're amateurs! And you tell me?! . . ."

Several of the magicians stepped between Houdini and the stunned Margules, and then Houdini wheeled around and stormed out of Riggs. The magicians watched him go, stupefied at his fit of anger. Flosso especially couldn't believe it. He thought he had seen it all out at Dreamland on Coney Island. But he had never seen anything like this.

Magicians realized how special this card genius in their midst was. New York was becoming the kingdom of magic and Vernon was effectively crowned the king. A column by Holden in *The Sphinx* in May 1928 served as the coronation. "The magicians of New York City seem to have the edge on other centers for original card problems," Holden declared. Vernon was "the cleverest man with cards in this or any other country. I must hand the crown to Dave Vernon when it comes to skill with the pasteboards."

But as brilliant as his effects were, as much as they were now reordering the art of magic and opening up new avenues of theory and technique for other magicians, Vernon wasn't making much money—the "long green"—off them. (In 1924, around the time he married Jeanne, he wrote a small book for magic shops called *Secrets,* but it included mostly standard items accessible to the average hobbyist. He sold the rights to it for only $20, and it stayed in print for years.) He still did most of his performing for other magicians, and seemed to have developed a blithe disregard for money that would drive Jeanne to distraction. "Hazard at play carries sensations that once enjoyed are rarely forgotten," Erdnase had written. "The winnings are known as 'pretty money,' and it is generally spent as freely as water." Vernon wasn't much of a gambler himself, but to him all money seemed to be "pretty money."

The situation changed somewhat in the summer of 1924 when Vernon was cutting silhouettes on the boardwalk in Atlantic City. He happened to be on a break and was doing a few spontaneous card tricks for a group of visiting engineers in the lobby of the Traymore Hotel when the famed booking agent Frances Rockefeller King happened by. She was impressed by Vernon's easy, sociable style and good looks, as well as by his impossible card tricks. They chatted, and she told him she could book him for private parties, both to do magic tricks and cut silhouettes, in the busy winter months ahead. Vernon demurred at first, protesting that magic was really only a hobby for him, but then he decided to take her up on the offer to handle him.

At first, Vernon didn't quite seem to understand what a break he had gotten. Normally, aspiring entertainers genuflected in vain before Frances Rockefeller King, who was the most powerful booking agent in show business. She had started her career onstage as a chorus girl, but had long since become the main agent for the Keith theater circuit, as well as high-society functions. She was a strong, straight-ahead woman who by the force of her personality had made it in a man's world. Vernon even thought her "rather masculine" and "horsey." She had little use for magicians, she made plain to Vernon, and handled only a small group of them, including Leipzig and the famous mentalist Joseph Dunninger.

King thought the vast majority of magicians were uncouth, socially inept bumblers. She used to tell Vernon that he was one of the "few magicians that she could trust with a knife and fork." ("Astonishingly," Vernon would add, "a lot of magicians don't know what that means!") Without planning to exactly, Vernon had suddenly become a professional magician. But the idea of performing before an audience for money filled him with dread. The man who had so calmly fooled Houdini suffered from stage fright. Vernon even tried to beg off his first engagement, a society celebration that also featured several big-name performers of the day, by offering it to Arthur Finley at the last minute. He promised Finley his full $100 fee, but Finley, intimidated by the prospect, too, said he wouldn't take it for $500.

Vernon's nervousness dissipated only when Frances White, the beautiful chorus girl, saw him practicing with his cards before the show and stopped to marvel at how calm he looked. "I hate magicians," she joked. "There you are sitting there so cool and collected, so relaxed, and here am I, a nervous wreck." Though Vernon's stage fright lessened as he grew more experienced, it never fully left him and he was known to need a quick drink or two to steady himself before going on. He was always much more comfortable performing for other magicians.

King arranged "hand artist" bookings for Vernon, too, and sometimes he did both magic and portrait-cutting at a gathering. It was a long way from the rushed cutting he used to do for the hordes at Steeplechase Pier. Now he was cutting portraits of the swells. Once he was hired to cut silhouettes of all twelve members of the Carnegie Steel Foundation, including the president, Charles Schwab.

Frequently, Jeanne would accompany him on these dates. She would dress as a pretty little girl, not hard for her, and after Vernon cut a silhouette, she would present it on a tray with a little flourish. At one ritzy function, Jeanne found herself sitting around with a group of wealthy wives when the talk turned to husbands. Each woman gave a brief, proud sketch of the high-powered position held by her mate. "Mrs. Vernon," a woman turned to Jeanne, "what does your husband do?" Jeanne didn't miss a beat. "He cuts paper dolls," she answered.

Dai Vernon was known to the general public as a silhouette artist long before he was known as a magician. As he progressed, and his reputation spread, he even achieved a measure of national fame. "A great deal of interest is being shown in the revival of this art, which is a very old one," *The Bee*, the newspaper of Danville, Virginia, proclaimed in April 1927. "And Mr. Vernon is the best artist of the kind in America." Vernon would go on to cut silhouettes of, among many others, F. Scott Fitzgerald, Thomas Edison, Woodrow Wilson, Franklin Roosevelt, and Jack Dempsey.

Silhouette cutting also put him on the road, allowing him to chase gamblers and their secrets once again. King frequently secured out-of-town bookings for him at carnivals, county fairs, local department stores, church groups, the Junior League. Suddenly, Vernon was traveling regularly around the country, mingling in the local gaming scene wherever he went. If he landed a job at a fair or a carnival, he was working the same venue the cheaters worked. This was like fieldwork following his Coney Island graduate school. If he did receive advance publicity announcing his arrival, like the glowing notice in the Danville paper, it was usually in the society pages and highlighted "D. W. Vernon," which was the name he tended to use as a silhouette artist. It rarely mentioned that he was a magician. Approaching cheaters as a magician was a sure way to get the chill.

Vernon rambled widely. He would regularly work the boardwalk in Atlantic City, a magnet for grifters. In addition to Virginia, he also traveled as far afield as Cincinnati; Chicago; Palatine, Illinois; Miami; Asheville, North Carolina; and Colorado Springs. He sessioned regularly with cheaters, importing still more of their tricks and ruses into his magic. And now he was no "fly-gee," an outsider who thinks he knows what's going on.

At the fairgrounds in Palatine, he finally got a close-up look at a three-card monte mob led by the legendary Pop Kelly. Vernon had first learned this old favorite of the Mississippi riverboat sharps from *The Expert at the Card Table,* but Kelly and his team had developed the little con to a high level. They were a "broad mob." Cards were, in gambling slang, "broads" and three-card monte was also known as "tossing the broads" or "broad tossing." When Vernon first heard the term "broad mob" he thought it meant a gang of prostitutes, or, as he put it, "a lot of girls of negotiable affections." "A little game from Hanky Poo," the broad tosser would announce, flicking the three cards down softly. "The black for me the red for you . . . all you have to do is keep your eyes on the little lady . . . 10 gets you 20 . . . 20 gets you 40 . . . now here we go . . . keep your eyes on the lady."

In Asheville, Vernon met an old retired gambler named Shock who showed him his technique for dealing "the punch." Using the punch, cheaters could mark desirable cards during play by pricking the backs with a pin hidden in their hand or fingernail. (Standard marked cards—"readers"—could be notoriously difficult to decipher, especially in low light.) If the sharp felt one of the punched cards while dealing, he could keep it for himself or his partner by dealing the second card instead. Shock also addressed one of Vernon's obsessions when he showed him a simple crafty method of marking the location of the top card after a legitimate cut. Shock would keep tiny, salt-grain-sized bits of rubber in his pocket, made by meticulously cutting up a rubber band, and under cover of retrieving his pipe or a cigar, he would dig a few under a fingernail. When he presented the deck for the cut, he would transfer a couple of the rubber bits to the top card. Once the cut was carried, it was still relatively easy to tell where that top card went. Vernon used the ruse in a magic trick and thought it worked beautifully. (The technique also found its way into the book *Cheating at Bridge* by Judson Cameron.)

Like the best of the cardsharps' work, Shock's ploy with the chopped-up rubber band was direct, utilitarian, and efficient. It "got the money," which was, after all, the main goal always for the cardsharp. But was it "artistic" in the sense that Erdnase had used the word? Or was it merely one of the "contrivances" he had touched on in the book but rejected in favor of pure sleight of hand?

When Vernon received Sprong's letter in Asheville, he had no doubt at all that the center dealer, if he really existed, was an artist ranking with *The Expert at the Card Table*. Just as Erdnase had labored to devise a shift that would work during a game, the center dealer would have applied great ingenuity, great virtuosity in trying to overcome it. Sprong was willing to pay $100 for even a shred of information on the center deal. A C-note. If the center deal was real, Vernon knew it would be worth a lot more than that.

The Depression brought the black curtain crashing down on Vernon's high-society assignments. The fancy parties started to drop away like Dust Bowl corn husks. Even Vernon's finishing school, his beloved Coney Island, began its own protracted death struggle in 1929, the year of the crash, when the brand-new Jones Beach on Long Island started to pull the crowds away faster than any broad mob's pitch could. It was a tough time indeed to try to lighten people's moods by asking them to think of a card.

Vernon and Jeanne responded to the uncertainty by hitting the road. Maybe on the move the hard times would have a tougher time catching up. Vernon kept his silhouette scissors close. He had discovered a reliable little secret about the quaint little shadow cuttings. No matter how bad things got, people still seemed willing to come across with their two bits to see their portrait cut in black paper. Indeed, Vernon did so well at Manitou in Colorado Springs that he was moved to stick a sign over his stand: "No Depression Here," it read.

Vernon wasn't going to lead this old, reliable art in any new directions. He wasn't even going to bother. He didn't care enough about it. What he didn't realize was that it was about to lead him to the most glorious secret of his other art, his true art. The art of magic.

5

MIDNIGHT

Allen Kennedy's boss was nothing like him. He was big-bellied and barrel-chested, whereas Kennedy was trim and wiry. His boss was often decked out in a suit and tie, complete with a vest and gold watch chain. Kennedy almost always wore the same simple outfit of light-colored button-down shirt, dark pants, and felt fedora. The boss was loud and blustery, even a practical joker. Kennedy was reserved, soft-spoken, laconic.

When he turned to cheating at cards and dice in Pleasant Hill, Kennedy seemed to stay just at the edge of the shadows, in the gray part of the world, as one card player put it. The townsfolk saw him around, certainly, but they could never quite get a bead on him. He lived near downtown, but they were never sure exactly what he was up to. His obscurity was in keeping with the ethic of the cardsharp. His boss, on the other hand, was a fixture on First Street, a backslapper who seemed to know everyone who came down the sidewalk. He seemed to be out there at all hours of the night and day, an unofficial mayor of the "many men and boys" that the *Republican* fretted were gambling their way to sure ruin.

Kennedy, who would train his hands to a high level of deceptive artistry, was certainly the more mysterious figure. While the boss was a gambler, he wasn't a sharp himself. He didn't manipulate cards and dice. Instead, he was the fixer, the manager, the impresario, as it were. He was a public face who put Kennedy the devilish virtuoso to work in their version of a close-up parlor, performing their own brand of larcenous, thoroughly invisible magic. Yet for all the mystery surrounding him, Kennedy had the common nickname Bill, a name that seemed suited to a wave and a friendly greeting while crossing the street in the midday sun. Hiya Bill. It was his boss, one of the legendary figures in the gambling lore of Pleasant Hill, who was tagged with the more evocative moniker, the darker handle. He was known as Midnight.

There were several theories floating around Pleasant Hill as to why James Wesley Underwood, who for a decade was the closest thing to a gambling kingpin the town had, came to be called Midnight. Most of these theories related to his prodigious appetites, which defined his life, and propelled it on what would be a relatively short yet extraordinary arc. Midnight Underwood had relentless appetites indeed –for money, for gambling, for liquor, for women. And these appetites butted heads with virtually every law that framed life in Missouri, or attempted to, in the early twentieth century. But like a backwoods brawler, Midnight's appetites always seemed to win out over the laws. For him, his appetites were the law. He made no attempt to hide them, or their effects on his life. It just didn't seem to matter to him what anyone thought.

For all their differences, there were actually some similarities in the lives of Allen Kennedy and Midnight Underwood. Both had been born into industrious, upstanding families on farms not far from town. Midnight was born seventeen years before

Kennedy, in 1880, and in the opposite direction from downtown Pleasant Hill, in an area known as Lone Jack. Neither exhibited much of an appetite for farming, and both turned their full attention to professional gambling after toiling at more traditional manual labor. And both had to endure trials, just a few months apart in the same courtroom over in Harrisonville, which would help set the direction of their lives in downtown Pleasant Hill.

Their legal cases were rooted in vastly different impulses, however. Kennedy's was, in the crudest sense, professional, stemming directly from those first, inartistic attempts at thievery. Midnight Underwood's was personal. Kennedy's case was disposed of quickly. His hearing, which came the same day he confessed to the sheriff, lasted just long enough for him to plead guilty and find out he owed the county $90. Midnight's case dragged on for months. And it was sensational, indeed. It involved the deepest of taboos, race mixing in the largely segregated town, and was highlighted by a gunshot blast in the predawn stillness of a late-winter night. It became one of the most notorious cases of the early Twenties in Pleasant Hill.

"Mass Gant Shot!" the *Republican* fairly yelped on its front page of March 18, 1921. It was just six weeks after Allen Kennedy had settled the boxcar case and returned to his parents' farm with his tail between his legs. The *Republican* didn't offer a lot of details of the shooting. It didn't have to. Because the paper only came out once a week, on Friday, it was offering its take on events that had occurred six days earlier. Most of the residents of Pleasant Hill had already heard the details, and they certainly knew the principals involved. The man who had been shot and wounded, Mass Gant, was a "pioneer Negro," as they said back then of a black person born before the Civil War, in the slavery days. Gant was a well-known figure around town whose exact age was undetermined but who was surely well into his eighties.

The man accused of putting a bullet into his hip was the forty-year-old James Underwood. In its story, the *Republican* offered up little more than his proper name. It was all that was needed. Midnight's background was familiar in Pleasant Hill.

What it lacked in details, the reliably moralistic *Republican* made up for with some hand-wringing. To the editors, the case that had exploded the Saturday before again pointed up the moral decay of Pleasant Hill. "Rumor says there are quite a number of boys around Pleasant Hill carrying guns," the paper warned in its overheated way, as usual not slowing for the niceties of punctuation. "It's bad business, better cut it out boys, and save yourselves and your families from the disgrace of criminal charges against you." The *Republican* advised parents that they "better talk to your boys and impress upon them the seriousness of 'toting' a gun, that an ounce of precaution may be worth more than a $1,000 in attorney fees and court costs."

Of course, the shooting of Mass Gant demonstrated much more than the need for stricter gun-control laws, as welcome as those might have been, too. The case represented the collision of Midnight Underwood's unfettered appetites and the mores and laws of the day. And it was also, quite simply, a family matter.

The roots of the case ran back twenty years, to the turn of the century when James Underwood first came in off his parents' farm in Lone Jack to downtown Pleasant Hill. Unlike Allen Kennedy, Underwood didn't become a failed boxcar thief. He wasn't out stealing chickens. Nor did he have any particular artistic ambitions with cards or dice, though he certainly came to have financial ones. Instead, he took gainful employment with one of the town's most expansive and successful businesses, the scale foundry. The Pleasant Hill scale foundry produced large, so-called pitless scales that could measure the weight of a fully loaded wagon at ground level. It was an early version of a weigh station, a necessary tool in an era when goods and farm produce were still delivered by cart. The foundry even had its own private electric power plant, an incredible advancement in a town that was still figuring out how to get wired up. The factory's whistles, loudly calling out the start and end of the shifts, reliably punctuated the Pleasant Hill days.

The work at the foundry was fierce. It was hot, dirty, and dangerous. The laborers there had to be as tough as the metal they shaped. When these big-armed men emerged at the end of a shift, they were usually filthy with soot and ash from head to toe. That aspect of his early work gave rise to one of the theories around town about how James Wesley Underwood had come to be tagged with his unusual moniker. In those days, Midnight was a nickname usually reserved for black people. But after a full shift at the grimy foundry, even the palest of workers could appear as darkened as any minstrel in vaudeville.

The scale foundry was one of the anchors in Pleasant Hill. The workers were part of establishment life in town, as Midnight surely was. It was a frenetic time, a boom period when the little farming community suddenly saw itself becoming, improbably, something of a manufacturing center. Kellogg's, the local greenhouse business, grew so much that it actually put in a paved road leading from its greenhouses to downtown. (Most roads in the area were still mercilessly dusty winding strips.) A new business, the R. R. Stillwell glove factory, opened in March 1902 and added its whistle to the growing daily chorus led by the foundry. The mighty Missouri Pacific railroad, which lost its Pleasant Hill depot to a fire in 1901, immediately started to rebuild, a project that dovetailed with the Rock Island line's arrival in 1903. The business district kept spreading beyond its original confines. From the fall of 1901 to the spring of 1902, downtown business lots doubled in price, from $250 to $500.

Workmen were everywhere. "What with the hauling of sand, etc., for the Rock Island, and the general boom in all lines of team work," the *Pleasant Hill Times* reported, "the like of hauling going on has not before been seen in Pleasant Hill in many a day.

Big teams are to be seen here, there, everywhere—all at work and the streets kept in a turmoil constantly." The Rolley Brothers Ice Cream Manufacturing Co., taking advantage of the presence of all the strapping young workers in Pleasant Hill, sponsored a baseball club with blue uniforms and the zippy name Rolley Brothers Blues. Midnight and his brother Fielding, who also worked at the foundry, joined the team, which played over at Sportsmans Park. Betting on the games was heavy, no doubt, for baseball was still one of the most popular wagering games going in that era. For his part, Midnight, a young man with regular, decent wages in his pocket now, was certainly developing his own powerful appetite for gambling. The boom in work around town was matched, of course, by the boom in gambling.

As tough as a shift at the foundry was, it didn't keep Midnight from gambling and drinking, and generally carousing after work. He was young and energetic and he found out early on he had a knack as an operator, an aptitude not just for playing in games, but running them. By organizing a regular game, he saw that he could, in effect, own it rather than just filling one of the seats at the table. And he could supplement his foundry wages quite handily. The percentage income from a steady game could prove as reliable as a factory pay envelope, especially if he threw in a good sharp who could manipulate the cards, and the odds, at key moments. Gambling partners were plentiful in Pleasant Hill, where the suckers would always come back for more action, win or lose. Midnight stuck with his foundry job. It was too good. But while working there, he began to stake out the approach that would lead him to his eventual status of local gambling boss.

As the economy of Pleasant Hill kept growing, so, too, did the scale foundry. It was a hummer, and kept attracting the attention of potential new owners. From the time the McDonald brothers bought it in the closing days of December 1900, it began to flourish like a cornstalk on a muggy July day. It did so well, steadily adding men and capacity, that by 1904 the McDonald Bros. Pitless Scale Company was being courted actively by towns across the heartland looking to create a manufacturing center of their own. Their efforts were like a cross between a poker game and a dowry offering. A group of businessmen from Keokuk, Iowa, put together an impressive offer of cash and bonuses, including free transportation on the Burlington Railroad for men and equipment. But then Pleasant Hill raised Keokuk by offering the McDonalds an astounding cash bonus of $5,000 and a guarantee of freight-rate concessions on both the Mo Pac and Rock Island lines. The McDonalds just raked in that pot and agreed to stick around in Pleasant Hill. Their foundry kept growing.

Fire was a persistent menace, an ever-present fear, in those days in Pleasant Hill. Local businesses were under the constant and real threat of sudden annihilation. Most of these manufacturing buildings were still made of wood, many of them made more flammable still through repeated baths of machine oil dripping everywhere. Summer droughts could be furious and unending. On July 21, 1901, churchgoing folk all over Missouri turned out for a special statewide day of prayer for rain. A week later, a tremendous downpour seemed to deliver a dramatic answer to the mass prayer and led to great rejoicing. But then, not another drop fell from the sky for the next eight months. When fires broke out in town, it was always a knuckle-biting race to get whatever water might be available, from Big Creek or one of the local ponds, to quench the flames.

Because it was, at its fiery heart, a forge, McDonald Pitless was even more vulnerable. In 1907, when fire inevitably attacked the factory, the inferno actually benefited from some cruel misdirection. Because it was July 4, the alarm was at first ignored in town because of the general clamor of bells and whistles already being sounded for the Independence Day celebration. By the time the alarm was sorted out from the rest of the noise and the horse-drawn fire engine could be assembled, it was too late. The foundry was destroyed. It looked as though the sixty laborers, the Underwood brothers included, were all going to be out of work.

Incredibly, owner B.T. McDonald Jr. had the factory rebuilt in less than three months, and by the end of September it was up and running again. McDonald Pitless was nationally known by then, with orders piling in from all over the country. By 1909, they were in operation 24 hours a day, scrambling to meet demand not just across the United States, but from around the world. The pitless scale foundry was the pride of Pleasant Hill.

The McDonalds continued to fend off more suitors than a pretty farmgirl at a Grange social. Finally, they could resist no longer. They were not so much lured out of town as snatched away by the richest of the eligible bachelors. At Christmastime 1911, the town of Pleasant Hill was shocked to hear that the McDonalds had sold out to the Moline Plow Company of Illinois. The entire works, including all the men who worked there, would be packing up and leaving within two months. Moline was relocating the company to Stoughton, Wisconsin, just north of the Illinois border. It was a devastating blow for Pleasant Hill. Even twenty years later, one newspaper referred back to the many families who left as the "hegira of foundry folk."

Midnight Underwood, at thirty-one, joined the hegira. He wasn't alone. His brother Fielding and another brother, Max, went along. Their parents joined because their father, Thomas, was also working at the foundry by then. For Thomas Underwood, who had been raised doing farm work and was still only in his early fifties, it was a good job, well worth relocating for.

And a woman, Midnight's woman, joined the hegira, too. They had an unusual arrangement, Midnight and this woman, whose name was Alice Gant, the granddaughter of Mass Gant. She and Midnight were not married, not in an official sense. But they were understood to be together. Most likely they had not even bothered to "jump the broom," as they said of a common-law marriage. Still, Alice Gant wasn't going to let her Midnight leave her behind in Pleasant Hill without him.

Everyone returns to Pleasant Hill. Ona Courtney and Allen Kennedy had certainly proved that, to their legal peril. Eventually, McDonald Pitless showed that even companies return. Twelve years after leading the "hegira of foundry folk" out of their hometown, the company led a return march back to Pleasant Hill, where they resumed operations in 1924. Midnight Underwood, however, was not among those returning refugees. He had already returned, after five years or so in Stoughton. He was definitely back by the time the United States jumped into the Great War, for he made sure to get his name on the call-up lists. Midnight was thirty-seven in September 1918, almost at the age limit for soldiers, but he did his duty and signed up with the board anyway. It was just a month after Allen Kennedy, who had still been a teenager when the foundry and the Underwoods left town, had added his name to the roll of aspiring soldiers.

When Midnight came back, Pleasant Hill seemed to be pretty much the same town that he had left a few years earlier. The downtown district, and its lively scene, had continued to grow. Midnight picked up scale foundry work again. In a neat switch, after the McDonalds left, the American Scale Co. had been enticed from nearby Harrisonville and had taken over the McDonald factory. As always, gambling continued to boom right along with the economic expansion.

In still another crucial way, Pleasant Hill remained unchanged. Midnight Underwood and Alice Gant, now that they were back in Missouri, could no longer live together openly as husband and wife. A white man and a colored woman, as they would have called her then, were not allowed, by law or social standards, to cross a divide that had been enforced for generations.

That was the second theory as to how James Wesley Underwood came to be called Midnight down on First Street. As he
became a man about town, it was pretty obvious to anyone who
bothered to monitor such things that James Underwood had a
decided preference for black women. Up north in Wisconsin,
which had always been strongly abolitionist, he and Alice Gant
could pretty much live their lives together out in the open.
Maybe they turned some heads among the Norwegian tobacco
farmers of Stoughton, but their relationship would have been
possible there.

But in Missouri, the situation was different. In the years after
the Civil War ended in 1865, Pleasant Hill's racial scene was
extremely complex, with a delicately metered, shifting scale of
conflicting laws, rules, traditions, and mores. The town sat on
the rough border between the North and South, in a strip of territory that had never been fully and decisively won over by either
side. (Missouri had always had something of a confused racial
stance. The 1820 Missouri Compromise enabled it to join the
Union, but as a slave state. Then, when the Deep South slave states
began to secede formally in the period leading up to the Civil War,
it decided against seceding.)

Ultimately, Cass County probably leaned more toward the
South and the Confederacy during the Civil War. Many of the
area's earliest farming settlers had come from Kentucky and
Tennessee, bringing their slaves along to work their new spreads.
During the war, the locally infamous Order No. 11 also helped
foster pro-Confederacy, or at least anti-Union, sentiment. This
1863 measure, issued by Union General Thomas Ewing (a
brother-in-law of the fearsome General William Tecumseh
Sherman), ordered all local residents living more than a mile
from Pleasant Hill and Harrisonville off their farms. The sweep-
ing move was ostensibly in retaliation for the bloodthirsty guer-
rilla operations of Quantrill's Raiders. But by confiscating or
torching many of the farms, Union soldiers helped create a

legacy of grievance that held for many years after the war ended.

Yet as Pleasant Hill grew, when Midnight Underwood was first following his appetites, blacks and whites found themselves all trying to eke out a living in the same area and often in the exact same ways. Aging Civil War veterans from both the Union and the Confederate armies shared the sidewalks with aging former slaves. Veterans from both sides of the conflict formed associations, which played a prominent part in the civic life of the town. One of their priorities was locating and placing headstones at the many unmarked graves of soldiers dotting the countryside. On Registration Day in the summer of 1917, when Pleasant Hill, with great fanfare, signed up its first enlistees for the Great War, veterans of the Civil War a half-century earlier were one of the main attractions of the grand patriotic parade through town. They sat in automobiles, which hadn't existed back when they were trying to kill each other off, and joined the line with the Boy Scouts, the ladies' patriotic auxiliary, and the visiting carnival performers.

Pleasant Hill's institutions remained strictly segregated well into the twentieth century. The town had separate schools, with the feisty Douglass School providing education for black children of all ages. It had separate churches. The local newspapers could veer from fairly respectful coverage to snide racist stereotyping. So-called pioneer Negroes or old-time Negroes, the euphemism for ex-slaves, were often referred to warmly as "Uncle" and "Auntie." They would be lauded in print for knowing their place. Items cataloguing blacks' supposed fondness for persimmons, which country tradition also oddly associated with possums, were offered up for the merriment of whites. Other items crudely and openly mimicked the "lawdy lawdy" speaking style supposedly used by blacks.

And yet there were important instances, even trends, of integration. The same newspapers that could stereotype so freely also included, without editorializing, the mundane comings and goings of the "colored" and "Negro" residents in their social columns. Pleasant Hill never had a racial lynching, and the newspapers didn't shy away from running wire items on the lynchings that took place down south. (In 1915, a white man, a suspected thief involved in a gun battle that killed Pleasant Hill's night officer, was lynched by an angry local mob.) Interracial friendships were quite common among children. Work, especially farm work, was often integrated. By the 1920s, the incomparable Sam Gipson, a black man, built up his plumbing and contracting business until it was the leading firm of its type in the area. Gipson was an extraordinary figure in the history of Pleasant Hill, winning municipal contracts, helping to sponsor the annual street fair, and even obliterating the color line in death when he became the first black resident to have his funeral in a white church.

But there was always one line that could not be crossed, not out in the bright sunshine of a Missouri farm day. The sexes positively could not mix across the color line. One episode in the spring of 1911 pointed that up with stark clarity. Pleasant Hill was stunned one Saturday afternoon in April of that year by the appearance of two wayfarers hailing from just north in Kansas. Even in a town used to hordes of train travelers and exotic strangers like gypsies, carnival workers, and hobos wandering in, this couple stuck out for the simple reason that the man was white and the woman was black. They even made the paper. The child with them was "almost equally black" as the woman, the *Pleasant Hill Times* reported succinctly. "Not understanding the association of Caucasian and Ethiopian," as the *Times* put it, city marshal Charles Bailey and deputy sheriff James Prater immediately braced the couple. The paper provided a melodramatic account of what ensued.

When the "strapping white man," John Turner, brought out a certificate indicating they were legally married the previous September, Bailey was unimpressed. "Got that in Kansas, didn't you?" he asked Turner. Kansas had been a free state, strictly pro-Union. Turner agreed that they had. "That's just what I thought," Bailey said before ordering the couple to "keep on walking" and not to let "the sun go down on you" in Pleasant Hill. Bailey and Prater were concerned, the *Times* reported approvingly, "that the presence of the two might contaminate the people of the city."

In early 1921, the Missouri state legislature passed a law "prohibiting the marriage of whites and Mongolians and of whites and persons having one-eighth or more negro blood." This racist law specified formal marriage, but the "Solons," as the newspaper headline writers dubbed the legislators, took the trouble in the same session to proscribe the type of consorting Midnight Underwood and Alice Gant had been doing up in abolitionist Wisconsin. They passed another law "providing that common law marriages shall hereafter be held invalid." No more jumping the broom.

Midnight Underwood certainly didn't care much about what the state legislature had to say. By 1921, he was heavily involved in running games downtown and making good money at it, money that he was starting to sock away and invest in real estate and even in the stock market. Midnight had an appetite for money. If he were willing to violate the very laws of chance, why would he care about all these petty laws of man? Prohibition had arrived two years earlier, but that hadn't stopped him from taking a drink, or offering up "white mule" at his games for anyone who happened to want it. Why should he listen to what a bunch of high-hatters over in Jefferson City had to say about a white man keeping time with a woman "having one-eighth or more negro blood"? He saw no reason at all to listen. He thumbed his nose at the whole idea by sparking the biggest scandal the town had clucked over in quite some time. It made Allen Kennedy's boxcar arrest look like a parking ticket.

If Midnight Underwood didn't care what people thought about his choice of companions, Mass Gant certainly did. Alice Gant's grandfather was past eighty but still stout and energetic, so much so that only three years earlier he had still been working as a farmhand just outside Pleasant Hill. It was all he had ever known—hard physical labor on the land. Alice, who obviously could no longer live openly with Midnight, was staying under her grandfather's roof at his small place in Pleasant Hill. There at least, Mass could seemingly have some say over her comings and goings. It was clear that Mass was no great admirer of Midnight, this loud, white, moonshine-swilling gambler with a practically advertised proclivity for black women. Early one Saturday morning in March 1921, at the doorway of Mass Gant's little home at Main and Jackson, Midnight Underwood came smack up against the stooped, bowlegged, but still hickory-tough form of Mass Gant. The resulting crash shook the town.

The facts of the case were straightforward and age-old. A man wanted to see a woman. Another man didn't want him to. Midnight had apparently spent all of Friday night drinking and by the predawn hours of Saturday was well juiced. Overcome with a hunger for Alice—his Alice, as he thought of her—he went to Mass Gant's house and began knocking loudly on the door. Mass came to the door but refused to let Midnight enter. They argued, rumbling back and forth, but Mass was steadfast. He would not yield. As he continued to refuse, Midnight's bile began to rise. But the angrier he got, the more resolute Mass Gant became.

Mass positively refused to let Midnight come into his home or see Alice Gant. Midnight, in his temerity, his drunkenness, his rage and frustration, his sense of absolute entitlement, finally broke the door down. But he couldn't break Mass Gant, who moved quickly to throw Midnight out bodily. The two wrestled at the threshold and then Midnight brought out a revolver. He fired at close range, hitting Mass in the hip. Even a bullet could not put the tough old Mass Gant down. He continued to stand his ground, despite a wound and the general shock of that blast going off in the early-morning quiet. Mass even managed to take the gun from Midnight, who was drunk to be sure, but still a tough man in his own right, and half his age. Mass put Midnight out of his house.

Midnight was arrested later that morning after Mass Gant swore out a complaint. He was charged with assault with intent to kill, a heavy charge, and taken before A. D. Prater, who was now serving as the local justice of the peace. Prater set bond at $1,000, the same amount Ona Courtney had been hit with just a couple of months earlier when he was hauled in on the boxcar thefts after returning from Chicago. Shooting an unarmed black man and stealing merchandise from the train yard came with the same price tag in Pleasant Hill. Unlike Courtney, Midnight made his bail immediately. He didn't even blink handing over the thousand (more than $10,000 today, but still a paltry bail for trying to kill a man). No scrambling around for funds to keep himself from being locked up. He didn't get that kind of money to throw around from just working at the foundry. After posting bond, he was set free pending his trial, which was marked down for the May term in the county circuit court in Harrisonville.

Depending on their exact location and their politics, the local newspapers all played the "Underwood Case" a little bit differently. The *Pleasant Hill Times* reported the case straightforwardly, giving just a dry, sparse account of the basic facts of the incident. Midnight and Mass Gant were both sons of the town, in their own ways, and the *Times* often put its desire to boost the reputation of Pleasant Hill before its obligation to provide truly detailed, unvarnished reporting. It was certainly true that the case didn't exactly gild the town's reputation, which the *Cass County Leader,* based in Pleasant Hill's perpetual rival, Harrisonville, couldn't help but point out. "Pleasant Hill again breaks into the lime-light as a center of crime for Cass County," the *Leader* crowed, "this time with a very disgusting case." The *Leader* was quick to stress the racial angle, as did Harrisonville's other paper, the *Cass County Democrat*, which jauntily brushed off the crime as a "shooting scrape." The incident had erupted, the *Democrat* confided, when Midnight sought "to visit a dusky maiden." None of the papers made anything of his unusual nickname.

In early May, prosecuting attorney George Chamberlin, who had been so disappointed a few months earlier when Ona Courtney deprived him of his chance for a juicy trial, upped Midnight's bond to $1,500. Apparently, he had some concerns that the defendant would flee, despite his obvious roots in the community. But again, Midnight didn't flinch. He went right to his bankroll and threw the extra five C-notes into the pot. In late May, the case was postponed until the September court term. Then, in September, it was put off until the October term. Finally, after numerous delays, the long-awaited trial of Midnight Underwood opened in Harrisonville on a Monday morning, October 3, 1921. And then it was all over in just a day and a half.

The courtroom was packed. Some fifty witnesses from both sides were listed, and Chamberlin announced that he intended to call twelve of them to testify to the defendant's character, or lack thereof. In response, Midnight moved to have the case delayed yet again, but Judge Ewing Cockrell turned him down flat. It was time to get to the bottom of this shooting of Mass Gant. The jury (all men in those days) was sworn and a portion of the evidence was presented before Cockrell adjourned the trial for the day. The next morning, the rest of the evidence was laid out for the twelve jurors. By midday, they retired to ponder Midnight's legal fate.

At one point during their deliberations the jurors sent a note to Judge Cockrell with an inquiry. They wanted to know just what the penalty ought to be in a case like this. Cockrell answered by saying that they were, in effect, putting the cart before the horse. You have to come up with your verdict first, he instructed, before you can decide what the penalty will be. Get to the verdict. A little later in the day, they did. They came back into court and announced that, based on the evidence, James Wesley Midnight Underwood had, indeed, assaulted Mass Gant with the intention of killing him.

The court system allowed for the jury to levy a punishment immediately and they did that now, too. For the crime of essentially trying to kill Mass Gant on his own doorstep, Midnight Underwood was directed to pay a fine of $100, plus some court costs. It was less than a tenth the amount he had so blithely put up as bail. The C-note would go, the court directed, into the county's "common school fund." Just eight months earlier, when Midnight's gambling pal Allen Kennedy had pleaded guilty to robbing boxcars, he had been fined $90. The $10 difference was presumably the value the jury put on Mass Gant's life. Midnight hadn't beaten any odds, of course. He had just played them wisely, as he always did. No white man was going to the state pen for trying to shoot a black man.

Still, the *Republican* saw some merit in the outcome of the Underwood case. "Heavy Fine" read its ludicrous, large-type headline. The verdict was the lead story of the week, naturally, but the paper kept its report brief, only four paragraphs. As usual, the *Republican* found a moral in the grim tale. "Such heavy fines," it intoned, "will, no doubt, have a good moral effect on the entire county."

No doubt? Moral effect? If the trial had any moral effect on Midnight Underwood at all, it was just the opposite of the one the newspaper was looking for. The stress to what the cheaters would call his "leather," his wallet, was so light as to be unnoticeable.

And the stress to his moral compass, to his opinion of himself, well, that was nonexistent. True to form, Midnight didn't slink away from the "very disgusting case." He didn't hide or leave Pleasant Hill. He continued to thrive, and he continued to feed his appetites.

Midnight headed right back out to First Street to hang around the venerable pool hall, always a reliable spot to hunt pigeons for his card games. He also liked to stop into the busy Hayes Restaurant by the depot, where, with great relish and fanfare, he would polish off the steak-dinner special (complete with fried potatoes, greens, eggs, pie, and coffee, all for 50 cents). When, just two weeks after his trial, Pleasant Hill held its annual street fair, the showcase event of the year that attracted some 16,000 people to the downtown area, Midnight feasted on that bounty, too.

The weeklong fair was always one of the most lucrative periods for the gamblers in town. "Wholesale Gambling," the *Republican* called the fair. The hordes who spilled into town to get a glimpse of the best peck of flaxseed or the best country-cured ham were always good for some action. But this year, Midnight went even further. For $10, apparently his lucky amount in those days, he had himself included in the fair program as an official sponsor of the event. He was on the list right alongside other top businessmen in town. It was an audacious move, but it made sense. With his games now expanding almost as fast as the McDonald scale foundry had, Midnight Underwood was one of the leading businessmen in Pleasant Hill.

Obviously, Midnight couldn't see Alice Gant anymore. But his trial did nothing to put him off women. He didn't bother to be discreet about it, either. If anything, his reputation as one of the best customers of the black prostitutes in town grew. He became a regular visitor to the Ashenhurst boardinghouse, where the women would take the trainmen they had picked up. One night sometime in the mid-1920s, Arch Hipsher, a large man who had succeeded Mose Mahaffey as night watchman, was standing down by the train depot. Arch was as familiar a denizen downtown as Midnight, only he worked the street from a different angle, as it were. He did a stint as night watchman from 1921 to 1923 and then returned to the job again in 1926. Arch Hipsher was a tough guy indeed. He knew all the regular nighthawks along First Street well.

When Midnight Underwood ambled up, they greeted each other and began to chat for a bit. As they talked, a young woman, a downtown hustler who went by the nickname Ginseng, strolled by. She was beautiful, light-skinned, and known around town to be half white and half black, a "high yellow" in the slur then common. She was obviously on the prowl for a railroad man. As she passed, Midnight licked his lips. He turned to Hipsher and smiled.

"Man," he said, watching Ginseng, "I'd sure like to go to bed with her." Hipsher eyed Midnight. He was pretty blunt himself, and he certainly matched Midnight now in directness. "You wouldn't go to bed with your own daughter, wouldja?"

This was the rumor downtown, that Ginseng was actually Midnight's daughter, the result of a long-ago, most likely long-forgotten encounter like the one he was now considering with her. (Ginseng's mother was a woman known in town as Step-and-a-Half.) No one could prove it, of course, but that didn't matter. It had become a First Street truth. Perhaps Midnight said what he did to Hipsher to put off the suspicions, a bit of gambler's misdirection. Or perhaps he didn't even know that Ginseng was his daughter.

And it wasn't just Ginseng. Other children in town, racially mixed, were connected to Midnight, too, if only by rumor and received wisdom. If the money he won downtown gave him the standing of a shadow city father, his other nocturnal appetite now gave him the status of a father in the shadows. For many years in Pleasant Hill, when people would spy a certain teenager walking down the street, they would say with certainty, "There goes one of Midnight's kids."

Midnight's apparent determination to violate the spirit of the anti-miscegenation laws (he never married formally) put him in direct, if unacknowledged, opposition to yet another social force that seemed to be growing in the decade. This one had a more immediate, and terrifying, local presence than the Missouri state legislators. In October 1922, the Ku Klux Klan appeared suddenly and dramatically in Pleasant Hill, holding a large initiation rally in a farm pasture near town. More than a thousand Klansmen attended to welcome a group of fifty local residents who were joining in secret. Like overgrown Halloween ghosts arriving a week or so early, white-sheeted figures materialized at several downtown intersections just after dark to direct cars to the gathering. In a grotesque twist, the Klansmen burned a fifty-foot-high cross in a field known as Happy Hill. The blood-red flames of their staple symbol could be seen easily from town for some forty minutes until it abruptly disappeared behind the trees. Apparently one of the Klansmen, trying to park his car in the darkened field, had run over one of the guy wires securing the massive cross and sent the entire structure crashing to the grass.

"The Knights of the Ku Klux Klan are in your midst," fliers left on the doors of local businesses warned. "Take notice. Bootleggers, gamblers, homebreakers, and all law violators are hereby warned that all law violations must cease. Our girls and boys must be protected. Married men, watch your step. Fathers, watch your sons. Mothers, know where your daughters are at night. . . . The man that patronizes the bootlegger is as guilty as the bootlegger. . . . No law abiding citizen need fear this 100% American organization. . . . Others have cause to fear." There they were, right at the top of the list of Klan targets. Bootleggers and gamblers. It was almost as if the flier had been tailored for Midnight Underwood. They didn't even need to mention traitors to the white race. It was obvious what the "Knights" thought about them.

The town took notice. "So they are here," the *Times* observed. "Deplore it all you may, they are here. Resent it all you please, they are here. Cry against them until you can cry no longer, yet they are here. Storm and rage and convert our courts into battering rams for their destruction, but still, ladies and gentlemen, they are here." The *Times* was clearly squeamish about the Klan, but it also hedged by arguing that the best way to wipe it out was by "removing the causes." It editorialized awkwardly that "when law is respected and the American Constitution upheld, then the final heat will have been victoriously run and the Ku Klux Klan become a thing of the past."

After that first intimidating flurry of activity in the fall of 1922, the Klan continued to gather sporadically in Pleasant Hill, mostly when the weather was accommodating to outdoor events. In May 1923, they held another rally up on Happy Hill. This time, they burned a smaller cross, thirty feet high, fastened more securely with several guy wires. This cross, made of gas pipe and covered with rags that had been soaked in oil, flamed enthusiastically. Some 2,025 people attended this time, and admission tickets were required just to get into the pasture. They listened to Zach Harris, a Klan lecturer from Kansas City, hold forth from the back of a wagon. Later that summer, in July, another KKK lecturer, Dr. J. W. Darvy, also of Kansas City, spoke on "Americanism" to another meeting in the pasture of some thousand white-robed Klan members. Darvy had, in fact, recently spoken to a large public crowd in town. In the spring, he had been the featured commencement speaker at the Pleasant Hill High School graduation ceremonies.

In the summer of 1924, the KKK seemed to shift its focus to Harrisonville, the county seat, and another town close by, Creighton. In July, a large rally was held in downtown Harrisonville, with the "rubescent glow of an electric fiery cross," as the *Cass County Leader* reported, lighting the menacing proceedings on South Independence Street. The *Leader,* Southern

Democratic in bent, seemed to be much less worried about the Klan than the *Times* had been. "Knighthood was in flower in Harrisonville last Wednesday night," it reported cheerily on the proceedings. A large rally in Creighton on a Monday night in July attracted 1,500 people. On Friday of the same week, the Klan burned a cross at an ice-cream social hosted by the Methodist Church Epworth League in Creighton. The *Leader* helpfully informed its readers that "the cross could be seen at a great distance. Over 250 people attended the social." (This in a town of about 335 people.) Later, in August, the Klan stepped up its anti-bootlegging push, contributing $10 to the Women's Christian Temperance Union at its county convention and offering a $25 reward per arrest and conviction of any bootlegger.

Eventually, the Pleasant Hill members of the KKK began holding small meetings on the third floor of one of the buildings on First Street. Just like the gamblers up and down the block, these "Knights" would come and go quickly and quietly. They would scurry up the stairs and then later, after their meeting, would hurry off into the First Street night. But they always wore their hoods and robes, even downtown, so that their identities were not immediately known.

Yet, despite the obvious sympathies of some of the townsfolk, the Invisible Empire never conquered Pleasant Hill. Their form of brutal, fire-breathing racist piety did not play on First Street. And Midnight? He didn't even flinch. They could never lay a hand on him. He would have stood on the sidewalk, hooked his thumbs in his vest, and let out a full belly laugh at these furtive white-sheeters before heading up First Street for another snort of the "white mule," another hand of five-card stud, and another squeeze from one of the "dusky maidens" at the boardinghouse.

No matter how outrageous his behavior, Midnight would have been immune from Klan intimidation and harassment. As "disgusting" as some of the locals might have found Midnight's manner of conducting his affairs, he was still one of them. The

Underwood name remained highly respected in Pleasant Hill, despite this black-sheep son. Midnight was of the town. He was as much a fixture in downtown Pleasant Hill now as the train depot itself.

By the late Twenties, Midnight was doing so well running card and dice games that he was able to expand into real estate. He even bought one of the prime properties downtown, the venerable Stillwell Building at 105 First Street, at the corner of Wyoming. It was just across the street and down the block from where the "Knights" of the Ku Klux Klan were holding their ultimately futile meetings. Midnight didn't have to slink up these stairs. He owned the whole building.

Since the days before the Great War, the Stillwell Building had always boasted two prime upstairs tenants: a doctor's office in the front and poker games in the back. (As early as the spring of 1912, the authorities, in one of their temporary fits of anti-gaming fervor, had broken up a popular running poker game in the rear, most likely the same suite of rooms that Midnight now took over for his games.) The Stillwell Building was as perfect a location to run a game as could be imagined downtown, looking as it did right over the train depot. Midnight and his crew could watch as fresh flocks of pigeons landed by the hour just below Midnight's windows.

It was here that Midnight put his friend Allen Kennedy, the budding card virtuoso, to work as the player at the table who could ensure that the returns on investments were always good. It was here in the Stillwell Building, which for a time was dubbed the Underwood Building in the local papers, that Kennedy would perfect what Dai Vernon was coming to think of as the ultimate crooked move, the most astounding sleight imaginable with a deck of cards. For Kennedy, the top floor of the Stillwell Building on First Street would be his vaudeville house, his parlor room, his version of Vernon's faraway society parties. It would be his unacknowledged stage.

Midnight's success at this chosen field gave rise to a third, and most enduring, theory about how he came by that resonant nickname of his. Well, old Midnight, folks used to chuckle, he got that name 'cause he conducts most of his business after dark. Others, usually those who dabbled in cards a bit themselves, had an even more specific twist on essentially the same line. They knew Midnight's reputation for somehow always doing well at the tables, always somehow beating the odds. They would shake their heads a bit and smile that, yup, Midnight always seemed to get his best hands after midnight.

What they didn't know was that Allen Kennedy was giving them to him.

6

SINGLE-O

A boy could see some amazing things down on First Street in Pleasant Hill. Magic was all around. It wasn't the rabbit-out-of-a-hat kind, featured by the occasional traveling magician at the People's Theater, or the vaudeville style of sleight of hand, snatching coins out of the air or causing billiard balls or cigarettes to vanish. It was the kind of unlikely, hidden magic that Dai Vernon chased after.

Gambling seemed to be everywhere in downtown Pleasant Hill by the end of the decade. And so were children; they, too, roamed pretty freely on First Street. But despite the rogues around, the kids were safe. Everyone kept an eye out for them, knew who their parents were, didn't let them get into trouble. Pleasant Hill was still a small town. People left their front doors unlocked. The gamblers didn't bother with these kids. As long as they stayed out of the way and didn't get all tangled up underfoot, the gamblers didn't even see them. But a lot of the children—the young boys, naturally—kept a close eye on the gamblers who came and went along First Street. If they hit it right, they could even learn something, too. The Pleasant Hill style of magic seemed to pop up in the most unlikely places.

When eleven-year-old Bob Shortridge stopped in at Burton's Restaurant on First Street one Saturday night in the winter of 1929, he didn't have gambling on his mind. Not just then. He had Burton's pie on his mind. He wanted a piece. He needed it. Young Bob, a sharp, serious lad, skinny and dark-haired, had just taken in a picture show, as they called them back then, and now he had to have a snack before he headed home. It was close to ten o'clock, getting a little late for him, and it was cold out. He made quick work of the pie.

Bob was alone in the restaurant except for the owner, Roy Burton, and maybe a dishwasher out back. As he approached the counter to pay Burton, he fished in his pocket for some change. He was still too young to be carrying folding money. Nestled in with the fistful of coins he pulled out of his pocket was the pair of white drugstore dice he carried with him everywhere. They sat openly on his palm as he counted out the money for the pie. Burton caught sight of them immediately, and barked, "What are you doing with them dice, boy?"

Bob, who despite his young age already fancied himself something of a gambler, didn't shy from Burton's question. He answered bluntly, telling him flat out that he liked to shoot craps. Burton reached out his hand. "I want to show you something about them dice," he said. Bob dutifully handed them over.

Burton took the dice in one hand and picked up an empty water glass with the other. It was one of those short, barrel-shaped glasses common at diners and lunch counters, round-bellied so that if it ever tipped over it would be less likely to hit its lip and break. Bob watched closely—he thought he was watching closely, anyway—as Burton dropped the dice in the empty cup and gave them a quick swirl. Craps was often played with a thick-lipped leather dice cup, which was supposed to pro-vide extra security against the possibility of manipulation. Bur-ton was simulating that style of play now. Bob could hear his dice clattering in the glass.

Burton tipped the glass and rolled the dice out on the counter. He hit the 2. Two 1's, what dice players call the aces, stared up from the counter. That was snake eyes. Bob leaned in now as Burton scooped the dice up and dropped them right back in the glass. A quick shake and he rolled again. This time the dice showed 3—a 2 and a 1. The 3 was craps, of course. Back in the glass they went for still another roll. Out came the 4 this time—Little Dick, the dice shooters called that combination, or Little Joe, or sometimes even Little Joe from Kokomo. Bob, wide-eyed, marveled as he watched Burton roll those dice—his own dice, which he had just taken from his own pocket—out of the glass again and again. Burton kept hitting the combinations in sequence: 5 . . . 6 . . . 7, the all-important number that could be either a winner or a loser, all the way up to 12, *boxcars.* Now there was a slang word that seemed tailor-made for Pleasant Hill. Burton had hit all the combinations possible with a pair of regular dice and he had done it in order. Just like that. As easy as the pie Bob had just eaten.

"Now, that's what people could do with dice when they know how," Burton announced as Bob took back his dice. "Just think about that." Bob pocketed the dice. He paid up for the pie and left, heading back home to his child's life of growing up in Pleas-ant Hill. But he did what Burton told him to do. He did think about what he had just been shown, this extraordinary demon-stration of dice manipulation. It wasn't difficult to think about, for it was memorable, truly stunning. Bob thought about it hard, so hard he came to a decision. At the tender age of eleven, Bob Shortridge decided he would never shoot craps again. He retired from dice. For good. It was a dramatic lesson, a lesson, in a way, in magic.

Pleasant Hill was not exactly what the con men would call a "right" town, a town controlled by a criminal syndicate, but it was in love with cards and dice. Gambling was, by the end of the decade, more than just accepted. It was firmly woven into the fabric of town life, a strong and colorful thread that helped define the picture of Pleasant Hill.

If only David Verner, with his extraordinary proclivities and drive, had been a boy in Pleasant Hill then instead of Ottawa at the turn of the century. He might never have left for New York. He might not have felt the need. He wouldn't have had to go riding for miles on his bicycle to see a simple gambling trick, or spend hours dodging the threats of the hucksters at the racetrack fairgrounds just to catch their latest scams. It would have all come to him. All he would have had to do was stroll down First Street and into Burton's for a slice of pie like young Bob Shortridge had done and he could have seen one of the highest expressions of the dice handler's skill possible. And Roy Burton wasn't even known as a sharp. He ran restaurants. He was really known for that pie.

And if Bob Shortridge had headed up the stairs at 105 First Street, the Underwood Building, as another local youth, Jim Wallace, did, he might have been frightened off poker as well. Wallace, who was born in 1913, came downtown hunting for a job when he was only ten, after his father died. His young mother, determined to hold the family together, had gone to work as an operator on the town switchboard, and Jim figured he was old enough to do something, too. At first he sold newspapers at the depot and onboard trains. Sometimes he pulled a little scam by taking a five-dollar bill and conveniently failing to make it back to the train on time with the change. Then he got a job as a "call boy" for the railroad workers. The train lines depended on strict schedules, and young Jim was responsible for rousing the workers who stayed at the boardinghouses in town. Jim was supposed to make sure the men were sitting up in bed, and then he could move on. Occasionally, one of them would fall back to sleep and miss his starting time. He would just blame Jim—"oh, that goddamn kid never did wake us up."

Gradually, Jim Wallace became something of a First Street regular, too. He wasn't a gambler, but he was bright and tough for a kid. He had to be. He developed a knack for getting close to the action without getting involved. Because he was still a child, nobody on First Street thought too much about him. But he was wide-eyed and saw what was going on. He kept tabs on the pool hall, the back-alley dice games, even the three-card monte games that sprung up along the street. They would appear seemingly out of nowhere, like on a Saturday when the street was crowded with farm families in to do their shopping, and then disappear just as quickly. Eventually, Jim started making a little extra money by working as a gofer, an all-around errand boy for the gamblers. That's what took him up the stairs of the Underwood Building, to the top floor back behind the doctor's office.

Midnight's suite of rooms wasn't fancy, but it was comfortable enough. Visitors weren't there to lounge. They wanted action. Midnight and the crew were a friendly bunch, and they had every reason to be. They wanted their "guests" to feel welcome. The noise level of the games was kept low, blending nicely with the jovial conversations held in that smooth-rolling western Missouri burr.

The rooms were furnished, of course, with a long dice table for shooting craps properly, and a few large card tables to handle six-handed games. There was a sink for washing up, and bathroom facilities. And it was a snap to send young Jim or another kid out for just about anything a crapshooter or card player might need or want during his hours of play. A sandwich? The all-night restaurants were just a door or two away. Home brew?

Something with a little more of a kick? One of the boarding houses on the small green just across the railroad tracks from the Underwood Building sold it out of the basement. They mixed it with a little fresh cherry juice there, just enough to make a boy sick, as they might say.

Allen Kennedy was up there in Midnight's rooms, too, plying his invisible trade. By then he was a full-time cardsharp, a mechanic, in Midnight Underwood's employ. Kennedy had turned thirty in June 1927, and he was now able to make his living with nothing but cards and dice. He did well enough to rent a small, white frame house a few blocks from First Street on South Campbell, where he lived with his wife, Mary, and his mother, Hattie, who had finally come in off the farm. Allen and Mary Kennedy had gotten hitched in 1922, when he moved into town after his father's death. Mary's people had come up from Oklahoma to Missouri, where she was born in 1891, six years before her husband. Allen, or Bill as he was known in town, seemed to have a thing for older women.

Midnight Underwood also lived not far from downtown. As befitted the boss, he owned his house, on Randolph Street just around the block from Kennedy. He didn't have a steady woman with him there, preferring as he did the gals downtown with their affections for hire. But he did move his parents, who had come back in the reverse foundry hegira, into the house with him (brother Fielding had stayed in Wisconsin).

Midnight and Kennedy were the gamblers with roots in the community. They kept up with their municipal taxes, stopping in promptly at city hall to have their payments logged in the book. They maintained running credit accounts at the Benson Brothers lumber yard, where they could pick up the supplies needed for repairs around the house or, in Midnight's case, for some of his other properties in town. They even made sure to pay their share of the street-oiling fees, an important service in a town where many of the roads remained unpaved. The oiling was especially crucial for Midnight's block on Randolph, which was topped by almost pure sand.

Most townsfolk didn't know exactly what Midnight and Kennedy were up to, but they knew it was no good. Yet the gambling pair was by no means shunned or labeled as outcasts. Far from it. Sure, there were the Bible-thumpers, the drys, the sheeted Klansmen skulking up First Street and occasionally roaring about gamblers and bootleggers and race mixers. But most folks looked on Mid, as he was also sometimes called, and Bill Kennedy as characters in the theater of their town. And most of them learned pretty quickly to stay away from their games. For their part, Midnight and Kennedy wouldn't hesitate to fleece a local player if he chose to get in their game. Kennedy once took the owner of one of the dry-goods businesses in town for a hefty sum. But they didn't go looking to trim the local nest.

They didn't have to. By that time there were about twenty-five trains each day coming in and out of the Pleasant Hill depot, bound both locally and beyond. Train passengers made the best marks of all. It was traveler beware, and if someone on a layover waiting for their connection felt like whiling away a few hours playing cards with some local hayseeds, well, that was their business. If they lost, well, as long as they had that train ticket out they could get home. The rail workers, too, were forever climbing the stairs at the Underwood Building. No matter how often they got taken, trainmen always came back for more. With the steady expansion of the rail lines, there were more of them now, hungry and thirsty men wandering downtown at all hours of the night with their pay jammed in the pockets of their overalls. They seemed never to tire of losing that money. Maybe, the locals used to laugh, they had just too damn much of it.

There were other games in town besides Midnight's. At various times, regular games were maintained above the pool hall on First Street. And several floating games moved around downtown. Dice were readily available at the drugstores, along with playing cards, both Bicycle and Bee-back. The Bees, which had no white border on the backs, were thought to be more deceptive for cheating moves. Eventually, some of the local businessmen even saw economic advantages to making a little room for gambling. In 1928, the popular Hayes Restaurant, where Midnight liked to eat, underwent extensive remodeling. The restaurant was enlarged, with the entrance to the dining room shifted from the depot side to the busy First Street side. The top story of the building was raised considerably to provide enough space for a second-floor card room. All these games dotting downtown were rarely molested or broken up by the night watchman. Occasionally a game would have to shut down temporarily, or move, when a wife complained to the town that there was no money in the house because her no-good husband was too busy losing his pay envelope at cards every week.

The town's tolerance for Underwood and Kennedy can be explained in part by Cass County's long friendliness to rebels. Frank and Jesse James, veterans of the bloodthirsty raids by Quantrill's guerrillas on the Confederate side, had rampaged through the area as bandits after the Civil War. By the Twenties, their memories were bathed in romantic myth, and geezers were still emerging from time to time in Missouri and Kansas claiming to be the real Jesse, still alive and looking for a little peace, quiet, and clemency from the governor. New Robin Hoods had also emerged by that time to inherit the James legacy. Probably the most popular in Missouri was Pretty Boy Floyd, who was said to freely travel the "outlaw trail" from the "right" town of Joplin near the Oklahoma border on his way north to the mob-run Kansas City.

Floyd sightings were common in small towns throughout the heartland and he, or someone who looked a lot like him, was spotted regularly in Pleasant Hill, too. One night an excited friend rushed up to Jim Wallace to say that Floyd was just then having his dinner in one of the twenty-four-hour restaurants near the depot. They ran down First Street and stood outside the window, gawking at the handsome, dark-haired bank robber just sitting there, eating his supper.

Perhaps the strongest cards both Kennedy and Underwood held at all times were their families. Everyone knew a Kennedy or an Underwood. Allen's mother, Hattie, was a member of the Baptist church, as were several of his sisters. His brother Mallory, who had been called up in World War I, worked at several legit jobs, as did another brother, Charles. (Still another brother, Scott, settled in Idaho after being based there when he was called up for the Great War. He broke the unwritten rule of returning to Pleasant Hill, though he did visit regularly over the decades.)

Midnight's parents were solid, civic-minded people. His father, Tom, had once served as the town's night watchman for eight years, from 1891, when Midnight was eleven, to 1903, when he was twenty-three and already raising hell. And Midnight's brother Max was a farmer with a solid business outside of town. Items on the various Kennedys and Underwoods appeared routinely in the social columns of the newspapers, even, surprisingly, in the grouchy *Republican* before it closed. (Conversely, whenever the carnival was in town, the local papers would rail against the carny workers and their petty scams, which were peanuts compared to the card games at the Underwood Building. But, then, those grifters were outsiders.)

Midnight liked to walk the oiled streets on the five-minute stroll downtown each afternoon, when he started his workday. But Kennedy used his winnings to buy a snappy Ford Model A coupe, which for a time became as much his trademark as the felt hat he wore everywhere. The boys in town kept their eyes on that car. Zipping by or gassing up the car at the filling station, Kennedy, with his dark hair, square jaw, and mysterious ways looked like someone out of a movie, the boys thought, maybe a little bit like Richard Dix from the westerns. To Kennedy, the car was a convenient cover for his cheating. He secured a business license at city hall for a one-man taxi service, stuck a sign in the windshield, and placed a few advertisements. But that was all a front. He may have provided the occasional legitimate ride to an out-of-towner visiting relatives or some salesman hustling down to the depot, but the whole taxi idea was really just "shade" for his gambling. It gave him a legal occupation to list when census takers and the like banged on his door and it provided him with a natural opportunity to mix easily with the train passengers forever streaming into Pleasant Hill, every single one of them a potential mark.

With his car, Kennedy also served, in effect, as an outside man, a "lugger" (also called a "roper" or a "guide"), steering the pigeons into his own games, where he could then turn around and cheat them with sleight of hand. It was easy while driving a customer around Pleasant Hill to bring up gambling. And if the passenger showed any inclination to get into a game, well, Kennedy happened to know just the place. As a matter of fact, he was heading over there to play, too, right over in that building on the corner of First and Wyoming.

The boys couldn't see the many amazing tricks Kennedy did up there in Midnight's gambling rooms for the simple reason that his magic was always hidden. Unlike the magician, the cardsharp kept not only his methods but his effects invisible, too. There was a trick going on, but nobody saw it. Kennedy was polished now, manipulating the cards or dice at will whenever necessary to tilt the game to his partners and himself. Cheaters had slang, dating back to the days when the game of faro ruled the West. The best of the mechanics among them were called "artists." The Underwood Building was, in effect, where Kennedy had his artist's studio.

If the dice action was heating up, Allen Kennedy would certainly be at the edge of the table working the cubes. Table crap games required that for a roll to be legal, the shooter had to fire the dice all the way to a backboard built in at one end of the table. Both dice were supposed to bounce off that backboard. This rule was intended to cut down on the controlled shots that were possible with regular dice, in which one of the dice would slide only a few inches while the other tumbled freely, creating the illusion that both had been thrown fairly. At a dice table, it was much more common for mechanics like Kennedy to switch loaded or mis-spotted dice in and out of the game as needed. These could hit the backboard recklessly and still come up with the right numbers.

With gaffed dice, Kennedy used an exquisite switching move known among cheaters as the "socket holdout." He got so good at this sleight that a family legend sprang up among his many relatives that he must have some kind of actual pocket or pouch in the folds of skin of his shooting hand where he could hide his crooked dice. His shots just didn't seem possible any other way. (For looser street games, Kennedy could apparently also rely on the difficult controlled shots with regular dice, which he had mastered beautifully, too. One of his favorite moves was to roll the bones apparently fairly, yet manipulate them in such a way that one of them always turned up the same number.)

Cards, though, were Kennedy's first love, just as they were Dai Vernon's. Poker games like the ones at Midnight's were known as "brace games" or "cold games." These were house games, but since the house was run by cheaters, everything was thoroughly fixed. And because Midnight and the boys were on their home turf, the games were also completely secure, for them, anyway. It was a vastly different setup than going into a strange game somewhere and then trying to cheat, as some roving mobs of cheaters did. A brace game was pretty much a "mitt's lock" for the cheaters, a sure thing. No matter how convinced he might be that he was being cheated, a visitor was not likely to "kick" about it when he was so outnumbered. Kennedy and the others thus had a certain luxury at the table, with many cheating options open to them. They would have taken full advantage of it.

The possibilities were vast in a brace game. Cheaters and con men often used the word *play* to refer to a particular scam, as in "What's the play?" It was the right word for these games, for at Midnight's rooms there was a show playing every night, a deceptive vaudeville act with a little magic thrown in on the program. To ring in a stacked cold deck, like those cheaters who had thrown cards onto the Ottawa train tracks, unknowingly donating them to young David Verner, would have been child's play. Or, cheaters working together could use a venerable scam called the "spread."

This was a nifty little melodrama performed by two cheaters at the end of a hand of draw poker, sometimes called the "showdown," when everyone was supposed to reveal their cards so that the winner could be determined. The spread would come during an apparent dispute between two players—actually the two cheaters working in collusion. The first would call his hand a winner and lay his cards on the table face up. But he would keep them bunched tightly together, because he was actually a card short, having just palmed one. The second cheater, feigning disbelief and complaining that he couldn't see all his opponent's cards, would reach disgustedly across the table and spread the cards out for himself. As he did so, he would slip, from his palm, the exact card the first cheater needed to complete the hand he had just announced.

The second cheater would know the card the first needed because they would communicate secretly during play. They would use a series of signals, known in cheater parlance as "the office" or "giving the office," or even "to office." During a game with more than one cheater working the table, there could actually be a constant silent din going on, the imperceptible dialogue of this invisible stage show.

The office was also useful for yet another strategy for milking suckers known as "crossfiring" or the "whipsaw." This play didn't even necessarily require manipulation of the cards. The cheaters, by conversing through a series of offices, would determine which one of them had the best hand. The others would then start betting up the pot furiously, hoping to drive up their eventual winnings and catch the unknowing sucker in the crossfire before cleaning him out. They might not win every single hand this way, but the straight advantage of playing as a team against a solitary player was huge. Crossfiring was even more effective if the cheaters did use sleight of hand to deal a good hand to the sucker, but a still better hand to one of their own. Then the mark would bet with even greater confidence, which would drive the pot up even more before he lost it all. For the cheaters, that was a lucrative play, a winner indeed.

Cheaters in a brace game were limited only by their greed, ambitions, and larcenous talents. In the secure environs of the Underwood Building, Allen Kennedy certainly could have gotten by with far fewer skills than the ones he developed. But he obviously wasn't satisfied with just getting by. He had a natural talent for card handling, he had seen that early on when he first started dabbling as a youth, and he let that talent flower now.

Kennedy most likely began his serious mechanic's career by mastering the bottom deal. Subway dealing, as the cheaters called it, was already a venerable sleight in gambling circles in the early Twenties, when Kennedy got serious about sharping after the death of his father. Indeed, it was an ancient move. Gambling lore held that a cardsharp by the name of Wilson was the one who first brought it to professionally deceptive levels in the United States sometime in the 1830s. The great S. W. Erdnase himself, in Dai Vernon's bible *The Expert at the Card Table*, had endorsed the bottom deal wholeheartedly as far back as 1902. "If requested to determine from what single artifice the greatest advantage is derived," Erdnase wrote, "we would unhesitatingly decide in favor of bottom dealing." Elsewhere in his book, Erdnase called it "perhaps the most highly prized accomplishment in the repertory of the professional." Indeed, dealing from the bottom of the deck afforded cheaters great flexibility in poker.

Once he got the pack in his hands for the deal, a top-notch bottom dealer working with steady-handed—and steady-nerved—confederates had great control. If he had a partner sitting to his right, he wouldn't even have to worry too much about Erdnase's (and Vernon's) bête noire, the cut. In gathering up the discards from the last hand—the "dead wood" or "timber"—the dealer would casually place the cards he wanted to use for the upcoming hand on the bottom of the deck. A false shuffle would keep them there, and it was not too tough for him and his ally to execute a false cutting sequence that would ensure the cards were still on the bottom when he started to deal. Whenever he needed them during the round of play, he would deal the cards off the bottom, usually to whichever partner was supposed to win that hand. (To divert suspicion, false dealers generally avoided dealing winning hands to themselves.)

Contrary to popular myth, there was rarely a need to deal a lot of cards off the bottom, or to deal bottom cards consecutively. Many times, all a subway dealer needed to do was deal only one card, or at most a couple of cards, off the bottom to a mark to "bust" what was shaping up to be a promising hand. Done in conjunction with some well-executed crossfiring, this was a devastating tactic. And a cheater typically only dealt off the bottom late in a hand, when the pack was much smaller, and therefore the illusion much better. In still another approach, the false dealer didn't even need to "cull," or gather, cards ahead of the deal. Using an efficient little sleight called the "peek" or "pike" (magicians called that one the "glimpse" and it was useful for them, too), the dealer could surreptitiously check the bottom card at any time and office his confederates its identity. If one of them wanted it, the dealer would office back and then send it over from the bottom.

The bottom deal was certainly effective in many situations. But it was a difficult move to acquire and called for constant practice, usually hours of dealing around a table, alternately taking a top card, then a bottom card in an effort to make the deal appear consistent. The technical requirements were exacting, and the best "subway dealers" fretted constantly about staying sharp. Tiny, seemingly imperceptible details could nag at them. They worried about whether the noise a bottom card made when coming off the pack was noticeably different than that made by a top card. Sometimes the bottom card seemed to make a slight popping sound that had to be eliminated. It was a dangerous "tell," a sure sign of cheating.

False dealers also lived in constant fear of two occupational hazards. The first, called "grabbing air," occurred when the dealer missed the bottom card completely and his hand came up empty. The other, called "getting a hanger," was related but had the opposite effect. Two or more cards would come out, rather than just the single bottom card. Both developments were tantamount to placing a sign on the card table reading "False Dealer Here." (However, Dai Vernon once met an ebullient and physically imposing false dealer in New York by the name of John Rakanakis who had a novel method for covering up when he missed and grabbed air on a deal. Rakanakis would instantly make a large fist out of the unexpectedly empty hand and start yelling, "Money on the table, boys!" while he pounded away on the baize. Erdnase probably would have approved of this audacious cover tactic. "The resourceful professional failing to improve the method changes the moment," he wrote, in what became perhaps his most quoted maxim.)

Kennedy mastered many other difficult moves that were useful for cheating at poker. Some complemented the false dealing
and others were used in entirely different strategies. He could
"run up," or stack, cards through a series of false shuffles so that
he would have the exact hands he needed for a winner. And he
could actually peek at cards while he was dealing, holding his
head cocked at a casual angle, which made for an especially
natural-looking and deceptive sequence.

Kennedy also developed a deft technique for determining
what cards the other players held even when he wasn't dealing.
He accomplished this devilish feat when the player to his left,
the dealer on the next hand, called on him to cut the cards. (The
rules required the deck to be passed on to the next player after
every round.) As Kennedy cut the top half of the deck to the
table, he would quickly glimpse the top four or five cards of the
bottom half by lifting them ever so quickly and slightly. When
the dealer completed the cut, those cards became the new top
cards of the entire deck. In five-card stud, the most common
version of poker played by Kennedy, the first card dealt to each
player went facedown. These were the "hole cards" or "down
cards" and they were supposed to remain secret, while the next
four cards were dealt faceup. But if Kennedy were cutting, he
would know everyone's hole card at the start of play without
even touching the deck during the deal. That was a tremendous
advantage. It was cardsharps' magic.

Despite these impressive skills, all of which could "get the
money," especially in the safety of Midnight's joint, Allen
Kennedy made the decision to create yet another move, an entirely new sleight of his own devising. It was a brazen sleight
that, as he imagined it, would eclipse the others. To him, even the
difficult bottom deal did not suffice. This new technique would
not only be much more difficult, but once he mastered it, if he

could master it, he could manipulate not only the cards but the game, and maybe even fortune itself.

There was a huge obstacle, however. The move was impossible. Kennedy was thinking about dealing a card not from the bottom but from the center of a deck of cards, while making it appear that it was coming from the top. Imagining it with a deck of cards in hand showed how ludicrous it was. How could a man possibly take the deck into his left hand, come over with his right and slip a card from the center without fumbling around like a drunken pickpocket? Creating the illusion with the bottom card was already tremendously difficult. Now, Kennedy wanted to go halfway up from the bottom, split the deck, and try to deal. It was fantastic, foolish.

It was a move that cardsharps, a skilled but practical breed, didn't even bother imagining because it was considered beyond reach. The whole idea of deceptively dealing a card out of the middle of the deck was absurd. There were sound reasons the center deal was a myth, something to chuckle over while sipping a bit of moonshine after a game. As a class, mechanics tended to reject out of hand all techniques considered impractical, flashy, or overly complicated. They were unnecessary, so why bother with them? Kennedy was certainly steeped in that ethic. And yet he still forged ahead with this audacious sleight that, as far as he knew, no one before him had ever conquered.

Why was Kennedy so foolhardy? He certainly had no need to take on the center deal, none whatsoever. He had already mastered enough sophisticated poker-table magic to serve him well for a lifetime of trimming the marks. And working with confederates, as he did most of the time, was "quite sufficient to answer all purposes," as Erdnase had put it with finality in *The Expert at the Card Table*. Kennedy knew how hard it was to hone a move to the point where it could get past fast company. He knew the years of arduous, diverting practice it would take to reach a goal that might, in the end, prove unreachable.

So why did he do it? For the same reason that Dai Vernon, hundreds of miles away in New York City, spent his nights hunched over a deck of cards endlessly practicing, with just a cigarette for sustenance. Why was Vernon forever tinkering with his tricks, to the growing consternation of his beautiful young wife? Why would he study the theory behind magic with the diligence of a physicist? When Vernon first arrived on the scene, there were several think-a-card tricks in circulation already, some of which were strong and could fool a paying audience. With his charm and ability to weave a story, he could have easily structured an act around these tricks. Instead, Vernon imposed ridiculously impossible restrictions on himself. He stripped the effect down to the point where he was simply laying five cards faceup on the table and then talking a person into thinking of the one he wanted. Vernon's approach was just like Kennedy's. The magician was as driven as the cardsharp.

Both the magician Vernon and the cardsharp Kennedy, just three years apart in age and burrowing into their card obsessions during the same era, were striving in their own ways to be artists. Allen Kennedy never would have used that word about himself, but he was now thinking creatively about sleight of hand in Missouri at the same time Vernon was in New York. Vernon was forever looking to solve card "problems," scenarios or sequences he proposed to himself that, if he could crack them, would mean ever more stunning, ever more natural magic. Kennedy's compulsion to create the deal that couldn't exist now meant he had a goal beyond just "getting the money."

The move was tailored for his world. If he could take a deck, place it on the table for a legitimate cut, pick it up and deal any card he wanted, he would, in effect, conquer that world. He wasn't going to leave Pleasant Hill. There he was, grinding out the games night after night in the Underwood Building. But through the cards, he could look beyond them. He could look to being the best, to doing the impossible.

Kennedy had no one to consult when he started his assault on the center deal. No one had done it before. And there was no manual to pore over. The possibility of the sleight had been vaguely mentioned in print long before he was handling cards, in references he never would have seen anyway. One was in a little book called *The Secret Out*, a compendium of magic tricks intended for the general public that was printed in the mid-nineteenth century. The book included a trick for simulating cheating at cribbage that suggested, without instructions, secreting the four 5's in the middle of the deck. The magician was then advised to take each 5 by "slipping one out to meet your right hand,"—but the book offered no details on how that was supposed to be done.

Another reference to center dealing came in a newspaper article in 1900, when Kennedy was three years old. It's slightly more intriguing in retrospect because the subject of the article, magician Alfred Benzon, eventually met Vernon, though not because of the center deal. The article appeared in the Cincinnati *Enquirer* on Sunday, October 21, 1900, and was called "The Latest Tricks with Cards." In an as-told-to format, Benzon described fourteen effects he performed regularly, though he refused to divulge any of his methods to the newspaper. (He did assure readers that none of the tricks were "beyond the digital dexterity of anyone who will devote time to solving and practicing them.") At the very end of the rather long list of tricks, Benzon mentioned some gambler's sleights. "Second dealing, as gamblers understand it," he said, "is the most dexterous accomplishment of any handler of cards. In spite of any vigilance, I deal from the top, bottom or middle of the deck and distribute the cards as I see fit, and no one can detect it."

Benzon was no center dealer. He was a master showman, a mysterious, self-dramatizing character who claimed all kinds of skills and powers he didn't really have. He was also great at whipping up publicity for himself. Vernon, who, like Kennedy also was not aware of the Cincinnati article, met the bearded Benzon years after it had appeared. It was not long after Vernon had arrived in New York at the end of war. "You're the young Canadian in the air force," Benzon had greeted him at Powers's magic shop, which "tickled" Vernon at the time because it meant that big-name magicians were already talking about him. Vernon proceeded to fool Benzon, who once had his hands insured for $250,000 as a publicity stunt, with one of his early think-a-card effects. Benzon, whom Vernon considered a "fabulous performer," eventually ended up pursuing mentalism. He made quite a name for himself by dressing up his tricks with "seventh son of a seventh son" mumbo-jumbo and spouting fake ectoplasm. But he never actually dealt cards from the center of the deck.

Kennedy decided, sensibly enough, that his hands were the foundation to the center deal. Since leaving his mother's farm, he had pampered them. They were not rough-skinned, or nicked and gnarled like the hands of the typical Cass County farmers and workmen. The constant sleights had left them unusually strong and supple, with each finger well muscled in its own right. Yet, as powerful as his hands were, he still handled the cards with a light, delicate touch, as a pianist or a violinist would handle his instrument.

Corralling unruly digits was a big part of mastering sleights. A mechanic's dependence on his hands was total. They were responsible for executing his desired actions as smoothly and thoughtlessly as blinking or breathing. The hands were the tools, but they were not necessarily always under control. They were like exotic carnival animals, capable of all sorts of spectacular feats but in need of strict training and constant drilling. And like animals, they could rebel. Specific fingers had nasty reputations for causing problems during particular sleights. In the shift, for instance, the left index finger could be a nuisance. It had a tendency, a tenacious physical habit, to wag like an overanxious puppy during the sleight, tipping off anyone watching that something was up. To master the shift, the card handler also had to conquer that index finger.

During palming, the thumb was the culprit. At the placement of the card in the hand, it could recoil instantly, almost as if it were displaying its moral disgust at what the rest of the fingers were doing and wanted no part of it. Vernon called that irksome phenomenon the "fishhook" and warned novice magicians to guard against it. The worrywart bottom dealers fretted so much about "flashing" a wayward finger that a myth sprung up about a subway dealer who had actually cut off part of a finger to eliminate the problem once and for all.

As Kennedy toyed with the deck, imagining how he was going to accomplish this new sleight at a poker table with all eyes trained upon his hands, he saw that the left hand especially would need training. The left would hold the deck at all times during the deal. The technique Kennedy began crafting called for him to buckle the bottom half of the deck with the middle, ring, and pinkie fingers of his left hand, which would then allow him to push the bottom card of the upper packet out with the middle finger into his right hand. Bending the cards was not so easy even under normal circumstances. But Kennedy would have to do it invisibly, with the hand appearing completely relaxed, the thumb resting gently across the top of the pack and the index finger held casually at the front. He could not allow even a flicker of tension in the hand, knowing, just as Vernon always preached to magicians, that everything had to appear natural. But as Vernon liked to say, "It's not easy to be natural!" As strong as his hands were, Kennedy saw that he would require even greater strength for the center deal. It occurred to him that there were some artists who might be able to help him. They weren't too far away.

Dai Vernon felt like New York was magic itself when he began to spin his tricks for the stars and the swells, dazzling them with moves faster even than the hot jazz that sauced the Manhattan nights. To Allen Kennedy, living and working in the bucolic town of Pleasant Hill, Kansas City must have seemed like gambling itself. And just as Vernon had been propelled to New York in the Twenties, the artists of Kennedy's calling were flocking to Kansas City. It was a dizzying, rollicking game room of a city, the rightest of all the right towns, a place with gambling and cheating as its birthright.

Grifters had handles for all the cities in which they worked their deceptions. Some seemed pretty obvious. New York was simply "The City." Others played off a city's name or reputation, like St. Paul, Minnesota, which got the charming little handle "The Sainty Burg." Others were derived from the characteristics of a place. Hot Springs, Arkansas, was "Bubbles," Boston was "Highbrow," and Washington, D.C., "The Cap." Kansas City, just thirty-five miles or so north of Pleasant Hill, was "Kaw Town." Like a grifter's come-on, the nickname was simple, quaint, and even deceptive.

Kaw was merely the name of the Indians who originally inhabited the area where Kansas City developed. They were also called the Kansas. After they were driven away both those names were used for just about everything in sight, from the town of Kansas, founded in 1838, which became Kansas City, to the Kaw River, which flowed into the West Bottoms area. But the grifters' nickname fit for another reason, for the Kaw left something besides their name. They left a legacy that would last, for even they had been known as gamblers.

Kansas City may have originally been built on beef and wheat, but it grew and pulsed on cards and dice. By the 1860s, the city could lay a strong claim to being the gambling capital of the entire country. It was certainly the liveliest. Cattle barons, army officers on leave, Western buffalo hunters, all flush with cash and wild-eyed with anticipation, descended on the city's Old Town section. At the time, the six-block area may have had as many as forty gaming establishments crammed into it, more than in any section of similar size in any city in the United States. These houses set the standard of opulence and became the model for many of the great gaming houses cropping up in the West in cities along the Kansas Pacific rail lines.

The best known of all the houses at that time was Bob Potee's Faro Number Three. Potee's place, which was on Missouri Street above Stein's restaurant and saloon, was lavish. He had it decked out with fine-carved mahogany furniture, rich-woven curtains and carpets, and, in what quickly became the signature of the place, two life-size sculptures of shapely young nudes dominating the entrance hall. The sports were encouraged to pick their favorite one and give it a loving caress for luck before heading in to the tables.

When the Missouri state legislature managed, amazingly, to actually ban gambling in 1881, it seemed that the glory days in Old Town were coming to an end. Many of the operators moved their houses across the state line to Kansas and picked up where they left off. One who didn't was Potee. In 1883, believing that he was witnessing the end of a golden age of gambling, Potee put on his finest silk hat and strolled into the Missouri River. He had left a note addressed to an old friend, another gambling chief named Joe Bassett, directing him to "plant me decently." Bassett obliged as soon as they fished Potee's body out of the water.

Potee had made a stunningly bad bet. All the law ever succeeding in doing was killing off the spectacular houses for a time and driving the games into smaller, more anonymous clubs. Faro gave way to "short cards"—poker. And by the 1920s, Kansas City was spinning like a roulette wheel once again. The Kaw River and the Missouri River, which met and knotted into each other down at West Bottoms, were like bright ribbons desperately trying to contain a fat, roiling present all wrapped in grit and glitz.

Twelfth Street was the heart, the stage upon which Kansas City played, like Vernon's Broadway in New York. (In fact, if Damon Runyon had landed on Twelfth in Kansas City instead of Broadway, he wouldn't have even blinked.) The lavish houses were back and Twelfth had clubs to rival Potee's on its best night. Baltimore Recreation, at Twelfth and Baltimore, specialized in blackjack and took in an estimated cool million a year. The Fortune Club took in half that on 10-cent bingo games alone. The famed Turf Club was the largest of the bookmaking joints in the city, which was saying something, and took action on horses, sports contests from all around the country, and even threw in craps besides. Those were just the best-known dens. The hundreds of basement games, second-floor card rooms, and floating crap games hummed around the clock, too.

Sex was one of the great chasers to gambling in Kansas City, and there were hundreds of "bawdy houses" clustered around Fourteenth Street downtown. These were nightclubs that offered a dizzying cocktail shaker of sex, booze, and hot music. The most infamous of all was the Chesterfield Club, just a block from the federal courthouse. Here the beautiful waitresses traipsed the floor in little more than their shoes. Some might have worn change belts, some just see-through aprons. Some were said to have their pubic hair shaved in the shape of the suits—clubs, hearts, diamonds, and spades. They were Potee's famous "lady luck" statues come to life.

———

Kansas City even had its own version of magic shops, though these were for the cardsharps. Vernon had his beloved Powers shop in Manhattan, with its cases of vanishing silk flowers, its linking rings and gleaming cups and balls, and best, its hushed back room where he got to trade secrets with other elite magicians. Kennedy had the Kansas City Card Co. at Twelfth and McGee. For crooked gamblers, KC Card, as it was known, was a cross between an outfitter and the front porch of a general store. In 1926, the management had taken over the third floor of 1118 McGee, the former living quarters of the late Louis Curtiss, the prominent Kansas City architect who had designed the building. It was a hushed emporium, beautifully appointed with its own fireplace, the perfect setting to trade in the wicked wares that were the company's specialty.

KC Card baldly presented itself as a supplier of legitimate "club room" equipment, and it did sell some of that. But its real business, behind the respectable sporting facade, was in the kind of props that could make it easier for a cheater to turn some larcenous magic. Both at the shop and through its catalog, which would become famous in the trade as the "blue book," KC Card offered every devilish gaff an operator could wish for. It sold perfectly milled and calibrated crooked dice with fine inlaid ingots in every size and color. The company helpfully provided two pair with every sale, one true and one doctored. Another specialty was marked cards, delicately worked by hand (the company would go on to win underground renown for the work of a bevy of Asian women who created these "readers") and matched to all the popular backs available at the corner drugstores. Both the dice and the cards could be shipped anywhere in the world.

Just as Vernon disdained props in his magic, the elite mechanics like Kennedy, who relied primarily on sleight of hand, tended to look down on much of the cheap gaffs that KC Card and other companies liked to push, the rigged Chuck-a-Luck sets and fixed punchboards. In fact, the low-level grifters who depended on such mail-order items were derided as "catalog men." Most of the top-level mechanics who relied on loaded "ivories" or marked cards crafted them themselves.

Still, the shop on McGee was a refuge, a reverse-world oasis where cheating was the norm and the customers could talk shop with the men who worked there and anyone else who happened to stroll in. Kennedy would drop in from time to time to catch up on the latest gossip, meet other card and dice workers, other artists from his and related fields, and swap moves.

One day at KC Card he got to fiddling with some holdout devices. These were complicated mechanical contraptions, made with straps and springs and pulleys, which a cheater could wear under his clothes to ring cards in and out of a game. Typically, these "machines," as cheaters called them, were operated by moving the legs slightly or expanding the chest. By the Twenties, machines were already seen as antiquated. (The most famous type was called the Kepplinger, after P. J. "Lucky Dutchman" Kepplinger, a big, tough San Francisco gambler who invented it in 1888. Kepplinger's machine became the state of the art in the late nineteenth century after he was jumped by a group of opponents who were suspicious of his incredible luck at the table. After they discovered his secret, they placed the first order for the machines.)

As an artist who favored pure sleight of hand, Kennedy had no use for these holdouts. But at KC Card he strapped one on and sat at a table, trying out the action and simulating holding out and introducing cards into a hand. An old machine worker who happened to be there that day watched Kennedy and immediately announced that he had never in his life seen such utterly natural handling.

But these unlikely artists of Kansas City weren't the ones Kennedy came to see for help with strengthening his left hand. The day Kennedy arrived at their studios it must have struck the faculty at the Kansas City Conservatory of Music as odd. He didn't come off as a farmer, exactly, certainly not a hayseed. He was a bit rough around the edges, not like the starched-collar musicians there. But he was friendly enough and polite, soft-spoken. And he had nice hands. That was easy to see when he turned their attention to them. He was interested in some exercises to strengthen his hands. They were puzzled. What instrument is it that you play? they asked. Piano? Kennedy, who couldn't exactly answer that his instruments were cards and dice, told them that, no, he didn't play any instrument. He just wanted some exercises for his hands. He wanted, he told them, to develop an "iron grip."

Whatever they may have thought of the stranger, they obliged him. They carefully showed him two exercises that were useful for fingering concert instruments. For the first, they told Kennedy to press his fingers against a tabletop or a wall and to hold the tension, first with each individual finger, and then all of them together. The second exercise was a little more elaborate. Place corks between your fingers, they instructed Kennedy, four in each hand, and then squeeze. That'll give you the iron grip you're looking for, they said.

Kennedy began working on these exercises obsessively. Midnight Underwood may have had his enormous appetites for all the immediate pleasures of life, but Kennedy's greatest appetite, as he began working on the center deal, seemed to be for practice. And there was no immediate satisfaction. He was looking ahead a few years. He was like Vernon that way, sitting for hours, boring in on his own movements, refining, calibrating his

sleight. Kennedy would work his fingers until they could uncon-
sciously follow his thoughts. But unlike Vernon, who would stay
up all night, Kennedy had to practice during the day. He worked
at Midnight's all night.

Because he practiced during the day, Kennedy began to take
advantage of those other denizens of First Street, the sharp-eyed
children of Pleasant Hill. The classic technique for a card handler to monitor his progress had always been to use a mirror.
"The only proper way to practice is to be seated in the usual
manner at a card table with a looking glass opposite," S. W. Erdnase had advised in *The Expert at the Card Table* in 1902, "and
much time and labor are saved by this plan." But practice before
a mirror created problems and ultimately could be deceiving. It
was difficult to check all the angles with a mirror, and the sight
lines could be skewed, too. During play, Kennedy wouldn't be
staring straight ahead at all times, as he would with a mirror in
front of him. He would have to be chatting, looking at the other
players, and so on. A mirror could create a false impression of
how good a move looked.

Kennedy's idea to sharpen his practice sessions was to recruit
children as observers, monitors of his progress. Here he was
again unwittingly paralleling Dai Vernon, who had hit on the
same approach in his magic. Children were cruel, Vernon liked
to say, which he meant in a good way. They were helpful to a
sleight-of-hand man because they were incapable of being cagey.
If, while a magician was doing a card trick, he palmed a card
and the children saw it, they would go ahead and announce it.
That was helpful to the magician, Vernon felt, much more helpful than most adults, who might see the card but be too polite to
say anything. If a trickster could fool some blunt kids with a
sleight performed right under their noses, he might be getting
somewhere, after all.

When Pearl Kennedy, the wife of Allen's brother Charles,
died, leaving Charles a widower with a pack of children to take

care of, some of them went to board with other families around town. Allen Kennedy's nieces Ruby and May worked at the Kapke Beauty Salon in town and boarded at the Kapke house. Uncle Bill would stop in regularly to visit them there. And sometimes, he would set to working with his cards.

One local boy who was sweet on May used to run into Kennedy regularly when he came calling. He would watch May's uncle the gambler sitting at the dining-room table dealing cards for what seemed to him like "hour after hour." Sometimes Kennedy would face a mirror set in the sideboard, but other times he would actually invite the boy to sit across from him and watch closely. The kid found it fascinating to watch for a while, but because he couldn't really detect Kennedy doing anything out of the ordinary, his interest would fade as the session went on. It just looked as if Kennedy was shuffling and then distributing the cards around the table. As far as he could tell, May's Uncle Bill seemed to be able to deal out any card he felt like. For a boy, that was interesting, maybe, but it wasn't much of a card trick. You never got to see anything. But for the cardsharp, it was the height of his magic. The center deal was reaching perfection.

By the end of the Twenties, Midnight Underwood's local empire, such as it was, had grown and he had begun playing the stock market, the ultimate game of chance. He had also moved up from being just a contributor to the annual street fair to being a special sponsor of cash prizes in the "Class A—Cereals and Seeds" competition. At the 1930 fair he put up the prize money for the largest individual ear of corn and for the six longest ears of corn, but fair organizers reassured entrants that the sponsors would not be picking the winners because "all corn exhibits shall be judged by an expert judge of corn."

But by the time he turned fifty, in 1930, Midnight's appetites had started to take a toll that they never had back when he was still young and swinging a sledge at the scale foundry during the day and drinking and gambling at night. And of all his appetites, it was the nocturnal one, the one that had drawn him to Mass Gant's door nine years earlier, that began to gnaw at him in a grim, new way. Somewhere in his carousing, he had picked up "The Old Thing," syphilis. He was now, as the grifters put it, "burnt." The disease had an appetite of its own, a ravenous one. If left unchecked, and there wasn't a lot to do to check it in those days, it could prove more insidious than all of Midnight Underwood's appetites put together.

On July 1, 1925, police officers from Pleasant Hill had conducted a raid in town on a house just north of the American Scale factory. There, they broke up a moonshine-bathed birthday party. The revelers were evenly divided by sex and race: seven white men and seven black women. Allen Kennedy was one of the men. It might even have been his birthday party, for he had just turned twenty-eight two weeks earlier. Three Gants were among the women.

The officers focused less on the celebrants than on what they were celebrating with—four gallons of "white corn" and eighteen bottles of "home brew." Police didn't even make arrests because the jail in town wasn't large enough to handle so many people of so many different colors and genders at the same time, which prompted some winking coverage in the papers and no doubt some rumbling within the local Klavern. The host of the party, who had gone on the lam rather than be picked up, now faced a heavy charge because Prohibition was in force. But the others escaped charges altogether and in a couple of weeks the whole affair was pretty much forgotten.

But the incident was actually a tell, a tip-off of sorts, of growing danger for Allen Kennedy. He had begun to develop a steady thirst for hooch. It was a common affliction, indeed an occupational hazard, among cardsharps, whose nerves were under constant assault. Pulling off moves undetected in a game, under fire, could bring on an intoxicating sense of power. Yet, even working in the confines of secure brace games, there was never any final sense of release for the mechanic of the crew. No matter how well the game had gone the night before, no matter how flawless his sleight of hand, the cardsharp had to be back at his practice the next day getting ready for the next night. White mule could help uncoil some of that anxiety, at least for a while.

But in March 1930, Kennedy's nerves were apparently so frayed that he decided to take drastic action, so drastic that he temporarily left the shadows where he spent most of his life in Pleasant Hill. His medical fears even made the newspapers, not so much for what they were, but for where he had decided to go to try to have them soothed. He was apparently so desperate, and so comfortable financially, that he wanted only the best. That meant heading all the way to Minnesota.

"Allen Kennedy has gone to Rochester, Minn., to the Mayo Clinic," the *Times* announced in its social column (in a small farming town in the Depression, where a visit to the local doctor was a rarity, such a development, even if it involved the local cardsharp, meant big coverage). The heralded clinic, which would someday be known for treating presidents and royalty, was expensive (its famous checkup alone could run over $100 in 1930, more than $1,000 today), and Kennedy suspected he would have to stay for weeks. The *Times* added a casual, telling detail about the plans. "In the meantime his wife is visiting her mother in Oklahoma," the *Times* wrote of Mary, who, while clearly a long-suffering woman, was content to let him endure his own suffering alone.

Yet, just a week later, Kennedy was back. That was all the time he needed away from the table to find solace and a clean bill of health from Mayo. "Allen Kennedy returned Sunday from Rochester, Minn.," the *Times* dutifully followed up. "He was most agreeably surprised, after being checked through the clinic, to be told that he might come home, take ordinary care of himself, go about his business, and that he would be all right." Of course, they didn't have to specify what his business was.

The *Times* added almost a note of congratulations to this unacknowledged virtuoso in their midst, as if the paper's editors were pulling for him a little bit. It was that Pleasant Hill solidarity again. "Mr. Kennedy had somehow convinced himself that he would perhaps be kept in Rochester six or seven weeks," they wrote, adding lightly, "Then to be told that he might come home at once—well, it was about what a fellow would describe as 'the thrill that comes but once in a lifetime.' "

The thrill of a lifetime. Despite the need to climb into a whiskey bottle or a pail of the home brew at times, Kennedy was living an artistic thrill with his new sleight now. It was a thrill that had to cause further jolts to his nerves, much more powerful than those attained in one of Midnight's games or shooting craps at a cattle sale. But once he had his center deal perfected, his masterpiece, he actually began to leave Pleasant Hill occasionally to work on his own. The mechanics dubbed the practice of going solo "single-o," and it was considered, like the center deal itself, impractical and foolish.

It was also dangerous, for obvious reasons. If something went wrong and Kennedy was caught out at the table in a strange game, he had nobody to back him up, no friends to help him talk or fight his way out of the jam. He wasn't the most talkative guy in the world as it was, couldn't reel out the patter like Vernon, and he surely was no fighter. Even with a crew, games outside of Pleasant Hill could get ugly as quickly as it took to turn up a hole card, especially in Kansas City, where gambling was locked tight by the mob. Once, Kennedy and some of his boys were in a game up in KC that was raided, either by cops eager for their rake-off or hijackers looking to make a quick score. Whoever it was, Kennedy and the crew didn't wait around to sort out their identities. They went out the window and down the drainpipe and were back in Pleasant Hill by morning. Though that story got around town fast and became something to chuckle about, it was a close call nonetheless.

As he worked single-o, Kennedy began, without realizing it, to spread the seeds of his own myth. He wasn't a show-off, far from it. A good mechanic couldn't afford to be. As Erdnase had put it, "Excessive vanity proves the undoing of many experts." But Kennedy couldn't resist. He knew how historic his masterpiece was, and he started to demonstrate it to other cheaters from time to time. Mechanics could be as cagey as loan officers and as coy as debutantes when it came to showing their stuff to other cheaters. They were like magicians when they sessioned, constantly hemming and hawing, proud but professing rust and lack of practice. A typical disclaimer was to announce a move, but then to protest a lack of nerve, an inability to use it under fire. But since the center deal was already assumed to be impossible, there didn't seem to be any harm in showing it off occasionally. That's how the rumors began, of a mechanic somewhere in the Midwest who could actually hit his "slug" right out of the center of the deck, those whispers that worked their way to magician John Sprong in Chicago, and then on to Dai Vernon by letter.

One time when he was visiting KC Card, Kennedy exhibited the deal for a guy called Old Man Lee, who ran the dice department. He let Lee cut the deck, even triple-cut it, and then he just picked up the pack and dealt out his desired cards. There they were. Lee was astounded.

When he worked single-o in Kansas City, Kennedy tended to

favor the nameless, rough-and-tumble second-story joints that had sprouted up after Bob Potee had taken his last swim in the Missouri River and now dotted the city like feed strewn on the floor of the chicken coop. They featured games similar in style to the ones Kennedy knew in Cass County, fast and a little looser than the layouts in the big, swanky clubs along Twelfth Street downtown. They weren't for swells but for more country types, like Kennedy, beer drinkers who worked with their hands and wanted some action to distract and excite them before they headed back to work. These joints also suited his style of play and his new move. And if he got caught there was more of a chance that he could escape with a beating rather than death, which would likely have been the result downtown. But Kennedy was never known to get caught.

One night in Kansas City he sat with another cheater, a friendly young guy named Amador Villasenor. Villasenor was originally from Old Mexico, as they called it in Missouri, and he normally worked out of Amarillo and Wichita. Kennedy and Villasenor happened to meet up in a joint popular with miners. They were like the trainmen, these miners, just as tough and just as ready to lose their money. They, too, made great suckers, and they flocked to Kansas City from several surrounding towns, including Creighton down in Cass County, which had a big coal-mining operation going. They liked to drink while they played and they attracted hordes of cheaters.

After the game, Kennedy and Villasenor got to talking, off by themselves. They were both soft-spoken and amiable, and they took a quick liking to each other. Eventually, they got around to showing each other a little of what they could do. Kennedy demonstrated his deal, which he had been using on the miners.

Villasenor couldn't see it. Even though he was still in his twenties, some six years younger than Kennedy, the Mexican was an accomplished card handler who had been around mechanics for a long time. But he had never seen anything like

Kennedy's work. To Villasenor's trained eye, hunting for every flaw, every tell, it looked like Kennedy was nonchalantly dealing cards off the top of the deck. He was taking them out of the deck at will. This man's work is invisible, Villasenor concluded. It was magic. Perfect.

Kennedy never saw Villasenor again. But what he didn't realize at their parting was that he was actually sending this friendly Mexican gambler out as his emissary, a messenger bearing witness to the deepest secret any card worker could imagine. Kennedy was dispatching him from this little roughhouse miners' joint in Kansas City to a meeting with a man neither of them knew, a man named Vernon, the greatest card magician of them all. The greatest, except perhaps for Kennedy.

7

THE BEST I'VE MET IN YEARS

Vernon had come within a week of missing out on the secret of his life. It was a stroke of luck that he gotten in to see Amador Villasenor at the Sedgwick County Jail when he did. Just a week after Vernon had the session with him in Wichita on a cold February night in 1932, the Mexican gambler was gone.

Villasenor had been locked up on a murder charge for six weeks, since the end of December 1931, not knowing from day to day what was coming next. All of a sudden, Judge J. E. Alexander sprang him. The habeas corpus writ Villasenor's lawyer had filed had done the trick, and now he was free to disappear from Wichita. Just a week, and Vernon would never have heard him describe the center deal or point him toward Kansas City.

Villasenor had certainly made a convincing witness for himself. That's what had guaranteed his release in the end. After he had lit out of Wichita with a friend in July 1929, leaving the crumpled body of holdup man Benito Leija lying in an alleyway outside a Little Mexico pool hall, the local papers had played up the story of the shooting. With no hard information on who had been involved other than the dead man, they built Villasenor and the friend into rampaging gangsters, a hard-bitten duo of Mexican gunmen nicknamed the "Tourist" and the "Weasel" who were loose in the Southwest. One report even said that police as far away as Waynoka, Oklahoma, and Bar Harbor, Michigan, suspected them in similar crimes. It was all nonsense and rumor.

In fact, it had taken the cops two and half years to track Villasenor to Amarillo. But when Deputy Marshal Fred Kaelson found him hiding out in the Mexican community there and brought him back to Wichita in December 1931, it had only taken them about five minutes to believe him when he said he had shot Leija in self-defense. Leija had stolen $95 from him, Villasenor told the cops, money he'd won in a dice game. And when he went to the pool hall to confront Leija, looking for $10 or $20 of it back for some food and gas, Leija had answered by slapping him in the face and going for the gun or the knife he had hidden in his belt. Villasenor had had to shoot, he told the detectives. He didn't want to, he swore he didn't. But he had to do it to save himself.

The way he told it, Villasenor's story made sense to investigators. The gambler was soft-spoken, sincere, and, more important, consistent in his story. What he told police matched what they had since learned about Leija on their own while Villasenor was on the lam. Leija had specialized in holding up games, and apparently was an expert knife thrower. The detectives could see that Villasenor was no murderer. He couldn't even bring himself to utter Leija's name while telling his side of the story. "The man who was killed," was the best he could do, as if Leija had somehow just magically combusted one hot day in the Wichita pool hall. The cops bought Villasenor's tale, representatives of Wichita's Mexican community bought it, and now so did the court.

Vernon bought Villasenor's story too, not about the shooting, which he didn't bother with, but about the miraculous card work he had once seen in Kansas City. Vernon had been careful and thorough with Villasenor at the jail. "You've been a gambler all your life, haven't you?" Vernon was a detective, too, in a way. He didn't lead Villasenor on. He had just let him answer the questions freely. "You've played cards all your life," he began, "have you ever seen anything you don't understand?" It was an open question. Vernon didn't tell Villasenor what to say to that one. He answered with his description of the center deal.

Villasenor was no John Sprong. He wasn't a magician reporting by letter from halfway across the country some vague rumor of a phantom cardsharp. Vernon had always found that cardsharps as a class exaggerated much less than magicians. They were low-key about sleight of hand, theirs or anyone else's. And they could be dismissive, downright withering, when it came to moves that were too complicated or highfalutin, not utilitarian. "How do you get into it?" a cardsharp would ask when Vernon would show off some slick move he liked and thought might work in a game. As much as he wanted these cardsharps' moves for his magic, sometimes he would also try to pass along a move from magic to gambling. "How do you get into it?" It meant, that's nice-looking and all, but show me a simple and direct way to use it at the table. Villasenor was a cardsharp, maybe not an artist, but he was clearly an experienced, practical worker. And yet he had raved, gushing like young David Verner backstage at the Bennett vaudeville house in Ottawa, about this man who could deal cards from anywhere in the deck.

"How do you know he deals from the center?" Vernon asked, leaning in. His need to establish the basic facts had reined in, momentarily anyway, the charge of excitement he felt. Oh, Villasenor assured him, they had been friendly. They had talked. And then the man had demonstrated what he could do.

How did it look? Vernon asked, again and again. He wanted to be sure. "Phenomenal." Villasenor's English wasn't perfect, but that was an easy one to translate from the Spanish —*fenomenal.*

"It just looks like an ordinary deal," Villasenor said, "but they come from the center of the pack."

Vernon shot questions at Villasenor as fast as he could sail cards across the table. The gambler didn't flinch at any of them. But he also couldn't, or wouldn't, give Vernon too many solid leads. Where did they meet? "Oh, in a little place," Villasenor told him. "A lot of miners came in and people, pretty tough people." What's his name? "No, I don't know his name," Villasenor had replied. Maybe he knew and didn't want to say? Maybe he had just forgotten? Where, exactly, was this? "I don't remember," Villasenor declared flatly. "Somewhere in Kansas City." That was a little better than what Sprong had heard—"out West somewhere"—but not by much. As far as Vernon knew, Kansas City probably had hundreds of places where a mechanic could cheat at cards. How'd the deal look? Vernon returned to that one again. "Perfect." Villasenor's answer never varied.

Villasenor may have been sprung from Wichita, but not Vernon. He was tied down in the city now, especially with the new silhouette job Ross had secured for him at the swanky Innes Department Store. As much as he may have wanted to bolt, he couldn't just drop his job to go running off after a mythic cardsharp.

Vernon wasn't so good at waiting, and he could be even worse when he didn't get his way. Almost like a child, it was difficult for him to put his obsessions on hold. Ross had seen that up close soon after Dai and Jeanne first arrived in Wichita in January. Besides the Innes job, Ross had also arranged for the Vernons to take the place adjoining his on the third floor of the comfortable Harrison Apartments on Seneca Street ("Five-room efficiency . . ." the classifieds hawked, "overstuffed furniture . . . soft water, laundry, on two car lines . . ."), owned by a local magician named Carter Harrison. Ross had met Vernon five years earlier on a jam-packed tour of the magic community in New York City with his good friend T. Nelson Downs, but now he practically had Vernon to himself.

For the first couple of weeks in Wichita, the two magicians did little but huddle together over their magic. They were like frat boys at final exam time, constantly crossing back and forth to each other's rooms at all hours. One day they began their session at three in the afternoon and didn't stop until eleven the next morning. They were building on their magical ideas, and building their friendship, too, which would last for the next fifty-five years.

For Ross, who was born in 1900, six years after Vernon, these sessions were graduate seminars. Originally from St. Joseph, Missouri, he had studied in Chicago with the talented card magicians Hugh Johnston and Arthur Buckley, but he had never seen anyone capable of the advanced insights Vernon reeled out on a minute-to-minute basis. Even Downs, the great vaudeville "King of Koins" who was now sixty-five and pretty much retired, wasn't at Vernon's creative level. (For his part, the cranky Downs seemed a bit put out that his former protégé Ross had found himself a new guru. "Ross has not sent me any dope on Vernon's stuff," he wrote a friend. "Just keeps romancing how Vernon invents a new trick every few minutes with a deck of cards. He invented a dozen one nite when he [and] Vernon had a session. Poker stuff.")

Ross was no neophyte, though. He was a generalist, incapable, it was true, of most of the advanced gambling sleights that Vernon loved so much. But Ross was also something that even the great Vernon wasn't anymore, a working professional. Handsome and friendly, with a straightforward, easygoing style, Ross was a diligent, practical performer who, despite the hard times, was still managing to scratch out a living as a magician. (He also supplemented his income by selling ads for the Wichita *Beacon*.) He specialized in a version of the old-style "spook show," a popular early-century form of magic act that typically featured pseudo-spiritualist illusions like the famous "spirit cabinet," in which the performer was tied to a chair in a curtained cabinet while all sorts of ghostly phenomena occurred around him. Spook shows were usually presented at night, sometimes even after midnight. Ross had based his act on a version he had enjoyed many years before as a youth.

He booked his spook show as well as a straight magic act throughout the area, at schools, church associations, business luncheons, anywhere he could scrounge an engagement. He strongly favored classic effects that had played well in vaudeville, the type of material that Downs and Leipzig had put over so well in their heyday. These tricks were reliable and always made a big hit with an audience. That, Ross felt, was the main goal of magic.

Ross had seen a lot, too, crisscrossing the heartland playing small dates. He had had some funny experiences. Once, at a chamber of commerce banquet in a hotel dining room in a small Kansas town, Ross put on what was for him a lavish show. He was getting paid well and he wanted to finish big, so he decided on a trick in which he produced a half-dozen live baby chicks from the pockets of two volunteers summoned onstage from the audience. The trick actually required him to palm a couple of the chicks at a time and then magically produce them. He positioned one volunteer to his right and one to his left.

After producing the chicks from the pocket of the volunteer to his right, Ross turned to the man standing to his left. He was dignified-looking, Ross thought, maybe even a little pompous. When he reached with his right hand, holding the palmed chicks, into the man's inside coat pocket, it immediately crashed into something heavy and solid. Ross instinctively unloaded the chicks into the pocket and drew out his hand gripping the object. It was a half-pint bottle of whiskey.

The audience went wild. They laughed and clapped, some even standing and yelling. Ross was jolted by the force of their reaction, but he was an experienced enough showman to register that this was, indeed, the note to end on. He thanked the volunteers, took his bow and walked off the stage holding the bottle high. When he came back out, some of the chamber of commerce members gathered around him to congratulate him on the show. "Ross, that was a great piece of business," one said. The best piece of sleight of hand ever done. We certainly didn't see you slip that bottle of whiskey into the minister's pocket." The dignified volunteer, it turned out, was not only the local minister but a strict prohibitionist as well. "That's what made it just great," the chamber official assured the magician. It was Ross's turn to be befuddled now as he scanned the room, looking for the minister. He noticed that the man had apparently pulled something of a disappearing act at the show's end. Ross was left to imagine how surprised the minister would be to discover the two chicks in his coat pocket.

Although Ross had seen a lot, he had never seen anything like Dai Vernon, who seemed a force unto himself. He did everything on his own time, following his whims and damn the consequences. Finances, family, none of the responsibilities that could shackle normal folk seemed to matter too much to Vernon. He and Jeanne had been married for eight years, and it was clear that she was growing bitter at her husband's blithe disregard for the responsibilities of married life, his haphazard approach to providing for her and Ted. That "pretty money" style might have been fun and romantic back in their Coney Island days, but these were darker times. And now she was pregnant with their second child. Ross could see that life with Vernon wasn't always such a magic trick for Jeanne.

One day, as he was preparing to leave on a three-day tour, Ross stopped over at the Vernons' apartment to say good-bye and found Vernon still lounging in his pajamas. It was early afternoon, but, typical of him, Vernon had only just rolled out of bed. When Ross told him he was heading out of town for the next few days, Vernon immediately perked up and announced that he'd like to tag along. "I don't have anything to do," he said, asking Ross to give him a minute while he got dressed.

Ross was delighted at the idea of Vernon joining him. But Jeanne wasn't. She came into the room just as Vernon said he wanted to go with Ross. Now she laced into her husband. "You're not going on any wild goose chase," she told him angrily. "I want you to stay here and look after your family." Ross stood uncomfortably on the sidelines as the two of them argued. Finally, Vernon, hangdog, and with what Ross felt was "ill grace," announced to his friend that he wouldn't be going along after all.

"But I'll tell you one thing," Vernon added dramatically, "how long you going to be gone?" Ross told him again he would be on the road for three days. "Now look at me," Vernon announced loudly. "You notice I'm wearing pajamas." Ross had noticed. "Well, the minute you walk through that door I'm going to bed and I'm going to stay in bed twenty-four hours a day until you return."

Ross didn't understand what his friend was driving at. "You mean you're going to sleep?" he asked. "Whether you know it or not," Vernon told him, "I can go to sleep for any length of time I decide." Even Jeanne agreed with this: "Yes, Dai does have a remarkable faculty for sleeping for long stretches."

Not really knowing how to respond, Ross left and headed off on his trip. The evening he returned to Wichita, he went over to the Vernons' apartment. Jeanne met him at the door. She seemed disturbed. "Where's Dai?" Ross asked immediately. "He's asleep in bed," she answered, motioning toward the bedroom. "Do you remember when you left three days ago he said he was going to bed to stay there while you were gone?" Of course Ross remembered. "Well," Jeanne said, "he is capable of sleeping for long periods, but I honestly believe he's been asleep day and night for the past three days. I've watched him very carefully."

Ross was skeptical. This seemed to be too much, even for Dai Vernon. He pressed Jeanne. "You mean he hasn't been up at all—hasn't eaten or drunk anything?" Jeanne said she had kept a close eye on the groceries and could see that there was nothing missing. "I haven't seen him even so much as go to the bathroom," she concluded. She seemed sure. Ross suggested gently that perhaps Vernon had actually sneaked out while Jeanne was asleep. "He couldn't possibly do it," Jeanne answered, explaining how she had gone so far as to lock both the front and back doors and hide the keys to the apartment. "He's certainly not capable of jumping from a third-floor window," she said. "Go in the bedroom and take a look at him," she suggested to Ross.

Ross went to the room and found Vernon "peacefully snoring away." Ross shook him, hard, and managed to get Vernon to open his eyes. "Haven't you started yet?" Vernon asked him, a startled look on his sleepy face. Ross told him that not only had he started, but he had just returned from his three-day trip. "Well," Vernon announced, "maybe it's time for me to get up." He got dressed. Without missing a beat, the two magicians then launched into one of their marathon sessions. It seemed the only logical conclusion to this series of unlikely events.

Ross didn't quite let it go, though. A couple of days later, he pulled Jeanne aside and buttonholed her again about Vernon's apparently having slept for so long. Was she absolutely sure he had never budged during those three days? Jeanne was adamant, positive—he had never left the bed.

Ross puzzled over this odd episode for another fifteen years before he finally learned the solution to the mystery. On a trip to New York in the late Forties, he happened to see Vernon's son Ted, who back in Wichita had yet not reached six. Ted was on furlough from the navy when Ross met up with him. While they were catching up, Ross happened to mention the incident of his father's "long sleep." Ted smiled. "I have an admission to make," he began, and then he went on to detail his role in an elaborate hoax conducted by his father. Vernon had "bribed" Ted, as he put it, to run to a stand next door and get some hamburgers and Coca-Cola packed up in a cardboard takeout box. Vernon had then run a string out the window of the bedroom. "I would attach the box and he would haul it up to the room," Ted said. He and his father had kept up the act for the full three days. Jeanne couldn't stay in the apartment the entire time, Ted remembered. The moment she went out, Vernon would run to the bathroom. It was all a trick, a petulant stunt to punish Jeanne for objecting to his plans.

The job that had lured Vernon to Wichita in the first place, and was now keeping him from leaving for Kansas City, was actually a comfortable, accommodating position. The Innes store didn't require him to come in and start cutting until eleven each morning, an acceptable compromise for a nighthawk like himself, and he could close up his stand by 5:30 each evening. That left plenty of time for working on card tricks with Ross and socializing with Loring Campbell, another Wichita magician who, like Ross, was hard at work trying to survive by giving performances throughout the Midwest. (While Vernon took to Campbell, he seemed to loathe magician Carter Harrison, who owned the apartments where he and Ross were staying. Vernon, apparently feeling that Harrison was uninterested in the higher subtleties of the art, refused to show him any of his tricks, much less how they were done. Sometimes he wouldn't even answer the door if he knew it was Harrison knocking.)

Innes, which billed itself proudly as "Wichita's Finest Store," lived up to the title. The city, with a population of only about 115,000, still boasted a handful of feisty department stores, but Innes was the gem of the bunch, a classic department store with big-city pretensions. It tried to feature a little of everything, from lingerie to furniture to health food ("Special Reduced Prices on the Kind of Foods Your Physician Wants You to Have to Get Well and Keep Well!") to houseplants. The store brought in the bargain-minded crowds with an annual "Capacity Day," when it slashed prices almost to cost. And it brought in the swells, or those who liked to think they were swells, by presenting representatives from the big-name cosmetics companies like Elizabeth Arden, "Straight from the New York Salon." It held seasonal fashion shows boasting "Living Models" in its elegant sixth-floor Tea Room and even exhibited well-known local and regional painters.

Innes proudly trumpeted Vernon as an artist, too, though not as a magician. Befitting its status as the finest store in the city, Innes had gone out and gotten the finest silhouette cutter in the country. "Scissor Artist Is Coming Here," declared a short piece in the *Wichita Beacon* heralding his February arrival at the store. "His silhouettes are startlingly correct," the paper wrote of "D. W. Vernon," the name he favored when doing portraits, "and his work has been recognized the world over. Persons who want to see an unusual likeness of themselves will be interested in Mr. Vernon's coming to Wichita."

Plenty were interested. Soon, Vernon was swamped with Wichitans who wanted their portraits cut in black paper—50 cents for one, 75 cents for two, or three for a dollar. He was suddenly a phenom again and the line of customers waiting for him on the main floor at Innes grew longer and longer each morning. The papers picked up on the trend, too. "Yes, that's my silhouette up there," wrote one columnist in the *Wichita Eagle* who covered the town's striving social and shopping scene. "And very well done by Mr. Vernon, who is at Innes now. . . . As a silhouette artist, Mr. Vernon is one of the best, and he's a conversationalist par excellence. . . . Go in to see him and let him do yours. . . . They're awfully good now."

"Conversationalist" was code for flirtatious. Vernon, a witty, debonair man, could handle the ladies as smoothly as he could handle the cards. And he could be as imperious as a Dutch master. If he didn't like someone's looks, he would refuse to cut their silhouette. At his Innes stand, he specialized in delicate portraits of the pretty, young marcelled maidens of Wichita. And although he worked amazingly fast—he advertised two minutes, but cut many of the silhouettes even quicker—he still managed to catch exquisite details. A tucked chin, a pouting lip, batted eyelashes. With these seemingly minor details he was able to illuminate his subjects despite the apparent limitations of the medium. "Wichita Society As Cut By A Pair Of Scissors," was the title of a stunning spread of portraits in a column in the *Beacon*, which also got in on the act. "Silhouettes have staged a popular revival thruout the world," columnist Jane Evans told her readers, "and we find these quaint little reminders of bygone days recording the profiles of the most modern miss." Evans changed her logo to a flattering Vernon silhouette, too.

"Wichita society" was, in fact, Vernon's natural market. They were just a fresher, western version of the Long Island society partygoers or Asheville country club set that Frances Rockefeller King used to send him to back east. The biggest difference was that Wichita was new money, in some cases brand-new money.

So far, Wichita had been pretty successful at holding the Depression at bay. A magic trick of geography was the main reason. In 1928, just a year before the crash, a series of deep oil pools was tapped in Sedgwick County in Wichita's backyard. Within a year, 116 wells were furiously pumping an estimated $24 million in "black gold." What had been wheat fields and fallow suburban plots were now, practically overnight, flowing plots owned by the newly wealthy. "The magic touch of oil has given a new skyline to great Sedgwick County," the *Wichita Beacon* exulted on the first anniversary of the discovery of oil. "Rich, peaceful farms remain, bringing forth the products of the soil; but they are dotted with towering structures, mammoth plants which are producing wealth in prodigious quantities."

A new class of small-city oil barons bubbled up, too. They were as obvious around town as those "towering structures" now dotting the Kansas wheat fields and they also attracted attention in the papers. "Two of the best known of the oil families are in the Colorado mountains enjoying a vacation. . . . The other two are building homes in Wichita," the *Eagle* reported. (From 1928 to 1929, building permits in the city surged from $3.9 million to just over $6 million.) Suddenly, no one was sure anymore who had struck it rich the day before. "Wichita Street Car Motormen Spending Royalty Money Now," the *Eagle* reported in August 1929. "Maybe your favorite street car motorman is an oil magnate. . . ."

Two other elements helped Wichita weather the tough times. Kansas had always depended on its wheat for survival and now it looked to the huge grain elevators north of town as a kind of municipal cupboard. As long as the weather held in growing season, Kansas could produce a staggering amount of wheat. In 1931, the Jones Milling Company in Wichita actually experienced a boom in business as charities like the Salvation Army and state and city agencies around the country turned to cracked wheat, which sold in the grocery store for about 5 cents a pound, as a main staple to feed the poor. It was estimated that a bushel of wheat could feed a family of four for a month. Soon, cracked wheat was becoming a culinary trend. "Downtown Diners," an ad for a new eatery declared at the beginning of March 1932, "A New Thrill Awaits You! . . . Announcing the Opening of Wichita's Newest Restaurant—the whEAT BIN." It promised "The End of Every Kansan's Rainbow . . . A Pot of Golden Kansas Wheat Which Is Really Good to Eat."

Publicity boosters of the city had struggled to come up with a good name for the other economic spark in Wichita, the city's emergence as the leading aviation manufacturer center in the West. They tried "The Gloucester of the Air" and the "Detroit of the Air." Finally, the "Air Capital" seemed to stick. Just as the oil fields became a hot news beat, so did anything related to the skies. Wichita was one of the first cities in the Southwest to institute daylight airmail service (which Vernon took advantage of to stay in touch with his magic buddies back in New York). Airplane manufacturers frequently debuted their secret new models in Wichita (the "Crested Harpy" monoplane by Sullivan Aircraft was a big hit of 1929). And because the city was a stopover point on the transcontinental flights from both coasts, celebrities frequently posed for news photos out at the airfield while they waited for their plane to be refueled. Wichita also played host to dangerous aviation competitions, including the continuous flight contests popular in the late Twenties and early Thirties. They were like dance marathons in the skies.

All this frantic business activity helped attract national conventions, which the Depression didn't seem to be able to slow down. In late 1931 and early 1932, auto dealers, beekeepers, stationers, and newspaper editors all flocked to Wichita for their association meetings. And just as the gamblers had followed the ranchers and cowboys who were trying to establish Wichita as the queen of cattle towns in the nineteenth century, the cheaters, grifters, and short-change artists now followed these twentieth-century pigeons. The city had had a lively tradition of gaming since General W. B. Hazen of the U.S. Army supposedly won twenty lots of prime "original town" real estate in a stupendous pot in a poker game in 1874. By the early Thirties, private gambling clubs thrived.

In the 2,000-strong Mexican community, in which Villasenor moved, monte was the main game. Also known as Spanish Monte, it had no connection to the famous three-card street swindle. (Three-card monte was "a misnomer if ever there was one," according to Herbert Asbury, who wrote a popular history of gambling, because the con game "had no more actual relationship to *Monte* than Old Maid.") Monte was a banking game, probably related to faro, in which players bet on the likelihood of a card coming up to match one of four random cards laid faceup on the table at the start of the game. Played on the square it could be a near-even proposition. But as Villasenor had shown Vernon and Ross, with a couple of smoothly executed sleights, it could be skewed heavily in favor of the dealer.

Innes was so happy with Vernon and the droves of customers he was bringing in, that he was asked to extend his stay. The store ran an ad letting its customers know that "Mr. Vernon" would be on the main floor in the stationery department "by popular request." The ad was illustrated with an unmistakable portrait of George Washington that Vernon had cut in honor of the upcoming Washington's Birthday. Innes also placed an article in the *Beacon* announcing that Vernon was being held over. This time they included a photo of him, too, and a single-word headline. The lone word was *"Artist."*

The great success Vernon was enjoying at Innes didn't make him feel like an artist, however. The silhouettes were irrelevant to him. What he wanted now was to go and find the artist Villasenor had crossed paths with in Kansas City. He wanted to see if that artist really existed, if he really could do the impossible, as Villasenor had testified.

But by keeping him in Wichita, the silhouettes allowed still another artist to find his way to Vernon. This artist was a kindred spirit who would in many ways match, and sometimes even exceed, Vernon's own manic genius. He would become, in the almost sixty years they would be friends, Vernon's Sancho Panza, his little brother, his comrade in sleight of hand. He first came into Vernon's life as a chubby but improbably graceful moon-faced man-child up from El Paso for a visit with Faucett Ross.

He and Ross had been corresponding for almost three years. One night he walked into Ross's apartment, took out a pack of cards, which he held lightly in his hand, and asked the two magicians to sit down.

For the first twenty minutes that Vernon knew him, Charlie Miller did card tricks, one after the other, a short program. When he finished he looked straight at Vernon and asked, "Am I using the right method?"

Vernon didn't get him right away. "These are the card tricks that Max Holden wrote about in his column," Miller added, "but gave no explanation. . . ." They were Vernon's own tricks. The columns in *The Sphinx* magazine were dispatches from the New York card front, sent out to the magical trenches around the country, and they helped spread Vernon's legend. For many of the magicians in the sticks who read Holden's columns faithfully, these tricks became legendary, too. They filled them with wonder, even jealousy, at what the big-city card expert could do. For Miller, they had served as inspiration. He had taken it upon himself to puzzle out his own methods for the tricks and now he had the cheek to test them on the great Dai Vernon himself.

Vernon quickly became delighted with the kid. Miller was absolutely amazing. He had not only doped out Vernon's own tricks, but as they went on to session, Vernon saw that Miller, who was only twenty-two, already had an encyclopedic catalog of his own routines and effects, original twists on sleights, all sorts of subtleties and creative new approaches to close-up magic. To top it all off, Miller was also a devoted student of Erdnase's *The Expert at the Card Table*. Vernon fell fast for him. It was artistic love at first sight.

As secretive and quirky as he was about his art, Vernon, who was thirty-seven when he met Miller for the first time, never hesitated to welcome someone who showed creativity and originality into the fraternity. He was proud, but he was rarely threatened by another magician. He didn't approach magic as a competitive sport. There were some magicians he just didn't care for, Houdini and Thurston being the two most famous. But he rarely expressed anger or played at the jealousy games so common in magic. By the time he met Miller, Vernon's standing in the art was as solid as the Lincoln Memorial. He reveled in other artists, and when he saw what Miller could do he took it upon himself to spread the news about a new star.

"The boy who has the 'real dope' is young Charles Miller of El Paso," Vernon declared in a letter to his good friend, magician Sam Horowitz back east. After their first meeting, Miller and Vernon had sessioned relentlessly for a few days. Now Vernon began a one-man publicity campaign on Miller's behalf. He promoted him, anointed him. He wanted him placed in the top ranks immediately. "Ross has hundreds of letters from him," Vernon wrote Horowitz, "and he is a genius considering the fact that he has been shut off by himself most of the time." It was that original sensibility of Miller's, his ability to overcome his own isolation through creativity, that probably impressed Vernon the most. Miller had been forced to think for himself. *Genius* was not a word Vernon threw around lightly. Usually he reserved it only for the greats of the past, like Johann Nepomuk Hofzinser and Jean Eugene Robert-Houdin.

"He has real ideas," Vernon continued, "manipulates coins and cards beautifully. . . . I would like to nominate him for the 'mythical Inner Circle' as he is really a No. 1." Just five days after this spectacular endorsement, Vernon, a notoriously lax correspondent, penned still another letter to Horowitz singing Miller's praises. He sounded almost giddy describing the talents of his new young friend, and he wanted to make sure the New York boys got it. He instructed Horowitz to alert John Mulholland, now the editor of *The Sphinx*, that when Miller "visits New York he's going to have them all talking. . . . Say that I think he's the best I've met in years."

As practical a performer as Ross was, he had his own obsession for collecting tricks. At thirty-two, he had already managed to strike up friendships by mail with many of the leading magicians in the country. Through a combination of friendship, flattery, gossip, a sympathetic ear, and the offer of his own and others' secrets, he had diligently induced many of them to send along their treasures. He kept them in meticulously organized files, and this goldmine was undoubtedly another attraction for Vernon when he came to Wichita. Ross gave him free rein to root around in the manuscripts. "This chap Ross has the most complete collection of secrets I've ever seen or heard of," the appreciative Vernon wrote to Horowitz, ticking off some of the names of the contemporaries who had contributed to the files. "Maly . . . Bowyer . . . Lorraine . . . Violet . . . Irvin . . . Tommy Downs . . . Eddie McGuire . . ." If the heart of the Inner Circle was in New York City, these were the regional masters of the art.

But none of their letters compared to the ones Charlie Miller had begun sending to Ross in 1929, when they first struck up their friendship. Miller had started by declaring his great interest in magic and how keen he was to learn from someone with performance experience. And then a steady stream of dizzying monologues to Ross commenced. His written voice was at once confident yet shy, audacious yet hesitant. In one line he would promise Ross some original card tricks. In the next he would hedge like an insecure child. "Don't expect too much," he warned, "because I am not very original and they may not appear to be so good." (They were, in fact, brilliant.) And Miller was always bringing up Vernon's name, sometimes several times in the same letter. He would almost badger Ross, wondering whether Vernon was really capable of these miracles he had read about.

In this written flood, Miller would pry gently, always looking for new secrets from Ross. He would run theories by the older magician, as well as his solutions to many of the vexing card problems of the day. When needed, he would even add charming little drawings to supplement his descriptions. Once he even offered his take on the second deal of Walter Scott, at the time one of the most prized secrets in the magical underground. Scott was a mysterious New England card handler who would come to be known as the "Phantom at the Card Table." The workings of his sleight were guarded and speculated on with equal fierceness. "I think that I know what it is, though," Miller wrote brazenly. "The cards are held in the left hand slightly spread. The right second finger pulls out the card. . . ." Miller didn't shy from tackling anything.

Ross, of course, had little use for the second deal. He didn't delve into the gambler's card sleights. But he kept encouraging Miller to write to him, and he and Vernon helped connect Miller with other magicians around the country. When Miller wrote to John Sprong in Chicago, it led to a funny mix-up. Sprong had never heard of a Charles Miller before. The letter from Miller was so insightful and the tone so similar to Vernon's, that Sprong concluded it really must have been Vernon who had written it. Instead of answering Miller, Sprong wrote to Vernon. He asked him why he had written from El Paso, Texas, using a different name. Vernon, greatly amused, wrote back to say that Sprong had made a mistake. There really is a Miller, Vernon explained, a magician writing to you from El Paso. Sprong refused to believe Vernon. The letter had sounded just too much like him. (Miller's letters became legendary in magic, and Vernon also urged his New York cronies to get on his list. "He describes things beautifully," Vernon advised Horowitz, "and types the clearest explanations I've ever read.")

What Ross could offer Miller in return for his relentless theorizing was advice on becoming a professional performer, which effects to choose, how to practice, how to stage an act, how to advertise, and so on. "If you treat magic as a definite selling game, such as insurance, you can get by and make a fair living," he wrote to Miller, "but if you string along like most magicians, just waiting for something to turn up, you're always going to be in the hole. . . . Depend on it, I'm giving you the straight steer." Ross also advised him, perhaps sensing the depth of Miller's growing obsession, to learn to turn his back on the art, too. "It's a good idea," he wrote, "now and then, to forsake magic for a period; allow your soul to enjoy a thorough cleansing. Then you can again approach it with re-invigorated enthusiasm and shed off all inhibitions."

Miller wasn't going to "forsake magic." He was just getting started and secrets seemed to drive him, just as secrets drove his new friend Vernon. And while Ross may have had "the most complete collection of secrets," as Vernon put it to Horowitz, now Vernon thought he had a lead on the greatest secret of them all. Yet he knew instinctively that this was not a secret for Ross, who, after all, didn't seem to see the significance of what they had heard at the county jail. Ross's main observation after seeing Villasenor was that his work was not as "clever" as Vernon's. What Villasenor had told them about what he had seen in Kansas City, if true, wouldn't fit so easily in Ross's files.

But it would fit for a sleight-of-hand master, for an innovator. It was a secret for someone who was willing to stay up all night—night after night—to practice a false deal until he got it to look like a regular deal. It was a secret for someone who had read, and memorized, *The Expert at the Card Table*, and who could watch a trick and come up with an instant improvement for it, or a better technique to achieve the same effect. It was a secret for Miller.

Max Holden had once written that New York had the edge

over other cities when it came to magic simply because that's where Vernon lived. And as great as the other members of the Inner Circle were, Vernon had always stood alone from them somewhat. Now that he was in Wichita, he was really his own Inner Circle. The arrival of Miller, with his devilishly talented pair of hands and wickedly inventive mind, led the delighted Vernon to widen that circle to include him. And once he had, he decided to include him in the hunt for Villasenor's friendly cardsharp.

Vernon spilled the details to Miller. He told him about how Ross had rushed over to Innes on a rainy evening to tell him that his friend Sheriff C. E. Grove was holding a Mexican gambler on a murder charge and that they should come over to see the guy do his slick moves with cards. He told Miller about the session, and how they had then talked with Villasenor. And he told him now about what Villasenor had reported.

"I'm going to Kansas City to try and trace this center dealer," Vernon announced to the young magician from El Paso. Miller had an immediate response, really the only answer he could give. "I'll go with you," he told Vernon.

The baby-faced kid was showing that he was a genius after all.

8

DICE MAN

"Charlie," Vernon commanded his new protégé, "don't . . . open . . . your . . . mouth . . . whatever you do." The two magicians were entering Kansas City, a mysterious, overwhelming world that was now the stage setting for their own improbable play. "I know how to talk to these people," Vernon said with authority. "I've practiced this. I'm not a racketeer myself but I know the talk and what goes with it."

Vernon had shared the Mexican gambler Villasenor's sketchy leads with Miller and agreed to take him along to Kansas City because the kid from El Paso had shown himself to be a magician after his own heart. Miller had demonstrated, from the moment he first spun Vernon's own tricks for him, an undeniable touch of genius. Beyond that, Miller understood the potential for this impossible sleight that Vernon was now so intent on finding. Miller seemed to grasp instinctively the complex currency of secrets.

But as their uncertain mission got under way, Vernon also realized that he was taking a big, soft, unshaped child into a hard adult world. Kansas City, Missouri, was a far different place than El Paso or Wichita, or New York for that matter. As he happily bounced in his letters to Ross from one topic to the next, Miller occasionally bragged, without much detail, about his social exploits. He once blithely mentioned a "girl in Los Angeles." But that was all bluff. Vernon, and even Ross, two smooth-talking, handsome men in their thirties, were experienced with women, with society, with the wider world. No matter how good he may have been at card tricks, Miller was still really a wet-nosed pup, a prudish mama's boy.

Magicians had to know about acting, of course, at least a little. It was a crucial part of how they presented themselves and put their effects over. One of Vernon's ultimate heroes, the nineteenth-century French conjurer Jean Eugene Robert-Houdin, who modernized the presentation of magic, left a much-quoted dictum to the effect that a good magician was really an actor playing the part of a magician. Just as he had done with most of the classic card tricks, Vernon now took Robert-Houdin's principle and gave it a new twist. For this foray into Kansas City, he was a magician playing the part of a cardsharp.

Vernon decided that the best chance he had of concealing that he was an out-of-towner asking a lot of prying questions was to pass himself off as an out-of-towner with legitimate standing to ask a lot of prying questions. Thus he chose to present himself as what the cheaters called a "boat rider" or "deep-sea gambler," a high-rolling sharp from back east who specialized in working the transatlantic liners. Heartland gamblers didn't see one of those every day. On the ships, which cheaters considered giant floating game rooms, the suckers were fat, happy, and lulled into submission by food, drink, and rolling waves. It was a lucrative grift indeed, and to the polished, urbane gamblers who worked them the boats might just as well have been ballasted with cash. ("A brilliant spectacle amid brilliant people," read an ad in the *Eagle* for the *Leviathan*, a ship that made regular crossings from New York to Cherbourg and Southampton. "If business summons you abroad . . . or you're following the sun to the Riviera . . . plan to go on this gala sailing.") To look the part of one of these rarefied workers, flush with cash, Vernon rented an expensive car, a Buick, for the trip with Miller into Kansas City.

But Miller's part was less clear. What role could this kid possibly assume among the hard-edged cheaters, the hooch-swilling, brawling miners, the gun-toting grifters of Kansas City? Miller couldn't pass for the muscle of the team, Vernon's bodyguard. Miller was large, all right, but he was roly-poly and cherub-faced. And what if something should really happen? Miller wasn't going to stand up to anyone physically.

Vernon didn't even want to take a chance on Miller trying to come on strong as a cardsharp. He only wanted him to suggest, by his presence, someone who was "with it." Vernon didn't want Miller to reveal himself at all. And he especially didn't want him to "crack out of turn," to say something stupid at the wrong time. Nothing could "rumble" or "bobble" a mark, excite suspicion, quicker than that. And the marks they were looking to fool in Kansas City weren't marks at all. They were the sharpest of the sharps in the country. Vernon decided that their best bet, basically their only bet, was for Miller to be a mute, a cipher. "Don't open your mouth," he warned him again, " 'cause you're going to spoil things."

If cheating comes up, Vernon advised Miller, stay quiet unless somebody talks to you directly. And even then, keep it vague. Vernon offered a simple rule of thumb. If the palaver turns to dice and someone asks you what you do, Vernon instructed him to say simply, "I'm a card mechanic." In a pinch, Miller could back that up with a false deal or some other slick move out of Erdnase. The reverse also applied, Vernon said. "If I'm talking about cards," and the attention turned to Miller, Vernon wanted him to say only, "I'm a dice man." No more.

Vernon would handle the talking for both of them. In a way, they were entering a foreign country now and, as Vernon explained to Miller, he already knew the dialect. Since his days as David Verner hanging around the racetrack in Ottawa, he had been collecting not only the moves but also the patois of these cheaters.

The golden rule, Vernon told Miller, was to avoid revealing, at all costs, that they were magicians. Cardsharps didn't really think too highly of magicians. Vernon knew that because he had occasionally sessioned with them using his true identity, as it were. They thought magicians were inexcusably screwy to put in all that time mastering sleight of hand and then not using their skills to "get the money." The cheaters' stance was that everyone was trying to steal from them, so they might as well get there first. If these gamblers in Kansas City thought that they were just two guys fooling around with card tricks, Vernon said, they'd clam up tight. Or worse.

Amador Villasenor had had a good reason, an incentive, to give up the center dealer. He had been sitting in jail on a heavy charge with no idea when he would be getting out. He needed to make nice with the sheriff and the guards. If they wanted him to talk to a magician, well then, that was fine with him. He was in no position to stand on the ceremony of the cheater's code by keeping his tricks of the trade tucked away. But these cheaters in Kansas City didn't have to open their pocket watches to tell someone the time of day if they didn't feel like it.

Vernon now brought their unlikely act to the greatest theater either of them would ever play. Kansas City in 1932 was a non-stop revue, staged by 430,000 people. It was a swinging, eye-popping cabaret that starred, depending on the hour and the city block, a revolving nightly cast of mobsters, fixers, politicians, strippers, cops on the take, prostitutes, bagmen. And artists. There were, in fact, artists galore milling all over Kansas City. Two types controlled the night, every night. There were the cheaters, of course, the ones Vernon and Miller were hunting for now, whose art was invisible. And then there were the jazz musicians.

"Oh my, marvelous town," a young pianist from New Jersey named Bill Basie had thought when he first found himself stranded in Kansas City in 1927. Basie, who had taken to the keys of a piano the way Allen Kennedy had taken to the pasteboards, was only twenty-three then. He was playing with the Gonzelle White road show when it made it to Kansas City and then promptly broke up there. Basie would go on to rise through the great Kansas City bands of the Twenties and Thirties, the Blue Devils and Bennie Moten's, before becoming the Count and leading his own band, perhaps the greatest of them all. As a young man, the city seemed to him to be nothing but "clubs, clubs, clubs, clubs, clubs, clubs, clubs."

Kansas City opened up Basie's eyes and his ears—wide. As he walked through the downtown, especially along Eighteenth Street, the main strip for the blazing clubs, the city seemed to shimmer and ring with music, his kind of music. He first heard blues, real blues, merely walking along the streets. The driving, soaring notes of the trumpets, the clarinets, the pianos, seemed to pour forth from every window and door he passed. It was the most remarkable, and the most beautiful, sound Basie had ever heard.

To Allen Kennedy, Kansas City was gambling itself. To Bill Basie, it was music itself. Two artists in their heyday in the same place, and they were both correct in their judgments. Downtown, it seemed that every empty storefront, every room behind a bar, every space larger than a root cellar was taken up with men either dealing cards and rolling dice or banging on the piano and blowing away on the horns. The saxophonists and the trumpet players had their all-night "head cutting" jam sessions, trying furiously, and loudly, to outdo each other. The cheaters had their "crossfir-ing," the silent machine-gunning of the marks, which was sub-sumed in the rhythms peculiar to their games. In Kaw Town, gambling and jazz went together like chicken and biscuits.

Most gambling clubs kept the music cranking, so the sports could keep swinging even as they dropped their mounds of cash. And most nightclubs, whatever the size, offered some kind of gambling, even if it was just a floating craps game upstairs. Some were tickling the ivories, some were throwing them. At the high-end clubs, no matter how great the music, or star-studded the all-night jam sessions, it was really the gambling that kept the money flowing in. There was certainly no tax on it, except for the skim that went to the mob boys. The legendary Piney Brown (immortalized in Joe Turner's "Piney Brown Blues"), who man-aged the famed Subway Club on Twelfth, may have cooked up the strongest, most artistic stew of them all. Brown offered con-tinual card and dice action at a spot he ran just next door to the Subway, and he kept an endless river of top-shelf bootleg hooch flowing freely. (Many of the jazz musicians actually preferred mar-ijuana, though. At the Reno Club, where Basie eventually had the house band, pot grew thickly in the backyard. Musicians would pick it and pass it through a window behind the bandstand.) Brown also drew the musicians—Basie, saxophonist Ben Webster, pianist Mary Lou Williams, among many, many others—in un-predictable, incomparable combinations every single night. It was a continuous party.

The mysterious club owner Ellis Burton, who was really a black gangster, had a rougher, less stylized approach than Brown. But he was just as much of an angel to the musicians. They loved to jam at his dangerous dive called the Yellow Front (the musicians called it the Yellow Dog), which was located above a feed store on Eighteenth. They kept up a steady beat to drive the gambling there, too. And when it came to pushing liquor, Burton was also pretty blunt. He just sold his whiskey by the glass, a quarter a shot, right out on a street corner over on Twelfth, just like soda pop. Burton was famous for the little glass he would use to serve up the shot.

Vernon had certainly been around a lot more artists of the cheating sort than the musical kind. But in a way, that jazz sensibility had been as much a foundation for his art as the cardsharps' moves. It was unconscious. The music had not been a literal accompaniment to his tricks, of course. It was more the spirit, an approach that allowed him to turn tricks that were so casual, so improbable that they seemed not to be tricks. He improvised freely. That's how he had first made his name in magic in New York. He had given card tricks, of all things, that same feeling of unlimited possibility that Basie and the rest of the musicians were now bringing to the Kansas City nights. Like a jam session that started with a standard melody ("Body and Soul" from 1930 was always a popular kick-off in the Kansas City clubs) and then riffed off into all sorts of exciting, uncharted new directions, a Vernon card trick would begin without him necessarily knowing where he was going to take it. Vernon would rely on his head, his hands, and his heart in equal measure to produce an effect he hoped was as thrilling to watch as it was exciting for him to execute.

Now that he was coming right into the eye of this stormy world of jazzmen and cheaters, all the while assuring Miller that he knew "the talk and what goes with it," Vernon figured he was going to have to improvise as never before. Sure, he was comfortable around cheaters, and had the moves to back up his sham line about being a boat rider. But he had never actually been a cheater himself, especially not in Kansas City. He may have tried a few times as a lark and he occasionally even told stories about cheating the cheaters. (In one tale, Vernon related how in the early Twenties he had once helped a couple of boxing trainers down in Havana win their money back from some cheaters who had taken them at the poker table. At first Vernon had been reluctant, too nervous to try, but the trainers had reassured him by putting heavyweight boxer Jack Johnson in the game to be his backup. At one point, the massive, dark-skinned Johnson took off his shirt because of the Cuban heat. With his sculpted physique, he looked like a "panther" to Vernon, who then "felt very brave" about moving at the table. He went ahead and won back the trainers' money.)

But an expedition into downtown Kansas City wasn't exactly the same as studying Old Pop Kelly's three-card monte mob on the fairgrounds in Palatine or spending the afternoon with the retired sharp Dad Stevens, who could riffle shuffle up any three of a kind called for, at the Waiters Club on State Street in Chicago. Vernon could play at mechanic all he liked. But it was no guarantee he was going to crack this city to find the one cardsharp he wanted to meet. To do that, he knew he was going to have to be more of a jazzman than he had ever been.

"How're you going to find out?" Vernon said to himself as he and Miller moved uncertainly through the streets. After a mild Christmas season, late February was raw. No matter how hot the jazz firing up on Eighteenth and Twelfth Streets, the two undercover magicians would have been bundled in dark overcoats over their suits, their hats tipped against the wind. Vernon ticked off in his head how little they really knew. "You don't know any names, you don't know . . ." How was he going to improvise if he had nothing to improvise with? Villasenor had mentioned "somewhere in Kansas City." Where should they start? Finding a cardsharp in Kansas City in 1932 wasn't like trying to find a needle in a haystack. It was more like trying to find a particular needle in a pile of other needles, a pile as big and bloated as the *Hindenburg*.

Vernon decided they would start small. Villasenor wasn't a gambling kingpin, and yet he had managed to see the center deal up close, right before his very eyes, as they put it in the carnivals. Or so he said. The place he had described wasn't swank like the lush Cuban Gardens out by the racetrack. And it also didn't sound like one of the bigger Twelfth Street joints, Baltimore Recreation or the Turf. Villasenor had remembered it as a rough-edged place, a rotgut-in-a-jar type of joint, probably with saw-dust on the floor. It was a place where miners came to throw their money away. To Vernon, this center dealer definitely didn't sound like a swell. He decided that he and Miller would first hit cigar stores and poolrooms, which dotted the throbbing down-town streets. It was as good a warm-up as any. A lot of cheating plays started in poolrooms. They were a way station in the land of the grift, a place where the sports congregated, swapping news and gossip.

But what to say? How was he going to get into it? Vernon knew the lingo, but he was going to have to ask some pretty pointed questions. He was looking not just for a man, but for a specific move. There wasn't even a slang term for the center deal. There couldn't be. As far as cheaters were concerned, it didn't exist. It was fairly impossible to come off as "with it" talk-ing about this move. It was a tricky proposition.

As they entered poolrooms, Vernon took the lead, and Miller hung back as he had been told to do. Just stepping through the doors of these dark, smoky places was uncomfortable. As two well-dressed strangers in dark hats and coats, Vernon and Miller stopped the room, everyone instantly on guard. Downtown Kansas City was enough of a village that outsiders were regis-tered immediately. These two didn't look like bumpkins, not the way they were dressed. They meant business, that was obvious. But what sort of business? They weren't detectives, at least not local ones. Many prominent Kansas City cops were on the pad by 1932, and any regular downtown denizen knew them on sight. Vernon and Miller could have been mobsters or holdup men.

Vernon, who thought he could charm anyone, tried to get the chat going. But even that was a struggle. These weren't the flirty daughters of Wichita taking a minute to be flattered while having their silhouettes cut at the Innes Department Store. Miller followed his instructions. He didn't say a word, keeping as quiet as one of his sleights.

Vernon started by casually confiding that he was a mechanic, that he played the boats back east. He had heard about some-one, he would say, someone in Kansas City he was anxious to get in touch with, another mechanic. Then, he would just come out with it. "Have you ever heard of a guy that deals from the center?" he would ask. He knew he sounded like a rube, but what could he do? There was simply no other way to get into it. Of the probably thousands of mechanics in Kansas City, it was important that he specify this particular one. He just had to put it on the table.

The hardened faces of these downtown hustlers would crease. Then the laughter would start, rising as it cartwheeled around the room. Then, they would add the dismissive waves of the hand. "These guys think you're crazy," Vernon would say as he and Charlie Miller took in the same mocking expressions, the same guffawing wherever they stopped. The scene repeated itself at each pool hall. Well, they were a little crazy. Vernon knew that already. He also knew they were getting nowhere fast.

Vernon and Miller didn't seem to realize just how much danger they were dancing with the minute they set foot on the frenetic streets of downtown Kansas City looking for a poker move that didn't exist. They were like the man in the silent movie walking down the block, oblivious to the bank safe crashing to the side-walk just inches away. For all the electric crackle of the jazz music and the gambling action, all the manic fun that Kansas City seemed to be having, just beneath it all was a steady pulse of menace and violence. The celebrated props of the Kansas City night were cards, dice, saxophones, glasses of hooch. But just as essential were the guns, the bombs, and the "persuaders," the blackjacks that the local heavies could apply as quickly and quietly as a good mechanic could office his partner across a table crowded with poker chips.

Kansas City may have been considered a wide-open town in 1932, an Oz of vice. But wide open didn't mean there was no control. The city was, in fact, tightly controlled. And there was, indeed, a wizard who oversaw it all. He wasn't some kindly white-haired guy pulling levers behind a curtain. He was a short, stout, hardheaded, bull-necked fellow with a volcanic temper who had risen from neighborhood tough down in the West Bottoms, the home of the slaughterhouses and rail yards, to become the absolute ruler of his city. He wasn't the mayor and he didn't hold any special elected position. He didn't need to. He was, simply, the Boss—Boss Tom Pendergast.

Kansas City mirrored its boss completely. It could dress itself up in an expensive suit and silk top hat and put a smile on its face. But underneath it was rough and, when it needed to be, decisively violent. If Kansas City had the greatest concentration of gambling action of any burg in the world at that time, well, that, too, was because of Boss Tom Pendergast. His machine, whose grip in 1932 was still unwavering, was founded, built, funded, and maintained by gambling. And Boss Tom never contented himself with just banking his share of the stupendous rake-off that those thousands of poker and craps games provided. (Pendergast was rumored to get up to a quarter of the skim from all the gambling in the city. Some estimates at the time, probably inflated, put his annual share at upward of $20 million.) To top it all off, Boss Tom himself was an epic gambler.

He didn't tarry at cards and dice, though. Pendergast preferred to lay his money, heavy money indeed, on horses. With the Depression on, his weekly bets were totaling in the tens of thousands of dollars and he installed a Teletype in the basement of his Ward Parkway mansion in the city's swanky country club district. (The influx of New Deal relief money later in the decade would push his weekly total of wagers into the hundreds of thousands.) Boss Tom Pendergast of Kansas City was known around the country as one of the greatest plungers, and biggest losers, in the sport of kings.

He was even creative about his titanic addiction to the ponies. Although horse racing was technically illegal in Missouri, he and a group of cronies had managed to open a racetrack called the Riverside Park Jockey Club. Riverside, which became known popularly as "Pendergast's Track," was the product of a novel argument made before the state supreme court that offered a way around the law barring racing. Riverside wasn't presenting racing, the Pendergast group contended. It was all really an effort to "improve the breed of horses." If a visitor to the track were so inclined, he could visit the "donations" window to give some money toward improving the breed. If his horse happened to improve itself faster than the other horses, well then, he was entitled to head right over to the "refunds" window to get back the original donation, plus interest. It's a testament to both the power of Pendergast and the gambling-inclined mind-set of Missouri that this argument somehow won the day (for a while, the statehouse in Jefferson City was known, both affectionately and derogatorily, as "Uncle Tom's Cabin").

The Pendergast machine, the empire, had been born way back in 1881, when Tom was nine. That was the same year the Missouri legislature tried to prohibit gambling, prompting Bob Potee to make that last, mournful walk into the Missouri River. Gambling got it all started, of course. Tom's brother Jim opened a saloon in the West Bottoms with the money he had won on a

Dice Man

horse race. Local legend had it that the name of the bar, The Climax, came from the name of the winning horse that had made it all possible. The saloon was the first institution in the Pendergast political dynasty. When Jim died in 1911, Tom, by then thirty-nine, inherited the machine. Over the next two decades he successfully consolidated and expanded it until he became the most powerful urban boss in the whole country.

From his modest second-floor headquarters at the Jackson Democratic Club at 1908 Main Street, Pendergast brought bossism to the level of a high municipal art. He ruled there like an ancient doge, dispensing jobs, favors, loads of coal, holiday turkeys—whatever was needed to keep the voters happy and in line. The poor loved him. He "paid them money," as they used to say in Kansas City. The bawdy houses, like the scintillating Chesterfield Club, came to be known as "Pendergast sin palaces." And although Boss Tom didn't know a thing about it, even the jazzmen fell in love with him. They credited him with providing the incubator—the endless nightlife at those downtown clubs—where they cooked up their new style of Kansas City music. To Pendergast, all he was doing was following the simple political credo set by his brother: make and keep your friends, liquor will always be good business, and fight reform with all your might.

But he honed and perfected it, too, beyond Jim's early-century ambitions. By the mid-1920s, Tom had engineered a complete takeover of city government, apparently legally through a voter-approved change in the city charter. And he craftily outmaneuvered and outlasted his opponents, like the fierce police commissioner Charles "Bring 'Em in on a Slab" Edwards, who had relentlessly hounded bootleggers and gamblers. Liquor law prosecutions ended in Kansas City for the duration of Prohibition. Through lucrative contracts that he steered to his Ready Mixed Concrete Co., Boss Tom even oversaw, and profited handsomely from, an era of frantic building all over the city.

But gambling was always the ultimate fuel for Pendergast. Here the machine exercised the exquisite control of a good card mechanic. Once, when a British journalist visited Kansas City (out-of-town writers were forever touching down and reporting back as if Kansas City were some exotic foreign kingdom), she asked Boss Tom whether he was organized by "bloc." He laughed and agreed that, why yes, he was organized by "block." It was true. The machine knew what was going on down to the very block. To a visitor reeling from club to club on Twelfth or Eighteenth in the middle of the brightly lit night, it may have seemed like anything went. But it didn't. There were costs and restrictions. In 1932, the fee for opening a regular card game, as common as planting corn down in Cass County, ran from $10 to $50 a month in payoffs. A failure to pay up brought a raid by police, who were also manipulated expertly by the machine through unnaturally low wages. Officers had a constant motivation to look for pay-offs, and they were a regular sight at all the gambling joints. ("If you want excitement with roulette, cards, dice, the races or a dozen other forms of chance," a reporter for a New York paper wrote in 1934, "ask a patrolman on the Kansas City streets. He'll guide you.")

Other police raids were usually plain fakes. Known as "water hauls," they were staged to soothe the occasional reformist impulses that flared up to the irritation of Pendergast and his minions. The tip would go out, conveniently early, that the police were on the way. Perhaps the only purely legit raid on a game in those days came when a wife or a kid went to the police or someone from the machine and complained that the man of the house was losing all the food money. Then they'd go right over and haul the guy out of there. It was the same rule that applied in Pleasant Hill.

"Wide open" also meant, of course, that criminals could be safe from harassment by the law in Kansas City. But there was a finely calibrated protocol. It didn't mean that just any outsider could stride into the city and start working the grift. Other mobs and machines around the country were aware of Kansas City's lucrative potential and, licking their lips, kept hungry eyes on it. Boss Tom and his boys, in turn, kept their eyes out for anybody who looked as if they might be trying to move in on them. Vernon and Miller would have been braced again and again in an effort to determine whether they were mobsters from one of the other territories, especially Chicago. Vernon's loopy queries about a center deal would have helped allay suspicions, pegging them as harmless eccentrics, the hustler's version of members of the Flat Earth Society.

Name criminals like Pretty Boy Floyd and Alvin "Creepy" Karpis got a special dispensation in Kansas City. They were in the pipeline, knew how to make arrangements, and were accommodated. Floyd was a regular at many of the downtown clubs. But unknowns crossed the hometown powers at their own peril. Locals knew to tie a red ribbon around their steering wheels to keep their cars from being stolen downtown. One night at the Chesterfield, a Texas cattleman made the fatal mistake of trying to defend the honor of one of the unclothed lovelies. He ran smack up against the club's team of enforcers. When they were done with his body, they dumped it over in Kansas City, Kansas, where it was picked up as a hit-and-run victim.

Election Day was typically an especially brutal holiday on the calendar in Boss Tom's Kansas City, with a handful of murders typically resulting from the machine's efforts to keep everybody voting the right way. Kidnapping was the tactic of choice during factional disputes. And business and union complaints were often expressed with "Italian footballs," bombs, lobbed through the front window of the appropriate establishment. Even federal agents would find themselves arrested as vagrants by the local police. Sometimes they were just given a beating to cool their investigative fervor. Holdups at games were common, and could be highly precarious not only for the players being robbed but for the stickup men, too, if they were ever caught by Boss Tom's boys. (Even the vaunted Baltimore Recreation was not immune from these reckless marauders. Bandits hit it for $800 just a couple of weeks after Vernon and Miller came calling downtown.)

Twelfth Street was home base to a gaggle of characters who would have made Damon Runyon's heart flutter with familiarity. Until 1930, when he was plugged in the throat by a frightened rival, the most famous was probably Solomon "Solly" Weissman, who also went by the menacing monikers "Slicey Solly," the "Cutcher-Head-Off Kid," and the "Bully of Twelfth Street." Other members of the fraternity were the well-known crapshooter Gold Tooth Maxie, the blind bookmaker Harry Brewer, who flawlessly added everything up in his head, and Tom Finnigan, the unofficial mayor of Twelfth Street.

To lord it over all these unpredictable characters and to keep a lid on the city, Boss Tom had felt obliged to turn over the police department to the mob. It was the smart play because it meant accommodating a man named John Lazia, who, like Pendergast, had risen from the streets to a position of power almost equal to that of the boss himself. (Pendergast was deft at bringing potential rivals into his operation, though the price was not usually as high as control over the cops.) Lazia probably inspired more immediate fear than the avuncular Pendergast, so much so that Boss Tom, who as a young man was something of a bruiser, took to carrying a gun whenever he had to deal with Lazia. Indeed, the mob chief was so feared in Kansas City that even fifty years after he and Charlie Miller had rooted around downtown, decades after Lazia's own violent end, Vernon still insisted on calling him by another name, a fictitious handle that he created. And Vernon had never even met Lazia. Though he now came close.

By appearance—Lazia was thirty-five in 1932—he made for an unlikely mob boss. He was slight, wore glasses, and chewed gum constantly. Sometimes he tried to cut a dapper figure, wearing spats and carrying a walking stick. He was clever, well-spoken, and polite, especially to women. His henchmen referred to him lovingly as Brother John. But Lazia's route to the top of the criminal underworld had been marked by ruthlessness coupled with an alarming audacity. A son of a respectable Italian immigrant family, he had seemed to be faithfully following the standard career track of ward gofer in the Pendergast machine when he launched a coup on his home turf, the Italian North Side, in 1928. Through a series of high-level kidnappings, Lazia had deposed the longtime Pendergast lieutenant who oversaw the district. Rather than go to war, Boss Tom wisely took him in, and in the next couple of years conferred increasingly broad powers on the resourceful upstart. Lazia's main job was to oversee the gambling operations in town.

Vernon never even tried to get near Boss Tom. (It's fun to picture him giving it a shot. Pendergast received supplicants three mornings a week from six till noon at 1908 Main. Everyone, no matter what their station, was allotted ten minutes, and Vernon may very well have gotten a hearing, if for no other reason than the entertainment value.) But after he and the silent Miller struck out yet again at another of the anonymous rough-and-tumble joints, Vernon was taken aside by a cheater and advised that the only way he was going to get a line on this unknown magician of a cardsharp was to ask John Lazia. Who the hell is that? Vernon practically snapped, betraying just how much he really was not "with it" in Kaw Town. Lazia's the boss of the rackets, this helpful hustler told him. He's the man who oversees all the gambling in town, the czar of crime, the "Al Capone of Kansas City." If anyone could, he would be able to run down this center dealer.

Vernon asked where he could find Lazia. "Well, you can't," the hustler shot back, his turn now to snap. "You've got to be sent in by the right guy." Actually, Vernon was closer to Lazia than he knew. Most nights the mobster could be found either at the Cuban Gardens, a casino-style club he owned out by the Riverside track (he had borrowed the seed money from a pal of Pendergast's), or at the Italian Gardens restaurant downtown. The Cuban Gardens, which took in about $2 million a year for Lazia, was a high-class, dinner-jacket-type place where the sports cavorted while a band in full Spanish getup cranked out "The Chant of the Jungle." At the Italian Gardens, on Baltimore right off Twelfth Street, Lazia would hold court until late each night. Seemingly unable to head home, he'd sit with his wife and a few select friends while a line of people gathered. They would shuffle their feet, waiting to see him for a minute or so. It was his version of Boss Tom's morning sessions over at the Jackson Democratic Club.

The cheater who passed along the Lazia tip to Vernon clearly didn't have the juice, the pull, to get him an introduction. But at their next stop, which he looked at as a kind of oasis amid all the futile hostility of the pool halls and gambling rooms they had visited, Vernon thought he might be able to finagle a way in.

The KC Card Co. must have struck the two magicians as a mighty hospitable place when they climbed up to its third-floor rooms at McGee and Twelfth. There might even have been a cheery fire going to fight the winter chill. The managers were friendly and helpful, and, because it was an emporium for cheating paraphernalia, were used to all kinds of inquiries that might have struck the average hustler as odd. Vernon and Miller could let their guard down a bit there. They could breathe again.

They met the manager, Elbert "Red" Langworthy, who was tall and, as his nickname denoted, carrot-topped. Langworthy had been with the company for several years, having started as a sales clerk when it was still known as Drake & Co., after owner Harrington E. Drake, and housed in a building on the next block. In 1926, the business had moved into the apartment at 1118 McGee that the architect Louis Curtiss formerly occupied, and Langworthy became the manager of the entire operation. He lived downtown and was known around the city as a prominent business figure.

While Langworthy oversaw the card sales, another experienced clerk handled the dice department. H. B. Lee, known around town as Old Man Lee, lived just over the state line in Muncie, Kansas. Like Langworthy, Lee, too, had long experience in this niche business and Vernon, still maintaining the conceit of his deep-sea gambler act, told him that he was looking for a special cardsharp. He also asked him if he knew John Lazia.

Lee was as dismissive as the hustler had been. "Nobody can contact him," he said, brushing Vernon's question aside. But as he and Langworthy talked with Vernon about the possibility of the fantastic dealer he had supposedly heard about, they did suggest some new joints for Vernon and Miller to visit. And while Lee couldn't get Vernon in to see Lazia himself, he did direct him to try a man with some connections to Lazia. Lee apparently even told Vernon that he could use his name, to see if that would grease any skids for them.

"Who sent ya?" a voice growled through the peephole of a thick, locked door on the second floor of a small, rough joint, the place where Lee had directed Vernon and Miller to make their outlandish inquiries. When Vernon didn't answer quickly enough, the voice repeated, "Who sent ya?" Vernon yelled back now. "Old Man Lee at the KC Card Company," he announced. He waited to see if the name was enough to open this door. It wasn't. "Who do you wanna see?" came the voice again, the growl just as sharp, the door just as closed. Lee's name hadn't cracked it a bit. "I want to talk to somebody in there. . . ." came Vernon's lame answer. He had no other. He couldn't start screaming through the barred door of a Lazia gambling joint about the center deal. "Who sent ya?" the voice growled yet again. "Mr. Lee!" Vernon roared, trying now to use the dice clerk's name as a battering ram. "Lee! . . . KC Card!" At last, the door opened. Vernon and Miller, still mute and faithfully following Vernon's orders, entered. They followed the man down a long, dark hallway and into a dingy back room. It was dark there, too. Vernon noticed that the wood floor was covered with a rough, dirty material, what used to be called "floorcloth." A couple of men sat off in a corner, apparently playing cards in the dim light.

Vernon was startled to see a man in a wheelchair roll out of the shadows and up to him and Miller. His approach was menacing and as Vernon took him in, he registered why. The man had no legs, normally a sight to elicit sympathy or pity. But the man also had a large .45-caliber revolver displayed prominently on the tray of his wheelchair. The fear generated by the gun more than nullified any advantage Vernon might have felt by the presence of his own legs. Wheelchair or no, this was one of the toughest-looking men Vernon had ever seen.

He was a celebrity of sorts, this fearsome figure, a luminary in the Pendergast-Lazia machine. Known by the quaint, somewhat nonsensical nickname of Peg, he was an enforcer and all-around muscle guy in the machine's street operations. No one seemed to know exactly how Peg had lost his legs. One rumor said war, another that he had somehow been hit by a train.

Whatever the cause, it had never slowed him down in the least. He wasn't a big guy, but he was clearly tough and capable, a redhead with arms like a smithy. Peg had even had special levers built into his car that allowed him to operate the pedals. He apparently had no trouble whistling around town, the wheelchair thrown unceremoniously in the back of his heap.

Sometimes, Peg would skip the wheelchair and propel himself on crutches alone, getting around under arm power, as it were. He would amaze the kids on the street, challenging them to races. Sometimes he even won, his crutches chopping down the street at an amazing clip, hurtling him along the city block. Other times, when he really felt like showing off, Peg would jump clear over a car, using his crutches as crude pole vaults. For all the gymnastics, though, he was always armed and had a reputation for being in on a lot of the machine's rough stuff. If something had to be taken care of, he'd take care of it. "What do you guys want?" he rumbled now at Vernon and Miller.

Vernon noticed that the men at the back of the room had stopped playing and were taking them in. "I'm trying to locate somebody," he began, feeling sillier than ever. How many times had he already said that in Kansas City? "There's a man here in town that deals cards from the center of the deck." Now he rushed it out. "I'm a mechanic," he explained. "I play on the ships. I'm very anxious to get in contact with this man."

The men looked at him quizzically. "What mail-order catalog have you been reading?" one of them piped up loudly, his voice dripping with sarcasm. It was a good question, given that Vernon and Miller had just come from the KC Card Co., which was known for its catalogs. If these guys were supposed to be close to Lazia, it obviously wasn't going to help. "What do you mean dealing from the center of the deck? It's tough enough to get the second card. . . . What do you mean?"

"Well, I heard there's a mechanic in town that does that," Vernon said, trying feebly to rally to his own defense. He knew the brush-off that was coming next. He was more than used to it. "Aaaa," the man snorted at him, dismissing Vernon's weak retort. "That's a lot of hooey. Nobody does that."

Somehow, though, Vernon's absurd introduction had managed to break the ice with these hustlers, and he and Miller were able to move further into the room. Vernon even huddled with Peg and the others, sitting at the table with them, talking about the absurd rumor he had heard. Miller stayed off to the side, leaning back against the wall in a chair. He tried to look nonchalant, relaxed. And he remained as quiet as a cigar-store Indian. Suddenly, one of the men seemed to notice him. Vernon had been doing all the talking since they first came in and now the man pointed to Miller and directed a question his way. "What's the fat boy do?"

Everyone turned to Miller. There was a long, silent moment. Vernon and this gang had been discussing cards, so Miller had his cue. He knew what he was supposed to say. He was on.

"I'm a dice man!" he fairly screamed. His voice was high and brittle, like the yelp of a dog whose tail has just been snapped in the porch door.

The room froze, deeply silent again as Miller's declaration settled. The men looked back to Vernon, the questioning expressions on their faces seeming to ask, What was that sound? Why had the fat boy just sent up a helium balloon like that? Vernon was stunned, too. He turned to the gamblers and made a little motion with his hand at his head. Don't worry about him, he tried to say with the hand, he's not too well. Then he got up from the table, grabbed Miller, and they beat a hasty retreat back to the street.

Vernon would always say that a good card trick should be constructed like a good play. It should have a beginning, a middle, and an end. A magician had to know how to be an actor playing the part of a magician. Miller, the precocious baby genius, was still learning how to play that role when Vernon rushed him along. He tried to have him fake the tougher role he himself was playing—an actor playing a magician playing a cardsharp. Miller wasn't ready for that one yet. He had known his line, memorized it, but he couldn't quite deliver it. He had blown their play.

The "fat boy" Miller, disgusted with himself, decided to leave Kansas City and return to El Paso.

Vernon decided to leave Kaw Town, too. He had to get back to Wichita. He was out of money again.

9

AND A LITTLE CHILD
SHALL LEAD THEM

Old Man Lee didn't really want to talk, but he seemed to have something to say. He was stalling, evading—doing a little dance of words.

Vernon waited patiently. Time meant nothing to him. Vernon was a man who could sit down with a deck of cards or a coin to work on a new sleight and the night hours would just slip away like the trails of smoke from his cigarette. He wouldn't even notice. He could do that for days, weeks, even months, however long it took to get the move right. He had waited three anxious weeks to get back to Kansas City, back to the KC Card Co., to search for his center dealer. He could certainly wait a few minutes longer while Old Man Lee tried to decide whether to open up. It looked like he just might.

Outside on the windy streets of downtown Kaw Town it was bitter cold. Though spring was only a couple of days away, it was as if the weather had decided to work in reverse in the opening months of 1932. December had been mild, but now the heartland shivered under constant bombardments of snow and ice.

The streets of Kansas City were also unusually chaotic in this third week of March. Boss Tom and his flunkies seemed to be working in their own odd direction, too. To settle what he saw as state meddling with his city police, Pendergast had apparently dissolved the department completely. Even the newspapers, bewildered by the unprecedented move, didn't seem to know whether there was any law, much less order. City residents were flat-out jittery. They had no idea at all.

KC Card was the same warm oasis, though, the same convivial magic shop for cheaters. And Vernon was playing the same part as before, the smooth-talking sharp from back east. He wore the role even more comfortably for this second act of his play. Unlike Miller, he had been unfazed by the reactions they had drawn in the first act, those waves of laughter and ridicule they had heard as they bounced like lost pinballs from one joint to the next. Normally, laughter was a balm and a boost to magicians. That lush, reassuring sound let out by an audience when a trick really surprised and stunned them could be more therapeutic than the crisp ruffle of paper money. It made magicians swell.

But the thunderous guffaws of the Kansas City hustlers, roaring like one of the eastbound flyers out of Union Station, had been something else again, harsh and dismissive. They had really shaken Charlie Miller. The laughter had made him shrink. It had been Miller's turn-out trip, his first real exposure to gamblers, and now he had vanished from Kansas City as quickly as he had first appeared at the door to Ross's apartment back in Wichita.

Those barking laughs had no lasting effect on Vernon, though. He had been around cheaters and tricksters long enough to know that a little laughter, a little ridicule wasn't going to slow him down. He was even chipper. That was his spirit. Vernon believed in taking each day for what it was worth, and following it along wherever it might lead. Often, it led to wondrous places.

Vernon worked his boat-rider lines effortlessly on Lee again, repeating the story of what he had heard, using the awe-tinged descriptions of Amador Villasenor to detail the unparalleled sleight of this mysterious cardsharp. As Vernon talked, he seemed to warm up Lee with his words. As far as Lee knew, they were both from the cheating world and as this handsome, amiable sharp from New York told of what he had supposedly heard on the ships, Lee's reluctance began to weaken. Finally, he began to crack.

"Think I know," he announced slowly to Vernon, "the only man in the world who can do this." The only man in the world. "He'll let you cut and replace, or even triple cut 'em," he said, echoing the Mexican gambler without even knowing it. "Yet any time he wants them, out they come."

Out they come. In the Sedgwick County Jail, Vernon had let his excitement at Villasenor's revelation show immediately. (Ross had been amazed at how wildly excited Vernon had looked and had even written to a friend about it.) But that was back in Wichita, where Vernon had presented himself as a magician and, after all, it didn't really matter to him what Villasenor thought of him. Here at the counter of the KC Card Co., he was supposed to be a hustler, a practical worker in search of a special tool. He couldn't jump up and down and start swinging his arms around. And he didn't. He leaned in and began to fire questions at Lee. Who is he? Where is he? What's his name?

Lee began his dance all over again.

While Vernon had waited to return to Kansas City, his trip delayed first by the need to make some more money cutting silhouettes and then by the harsh weather battering the area, he apparently made the decision that aimless improvisation along the downtown streets was not going to do the job. Like a magician trying to determine which sleight would work best for the effect he wanted, he saw that he needed another approach.

Improbably enough, word of his search for the center deal had already started to leak out among the underground of elite magicians around the country. In one of his regular letters to his confidant Horowitz, Vernon had mentioned what Villasenor had told him. "I'm sure going to make a real effort to locate this fellow and have a look at it," Vernon wrote, with extreme understatement, to his friend at the beginning of March. (He was already keeping some of the story to himself. While he made sure to extol Charlie Miller's unique genius to Horowitz, he didn't tell him that the two of them had already made a run into the heart of Kansas City's downtown gambling district.)

Ross, too, had already let word slip, to his old friend T. Nelson Downs over in Marshalltown, Iowa. Downs, who was eager to get what he called the "dry bones" on "Vernon's stuff," wanted the two younger magicians to come to see him for a session. He had even invited John Sprong to come over from Chicago. But when Vernon and Ross demurred because of Vernon's plans, Downs was irritated and unimpressed. "It seems Vernon wanted to see some one in K.C. who Ross said could deal from the center of the deck," Downs wrote to his friend Eddie McGuire, the man who had introduced Walter Scott and his great second-deal work to New York's Inner Circle. Downs had dabbled in gambling, too, in the past, usually with unsatisfactory results. Now sixty-five and crotchety, he was dismissive of the object of Vernon's search. "This was also done by gamblers to my knowledge 45 years ago," he wrote to McGuire.

Vernon wouldn't have minded the top magicians discussing the idea of this secret. They all kept in regular contact by letter, gossiping like schoolgirls, and it was pretty typical for a new trick or technique to attract a certain amount of carping and envy. The problem here was that Vernon didn't have the secret yet. He hadn't uncovered the move and he was already getting doubting reviews. Anything Vernon did, anything he even planned, was worthy of comment.

Vernon had another, much more pressing reason than magicians' gossip to spur him to come up with a new tack for his search. It was no longer wise, by March 1932, to be lurking around in an expensive car with out-of-state plates while wearing a well-cut suit and pretending to be a criminal. Just two weeks after Vernon had returned to Wichita from his trip with Miller, a stupendous crime back east had managed to send tremors through even "right towns," those areas in the Midwest considered hospitable to gangsters and cheaters.

For many Americans, it was absolutely the crime of the still-young century. On March 1, Charles Lindbergh's infant son was snatched from his upstairs bedroom on the family's wooded estate in rural New Jersey. The kidnapping convulsed the country with shock and horror. By mid-March, with the boy still missing, it seemed to reconfigure some of the criminal equations even as far away from New Jersey as Missouri. Kidnapping had become frighteningly routine in Missouri, a regular tactic employed by the underworld to raise quick cash, exact revenge on rivals, or tip the scales during criminal or municipal power struggles. The St. Louis mob in particular had branched out with kidnappings well beyond its usual territory, which in turn was making the Kansas City mob antsy.

But the Lindbergh kidnapping dwarfed all that. In 1932, Lucky Lindy was still an uncontested national hero, a beloved icon. In the fallout from the stunning abduction, gangsters everywhere started to feel an intense heat. In the first days after the crime, it was just assumed that some mob-connected gang had taken the boy. As a consequence, police across the country started to crack down on everything—rum-running, shakedowns, bank jobs, and the like. The situation had become so uncomfortable for mobsters nationwide that the recently incarcerated Al Capone, "Scarface Al" himself, had offered to put up his brother as a jailhouse stand-in if the authorities would only let him out to hunt down the Lindbergh kidnappers. (They didn't take him up on this creative parole offer.)

Rumors ran rampant and the public mood veered wildly between optimism and pessimism. "Listen for the bombs!" the *Wichita Beacon* cried on March 4, just three days after the Lindbergh boy was taken. "With hope reviving for the early return of the kidnaped [*sic*] Lindbergh baby The Beacon's plans to announce the glad tidings are complete. Immediately after the news is flashed by direct wire from Hopewell that the baby has been returned bombs fired over the downtown business section by The Beacon will herald the news to the waiting day. . . . Listen for the first announcement by the Beacon bombs."

Yet just two days later, the *Eagle* had a darker report, advising its readers to "Keep Eyes on All Suspicious Cars": "With the Lindbergh baby gone long enough that it may appear in any part of the nation interested Wichitans have taken to noticing all suspicious looking cars in the faint hope that they may get the clue that will solve the mystery." The paper reported on a laundry driver who, thinking he may have inadvertently crossed paths with the kidnappers, had trailed a strange car through the city.

In Kansas City, this general anxiety was heightened by the sudden uncertainty over the police department. Amid complicated maneuverings, Boss Tom had finally nullified any state influence on his city police, a stunning bit of machine sleight of hand that was sold to the populace as a victory for home rule. ("Police Cling to Duty," the hopeful *Kansas City Times* headlined its report on the situation. "City Must Not Be Without Protection Is the Spirit.") But police officers, themselves unsure about the status of the department, were "going about their duties in only a half-hearted manner," the *Times* reported. It didn't take long for a new urban legend to spring up—tales of residents calling their local station houses only to hear the comforting tones of John Lazia's voice on the other end of the line.

Because it was even dicier now to move through these streets pretending to be a grifter, Vernon decided instead to rely on a different time-tested trick in his bag. His style of improvisation had been built from many elements—chance, circumstance, observation, coincidence, mood, and so on. But it was Vernon's ability to read a person that was perhaps his most powerful weapon. Since his boyhood days in Ottawa, when the intense J. Warren Keane had first made him aware of how the principles of psychology could be applied to magic, Vernon had honed his techniques for applying them to his peculiar art. He had studied the writings of William James, and he had made it a practice from early on to observe people closely in order to divine the best way to fool them. He had developed an uncanny ability to take aim.

Often, his techniques worked best with other magicians. They thought they were forearmed with the knowledge of how tricks worked. But that confidence could actually lull them, Vernon found. When he was still a teenager, still David Verner, Vernon had met another gifted Ottawa magician named Cliff Green, who was a couple of years younger but already a fine card manipulator. David had seen Green around town, always impeccably dressed and walking with what Vernon took to be "an air of disdain." He decided, before he had even met him, that he hated Green. Of course, once they met, at Ottawa's Russell Hotel, they became fast friends. And then, when they got around to showing each other what they could do, Vernon trounced Green.

"What kind of work do you do?" Green had asked David with a challenging note in his voice as he handed him a deck of Texan-brand cards. Already experimenting with his high-wire style, David was unsure of what his trick would be. When he shuffled the cards he happened to catch sight of the three of diamonds on the bottom of the pack. He then cut it to the middle of the deck and held a break over it. Green, too, had noted the three, but he hadn't seen David noticing it. "Now what?" Green asked. David directed him to just think of a card and then name it. It was his riff on the simple but memorable effect that Keane had fooled him with. "I got one," Green announced. Incredibly, he then named the three of diamonds.

David placed the pack on Green's outstretched palm and cut the deck, turning over the three. Green's face flushed, then turned white. "Now what do you do?" David asked innocently. Green, who later also moved to New York, would tell this story of their first meeting, always stressing how utterly fooled he had been. Even four decades after Vernon pulled the trick on him, Green still remembered that the card was the three of diamonds.

(Vernon's ability to successfully challenge people with cards by reading them became legendary in magic. Many years later, he did a trick for a tough pit boss at an illegal gambling club in New Orleans. He had the man pick a card and return it to the deck. Vernon shuffled, but then he handed the pack to the pit boss and told him to deal the cards one at a time onto the table and stop whenever he wanted. The man dealt through almost the entire deck and only stopped when he got to the fifty-first card, second to last, which he held facedown in his hand, a smug look on his face. Vernon asked him to name his card. It was the six of clubs. When the pit boss turned over the card he was holding, there was the six. When an astounded friend, who had watched the seemingly impossible trick, asked him about it later, Vernon replied that he "just knew the son of a bitch would stop at the fifty-first card.")

Sometimes, Vernon drew a person close to him during a trick, familiarity establishing the best path to deception. He loved women and he adhered to the strategy of another of his great heroes, the nineteenth-century Viennese conjurer Johann Nepomuk Hofzinser, that magic tricks should be crafted to appeal just as much to women as to men. (Hofzinser was also apparently the originator of the cherished statement that card tricks were the "poetry of conjuring.") In another of his classic card routines, known as "The Fingerprint Trick," Vernon would pretend to locate a spectator's chosen card by matching their fingerprints to it. The buildup involved examining the fingers of the person who chose the card. If a good-looking woman was in the gathering, Vernon would invariably ask her to select a card.

While pretending to inspect each card, looking for the correct one, Vernon would take the woman's hand in his, eagerly yet gently, and make a show of examining her fingerprints. "You have beautiful hands, by the way, young lady," he would say, holding on for perhaps a second longer than he needed to before going on to reveal the card. "But anyway . . ." It was pure psychology.

Like Allen Kennedy, Vernon generally avoided props in his magic, preferring to rely as much as possible on pure sleight of hand. But when he made his return foray into Kansas City, focusing on the KC Card Co. as the richest vein to mine for information on the center deal, he did bring a prop of sorts. To Vernon, it was a much beloved possession, one with the force of a talisman. It seemed to have a unique, evocative power.

A few winters earlier, when he was down in Florida with Jeanne and Ted on the silhouette-cutting circuit, Vernon had managed, after much pleading and finagling, to pry a beautiful antique faro box out of a Miami pawnbroker. The old faro dealer who had hocked it had long since left Miami, but the pawnbroker, despite Vernon's many entreaties, steadfastly resisted giving it up. On the day Vernon and Jeanne packed their car for the return drive north, he parked outside the pawnshop and then marched in with little Ted. Vernon placed five crisp $10 bills down on the counter. Although the pawnbroker had earlier turned down the $50 offer, he now was finally convinced of just how much Vernon wanted the box and agreed to sell it.

The box, which was gaffed for cheating, became one of Vernon's prized possessions. It had been made in the nineteenth century of fine German silver and came in an expertly turned leather case. The typical legitimate faro box held a deck faceup for dealing, the top card visible at the top of the box. Vernon's, known as a "brace box" or "screw box," had delicate spring works expertly set in its thin silver walls like the inner mechanism of a fine watch. It allowed a crooked dealer to know what the second or even the third card was while he seemed to be simply dealing one card out at a time. The box could also be set so that the dealer could deal two cards in perfect alignment at the same time, putting an extra, secret card into play.

Faro was the leading card game of the sporting set in the nineteenth century. It had been wildly popular, especially out west. In its heyday, establishments that featured faro typically hung a sign out front with a picture of a Bengal tiger, which became the symbol of the game. Those who played regularly were said to be "bucking the tiger." (Though he didn't detail any techniques for cheating at faro, Erdnase did mention in passing in *The Expert at the Card Table* that he had "bucked the tiger voluntarily.")

Eventually the game became rife with chicanery and faro dealers became the elite among cheaters. They used to refer to a gaffed box like the one Vernon bought as the "old thing" (which was, oddly, also the early underworld slang term for syphilis). Vernon, who had something of a mania for all boxes, was absolutely delighted to have won over the pawnbroker. He referred to his faro box as the "box of boxes," and reveled in showing it off to people, deftly taking it apart to reveal how intricate and finely crafted the mechanism inside was. When he finally caught up with the old dealer who had previously owned it and began asking him about the finer points of handling it, the past master looked at him and asked, "Have you got the old thing?" Vernon was thrilled.

He even featured his faro box when he was asked to do exhibitions on crooked gambling. He would demonstrate how the dealers had used it and then give a lecture on the finer points. Except for some remaining short cons built around the game (which were said to still fetch touches of up to $50,000 from some wealthy marks), by the Thirties faro had mostly given way to craps and poker. So when Vernon brought out his box, it had an instant antique allure to it. He always noticed that the "old thing" never failed to draw a small crowd of curious men to it.

Gambling equipment establishments like the KC Card Co. still sold modern-day versions of these brace boxes. But Vernon was sure that even they had never seen as fine a piece as his faro box. The catalog stuff just couldn't touch it. Vernon felt it would be like comparing a pair of fine Parisian gloves to a throwaway pair from Woolworth's five-and-dime.

In targeting the KC Card Co. again, Vernon was like a detective coming back to reinterview the same close-mouthed witnesses to a crime. He hoped, if possible, to elicit a detail, a fact, some piece that might help him solve this vexing puzzle. And he apparently hoped that the faro box would assist him by working its unique magic on these men who had made their livings around such contraptions. They were his marks now and he wanted the box to charm them. He hoped it would somehow unlock memories the way a fine old grandfather clock could spur family stories from the past. It was a naive wish, a magician's wish really, but not a wrongheaded one. Thus he climbed the stairs at 1118 McGee once again.

Red Langworthy, the manager, was out when he arrived. Vernon met a couple of the salesclerks and began his act by trying to get to know them. He had no "fat boy" in tow this time. He could play the scene as he saw fit, not worrying if Miller would chime in. He didn't want to come on too strong, determined only to give the casual impression that he was a "right" guy, just like them. Vernon wanted to put them at ease. He showed off his pride and joy, the "old thing," and they in turn pulled out some of the complicated hold-out "machines" used for introducing and removing cards secretly in a game. Though some cheaters still relied on these devices, their use had dropped off since the turn of the century. In 1932, they were almost as much mementos of the horse-and-buggy days as Vernon's faro box. The clerks earnestly tried to demonstrate to Vernon how the hold-outs worked, though they didn't seem to know too much about the intricacies of handling them. But as Vernon knew, a hustler interested in buying a "machine" didn't need any instructions.

Vernon worked his way to the dice counter, angling to speak with Old Man Lee in private. Lee had potential. He had gotten his nickname for obvious reasons, because he was an old-timer who had been around gambling, cheaters, and gaffs for years. Laconic and reserved, Lee clearly had not gotten as far as he had by talking a lot about his clientele or the secrets of their trade. Still, Vernon was convinced that if anyone at KC Card would know anything about the center deal, it would have to be Lee. Vernon bet that his silence was covering a vast store of knowledge. Surrounded by dice in all colors and configurations, marked cards, props of the grift and the carny world, he took aim at Lee now.

Vernon showed off his beautiful brace box, a potent item for Lee because his involvement in the gambling world dated back to the faro era. As they chatted on, Lee began to warm up, his reserve fluttering a bit. Whatever suspicions he may have had about Vernon were apparently fading. As they talked further, Vernon reminded him again of how he was looking for a wondrous card worker who apparently operated in the city, a man who had defied all the logic that bound their unusual profession.

Lee finally announced that he thought he might know the man Vernon was talking about. He wasn't sure. A man had been in from time to time, a mechanic, and one day he showed Lee some deal work. It might have been the same deal Vernon had heard about on the boats. But it looked so natural, he couldn't really be certain. The man had had Lee cut the cards several times, legitimate cuts, but he dealt the cards he wanted just the same. Maybe that was the same man.

When Vernon, keeping his calm, began to press Lee for the man's identity, Lee began to dance again. He wouldn't give Vernon the name right away. Maybe Vernon could just call the guy on the phone? Lee suggested. It made for an absurd picture—Vernon trying to convince a mechanic over an open phone line that he should agree to give up his secret move. How about a wire? Lee tried next. Even worse. No working cheater would ever respond to a wire like that. Lee had spilled too much, and now he seemed to be trying halfheartedly to get it back. Vernon wanted to meet the man in the flesh. The phone, a telegram, weren't going to cut it.

Finally, Lee dropped his defenses and Vernon won the hand. Lee surrendered the name. He explained that though he didn't know an exact address, he did know the town where the man supposedly lived. Actually, it wasn't so far from Kansas City, just south. The town was called Pleasant Hill. The man's name was Allen Kennedy.

When Dai Vernon stepped into the Citizen's Bank on First Street in Pleasant Hill on a frigid Saturday morning, March 19, he had no idea that he was just across the street and up the block from where Allen Kennedy worked every night. Kennedy wasn't over at the Underwood Building during banker's hours, of course. He was at Midnight's poker table through the night, especially on a Friday when the weekend got under way. Vernon had left Kansas City early. After reaching this little farming community that Old Man Lee had directed him to, he had headed straight for the bank.

It was an illogical play, at best, though Vernon probably thought it was clever. As he joined the line of farmers and others who had come downtown to do their weekend banking, he thought he would approach a teller and ask if a man named Kennedy banked there. He figured he might get an address that way, or some other information. But it was absurd. "I'm sorry," he was dismissed quickly, "we don't give the names of people who have deposits here."

When he crossed First to the Pleasant Hill Banking Co., on the same side of the street as Midnight's building, Vernon got an identical answer. Vernon should have expected it, of course. He had no business marching in and asking for something like that. Banks were already nervous, teetering from the Depression and an epidemic of holdups. They would never give out the personal information of their customers, especially to a well-dressed stranger, a city slicker. Beyond that, cheaters were not known to use banks anyway. Their bank was their front pants pocket, where they stashed their rolls, their "pretty money." Vernon handled his the same way, for that matter.

Just a few blocks away, Allen Kennedy was sleeping off his night shift.

Vernon's next play was a bit savvier. Figuring that this Kennedy probably drove a car, he made the rounds of the filling stations in town, the Phillips on First, the Shell station, the Cass County Produce Co., which also had a pump. "Do you ever sell gas to a fellow named Kennedy?" he asked at each one, without adding why he was inquiring. He wasn't hit with laughter, but he got the same discouraging answer at each—a flat no.

He didn't realize it, but Vernon was seriously misreading Pleasant Hill. As skilled as he was at taking aim at people, he was missing in this little town. It wasn't his fault, really, for he was judging it by its looks, which were deceiving. Certainly, at first blush, it looked to an outsider like a sleepy little farm hamlet, especially during the day. There were cornfields surrounding it, church steeples, fresh country air. Pleasant Hill instantly conjured up images of wooden milk buckets, gingham, pies on the windowsill. Vernon had no way of knowing that that was only one side of the place.

He didn't know about Midnight Underwood, about First Street, about the back-alley craps games. He didn't know that if he just hung around the rail depot or, even better, the train yards, he could be roped into a game in no time. There was no Peg down here, no Boss Tom, no John Lazia. But still, this little town had its own streak of Twelfth Street, too. Vernon just didn't know it.

But Pleasant Hill read Vernon correctly right away. That was for sure. He was an outsider, plain and simple. The local authorities always had their eyes out for "floaters," drifters who could run the gamut from harmless hobos looking for a bowl of soup to "dips," deft-fingered pickpockets trying to work the First Street shopping crowds. To the townsfolk he encountered, Vernon could have been almost anyone. He was handsome, well-dressed, smooth-talking, friendly, and charming. But he was not one of them. And he was mighty inquisitive. They would have smiled, chatted a bit even, been courteous to a fault. But they weren't likely to tell him much of anything at all. They had no idea who he was and why he was asking.

The town had another reason that third week of March 1932 to be on guard about strangers, especially those wearing suits and driving big dark cars. The peaceful-looking farm community had its own crime of the century to face, which was unfolding in a wooded area outside town known as Devil's Ridge. Just a few days before Vernon arrived, the body of Tom Alexander, a farmer, had been pulled, along with two prized hunting dogs, from an old well out there. Alexander's head had been bashed in. He was found not far from where Emmet Howard, a friend of his, had been discovered in December, beaten and on the brink of death. Alexander had been the chief suspect in the murder of Howard and a nationwide alert had gone out. But with the ghastly discovery, the alert was canceled and suspicion turned to what the papers called a "band of thieves," "gangland fugitives," or a "party running counter to law." To the Pleasant Hill townsfolk, Vernon would have fit the description perfectly.

As Vernon began to walk the streets of the town, he was actually walking into an illusion. In Kansas City, he had expected the cheaters to be close-mouthed, tough to warm up. He had even expected trouble. But not in Pleasant Hill. He had expected easy pickings here, so he was confused as it slowly started to dawn on him that he was actually getting the runaround.

Kennedy's local nickname, which was rooted in the farm he had left ten years earlier, also threw Vernon off. He took to stopping people on the street to ask if they knew Allen Kennedy in town. You must mean Bill Kennedy, they would answer. Bill? Allen was the name he had, Vernon would insist. That is Allen, they would say. People here call him Bill. Okay, then, Bill Kennedy. Any idea where he lives? he would ask next. No, sorry. No one seemed to know.

Vernon was vexed, but not discouraged. It was a small town. Someone had to know where this Bill Kennedy was. They certainly all seemed to know who he was. Finally, someone gave him a hot tip. Kennedy lived in a small apartment above one of the grocery stores downtown. Vernon began to get excited as he set out to find the place. It was his first ray of hope. But when he got there, he found the apartment unlocked, deserted. No one had lived there for a while. It seemed like a crude, but effective, trick.

They played other tricks on Vernon now, sending him in all different directions. Everyone, it seemed, was telling him something else. It was starting to make those dismissive gales of laughter from the cheaters up in Kansas City look downright helpful. Another person he asked on the street told Vernon that sure, Kennedy lived behind a print shop downtown. When Vernon got there, he saw right away it was another false lead. No one lived there either.

Still, Vernon managed to pick up a couple pebbles of information about Kennedy. When he stopped one man he thought was "wise-looking" and asked him about Kennedy, the man answered quickly, "If you find him it wouldn't do you any good." What did he mean? "He never talks to anyone," the man added. That sounded to Vernon like a cardsharp. Suddenly, the man had a question for Vernon. "What does that guy do anyway?" he demanded. "Sometimes you see him driving a taxi, and the next day he's a printer or an automobile mechanic. . . ." In its vague way, this all sounded promising. Kennedy seemed to have managed to stay in the shadows here. But where was he? Vernon, following up on the man's "mechanic" comment, headed down to Lake Street to the Livingston Garage and then over to Bricker's. Sure, they knew Bill Kennedy there. Where does he live? Vernon asked. Sorry, no idea.

Vernon began to see that this quaint little town of Pleasant Hill was more "with it" than he had realized. He was feeling as though his troubles had only started.

Vernon returned to Pleasant Hill the next day, Sunday, March 20 (most likely after going back to Kansas City overnight). It was Palm Sunday, a religious milestone that probably never registered on him. Though spring was arriving officially at noon that day, it was freezing again, and cloudy. Winter didn't seem ready to leave yet, regardless of the calendar.

First Street was not as hectic on Sunday as on Saturday, with most of the businesses closed for the day of rest. But the drugstores were open, and the luncheonettes. Churchgoers were milling about. There were enough people around for Vernon to try to get a new line on Bill Kennedy. He certainly kept trying. But even with the new day, it was the old story.

Unlike the way he had cracked Old Man Lee, Vernon couldn't seem to get Pleasant Hill to spill. His faro box wasn't going to work here. By early afternoon, he was sitting back in the Buick downtown trying to figure his next play. He knew he should probably get back to Wichita. It was a long drive, over 200 miles. He wasn't beaten, but he was vexed. He had confirmed that there was a Kennedy in town. That was something. And he thought that he must be close. But he also saw that these good people of Pleasant Hill were not opening up so easily. In their own polite way, they were as closed as the Twelfth Street gamblers. They were not giving up one of their own. Vernon was starting to think that he might have to concede this round. He could come back to try again later. Then he noticed a little girl standing on the sidewalk near his car. She had just come out of a store and was finishing an ice-cream cone.

As he turned his situation over in his mind, Vernon, almost absent-mindedly, watched the girl, one of the children of First Street. He noticed that she seemed to be upset. He could see it on her face. She looked to Vernon as if she might start crying because she was running out of ice cream. He called over to her.

"C'mere," he motioned to the girl when she looked to him. She didn't budge, obviously afraid to come too close. She wasn't more than six or seven years old.

"Little girl, c'mere," he repeated, still trying to coax her toward him. "I'm not gonna hurt ya," he called in a light singsong, "I'm not gonna hurt ya." Her parents had probably told her to stay away from strangers, he figured. She moved a little closer now, but she wouldn't come all the way up to the car. Vernon took out a quarter and flipped it out onto the sidewalk toward her.

"Buy yourself another cone," he instructed. She picked up the coin and disappeared into the store. A couple of minutes later she came out, working on a new cone. She came closer to Vernon's car this time and thanked him. She was all smiles. Without really thinking what he was saying, he asked her, in the same singsong, "Do you know where a man named Bill Kennedy lives?"

The girl didn't skip a lick. "Mr. Kennedy lives in that white house at the top of the hill," she said, pointing up away from downtown.

As he drove up the small rise and found the simple frame house the girl had pointed toward, Vernon had two thoughts. Though he wasn't a religious man at all, he found himself recalling a line from Scripture, "And a little child shall lead them." His other thought was less lofty. "She can't be right. . . ."

"You're not the man I heard about on the Atlantic?" Dai Vernon announced to the rugged-looking, dark-haired guy in overalls standing in the doorway peering out at him.

Allen Kennedy looked over the dapper stranger in a suit and hat who had just knocked on his door. He didn't recognize him and he didn't quite catch what he was saying.

"What . . .? What . . .?" Kennedy seemed genuinely confused. "Heard on the . . .?" A faint note of excitement seemed to creep into his voice now.

"I heard about you on the Atlantic," Vernon cut in forcefully. "You're not the man, are ya?"

"What do you mean?" Kennedy asked. He stared at Vernon.

"Can you," Vernon began, his voice level, measured, "hop a card out of the center of the deck?"

A moment passed, then a tremor of recognition shook Kennedy's voice, which he dropped instinctively almost to a whisper as he answered Vernon.

"Yes . . . yes . . ." he said, waving his hands quickly now, motioning to the stranger to come in.

Vernon followed Kennedy into the house.

By 1932, Dai Vernon had been chasing cheaters and their tricks for almost three decades, since he was a small boy in Ottawa. He had met and learned from some of the best cardsharps on the grift, men with colorful handles like Nightingale, Mr. Shock, and Dad Stevens. He had befriended and swapped tricks and techniques with most of the greatest magicians—Leipzig, Downs, Jarrow, Malini, Elliott. He had fooled the legendary Houdini himself. He had performed for the elites of society, turning the salons of their ritzy apartments, the patios of their summer estates into halls of wizardry ringing with the natural sounds of wonder and awe.

And later, Vernon would go on to mine still more miracles. He would appear at Radio City Music Hall and the Rainbow Room. He would entertain the most famous figures in the celebrity universe in New York City and Hollywood. The incomparable Muhammad Ali would declare, when greeting an elderly Vernon, "Finally, the two fastest hands in the West meet." Vernon would astound royalty, too. When he met King Carl XVI Gustaf of Sweden, he laughingly asked him, "Did you know that I shot craps on your grandmother's lap?" And it would be true. Vernon would one day instruct the plucky Queen Louise herself in the finer points of "rolling the bones" on the surface of the royal gown she would pull smooth across her lap.

But of all these wonders he had seen, all the secrets he would track, create, or divulge in his century-long life, this first session with the soft-spoken man in overalls standing in his modest living room in a small town in Missouri farm country was the only one that Vernon would liken to discovering "a new world."

"You heard about me on the Atlantic?" Kennedy asked Vernon incredulously as they faced each other in Kennedy's living room. The cardsharp was obviously excited, but skeptical, too.

"Yes," Vernon responded evenly now, settling into his part for the dialogue ahead. "I was talking to some gamblers on the boat and they told me that this man, that you could do it . . . a man named Kennedy. . . ."

"They heard about me on the ships?" Kennedy asked again. Vernon could see that Kennedy was pleased. He sounded almost like a little kid himself.

"You know," Kennedy practically blurted, "the ambition of my life is to go on those ships to Europe and be able to play cards." The picture of it in his mind seemed to thrill him. "I could win fifty, sixty thousand dollars from wealthy people . . . people that have money." But then he added, "A guy like me . . . couldn't get on a ship, could he?"

"Why not?" Vernon answered cheerfully.

"Well, you know . . ." Kennedy said, gesturing toward himself, taking in his surroundings. "I'm just a farm guy really. . . ."

Vernon's play was turning out better than he had rehearsed it in his mind. He bucked up Kennedy immediately.

"Listen," he said helpfully, "you could go on there as a Texas oil man. You could wear a cowboy hat"—he pointed to Kennedy—"you could dress in overalls." Vernon made it sound like a snap. "They'd think you're an eccentric millionaire, that's all." He reassured Kennedy, "You don't have to dress. You could be a millionaire," he repeated, ". . . from Oklahoma, or any oil country."

In a sense, Vernon had just won the opening hand with Kennedy and the cardsharp didn't even know it. Kennedy had bought his act unhesitatingly. The flurry of excitement ignited by a fellow mechanic coming so far to find him had caused him to reveal himself.

But as they sat in the living room and continued to chat, Vernon saw that Kennedy was making no move to get to the cards. And he didn't mention the move that Vernon had invoked to get through the door.

They talked on. Vernon had to wait. He couldn't steer the play now. He had to follow Kennedy's lead.

Suddenly, apparently satisfied, Kennedy called out to his wife, Mary, in the next room. "Put a deck of cards out on the table," he said, "and see that everything is cleared away."

Kennedy led Vernon into the small dining room. He pulled up a chair for Vernon on one side of the table and then sat down across from him. Vernon noticed that there was a tablecloth on the table. He also noticed some dice cups on a bracket on the wall.

Vernon took the cards first. Cheater's protocol. He was the visitor seeking another man's move, his stock in trade, so he had to establish himself, show what he had to offer. He also had to demonstrate that he was who he said he was.

Vernon began with a shift, his old obsession, a pet version he had dubbed the VF, or Vernon Forward, shift. Kennedy seemed to approve, but he immediately made a suggestion to Vernon about how to make it more suitable for the card table. The cardsharp, without knowing it, was tutoring the magician.

Vernon then moved, wisely, to the most powerful sleight he had mastered—his version of the second deal of Walter Irving Scott, the mysterious "Phantom at the Card Table." Scott, who was rumored to be a sharp, had fooled the elite magicians in New York and the details of his second deal had been circulating in the underground. It was Vernon's biggest gun.

Kennedy watched closely as Vernon dealt seconds. He was enthusiastic, complimenting Vernon by saying that it was "one of the best I've seen." But he immediately added, "If you can do it without the seesaw . . ." This was a common habit of magicians when they attempted false deals. They would tip the deck up and down continually in an attempt to hide the sleight, a practice called "neck-tying." Kennedy had homed in immediately on one of the flaws of Vernon's technique, a savvy observation.

Next, the cardsharp focused on Vernon's "take," the way he

inverted his right hand to remove the second card from the deck and turn it faceup. This was a useful move for stud poker, Kennedy's main game. He had Vernon explain the details of his method, the magician instructing the cardsharp now.

When Vernon was finished, Kennedy at last took up the deck and began to work the cards. He started by giving them a simple riffle shuffle, the pack on the table, the bedrock move of all card dealers. That's all it took for Vernon to see that he was sitting across from a master. Kennedy's hands were muscular, blunt-fingered, but he had a light, fluid touch. His handling was soft, smooth, completely natural. It was like watching as Heifetz tuned up before a concerto.

Kennedy removed three kings from the pack, showed them to Vernon, and made a display of putting them at the bottom of the deck. He put the deck on the table and asked Vernon to cut. Vernon did, separating the cards into two roughly equal piles. Following standard card-table procedure, he didn't carry the cut, but left the top portion resting on the table. Kennedy was the dealer and the rules called for him to finish cutting before dealing. Kennedy picked up the bottom half of the deck and placed it on the top half, burying his kings in the middle. He then placed the deck in his left hand and prepared to deal around. Vernon bored in on his hands now. So far, everything looked perfectly innocent to him.

Kennedy then began to deal out four hands of five-card stud poker. One hand went to Vernon. Kennedy dealt the hole cards, the facedown cards, first. Then he dealt around one faceup card to each hand. Before dealing the next faceup card, called the "turn card," he paused and looked up at Vernon. "Did you see anything?" he asked. Vernon said no. Everything looked right to him. "Watch *now* and tell me if you see anything," Kennedy announced. He began to deal again, sailing the third card across the table to Vernon. He saw right away that it was one of the kings.

Vernon had no real way of imagining the center deal. Since he had first heard of it from Sprong, he had tried to picture how it could be done. But as skilled as his own hands were, as experienced as he was with the most advanced sleights, he still couldn't perceive the center. It remained an abstraction, an impossibility. And watching Kennedy now at his dining-room table didn't really help him. As Vernon leaned in, concentrating intently on Kennedy's muscular hands, all he saw was a man dealing hands of poker off the top of a deck of cards.

"Well, what happened?" Vernon asked meekly, looking at the king staring up at him from the table. "Well," Kennedy replied evenly, "that one came from the center." Vernon stared back at the king. To hell it did, he said silently to himself. As Kennedy began to deal the next round, Vernon thought, "I'm watching like the devil . . . I'll catch it this time."

Kennedy played a little trick on Vernon now. For the fourth card in the hand, he dealt an "indifferent card," not one of the three kings he had buried in the center of the deck. For the fifth card, the last one in a hand of five-card stud, another king came across and fell in front of Vernon. Now two kings stared up at him.

"Go ahead," Vernon nodded. He wanted Kennedy to continue dealing beyond the five cards so that he could try to catch him dealing the third king. It was an exhibition, so it didn't matter if they didn't follow procedure. Vernon wanted to watch the deal.

But Kennedy's hands remained still. "You've got the other one in the hole," he said, motioning toward Vernon's facedown card, the first one he had dealt to the magician. Vernon turned the card over. It was the third king.

Vernon felt a charge run through him. He was astonished. Kennedy had dealt the first card out of the center of the deck before Vernon even knew he had started. He had just dealt it out, right under Vernon's nose. This was the move that mechanics had whispered about for years, that Sprong had written him about, that Villasenor and Old Man Lee had gushed about. It truly was invisible. Vernon fairly swooned.

He asked Kennedy if he would please do it again. Sure, Kennedy said. He gathered up the cards and ran through the sequence again. And then again. Kennedy performed his magic for Vernon over and over, hitting the cards seemingly at will. There had been no exaggeration in the reports Vernon had heard, he saw that clearly now. Kennedy kept dealing around, skimming the three kings to Vernon across the table. Vernon knew that, in a game, with money on the table, all Kennedy might need is one well-timed card, one card all night. Vernon was watching a magician.

As their session continued, the magician and the cardsharp examined Kennedy's masterpiece like craftsmen. Kennedy began to break down the deal into its components for Vernon. He showed him how to position the cards and the way he could effortlessly bow the bottom portion of the deck. He stressed that the left hand, which did almost all of the work, had to have a crushing grip, and he described for Vernon the exercises he had learned at the conservatory of music in Kansas City. The instructors there had thought he was a piano player, Kennedy said. Kennedy told Vernon that it had taken him a full five years to perfect the deal, and that he had heard from a "reliable source" that the only other person who had ever done it was a gambler down in Joplin, Missouri, fifty years before.

Then Kennedy showed Vernon some other moves he had perfected. To Vernon, even these techniques seemed to surpass the card-table artifice he had witnessed previously in his life. Kennedy could peek at cards while he dealt, his posture completely natural and unassuming, his head tilted a little to the left as he leaned back slightly. He showed Vernon how he could glimpse cards when cutting the deck so that he would know everyone's hole card even when he wasn't dealing. The cardsharp admitted that that one took a lot of practice, too. Vernon was fond of saying that perfection was unattainable, but as he watched Kennedy, he felt that he was, indeed, seeing it at last.

Then, like a true professional, Kennedy outlined the one drawback to his great masterpiece that he had been able to identify. Occasionally, he warned Vernon, two cards would come out instead of one. Kennedy said he had tried mightily to eliminate the danger, but he hadn't succeeded. Yet when he tried to demonstrate the hazard for Vernon, he couldn't make it happen. He just kept dealing a single card flawlessly. At one point later in the afternoon, Vernon ran out to his car to fetch his faro box to show it to Kennedy. In the car he spied a new, unopened pack of cards and he brought that in, too, intent on asking the cardsharp yet another question on how to work the center deal. When Kennedy took this new pack to demonstrate in answer to Vernon's question, out popped two cards. An older deck worked better for the center, Kennedy explained.

It's a daunting fact about sleight of hand that while it might take just minutes, maybe an hour, to outline the workings of a move, and seconds or split seconds to perform it, it can take years to master it. As Sunday afternoon gave way to Sunday night, and dark came on, it was getting closer to the time for Kennedy to get to work. Vernon had to begin his journey back to Wichita, and the journey toward his own mastery of Kennedy's extraordinary creation. The magician and the cardsharp had collaborated all afternoon and by the time he left the little house in Pleasant Hill, Vernon felt that they were friends.

As he worked his way by car back to Wichita, Vernon remembered that he owed someone word of the outcome of the search for the center deal. "Have just spent the entire afternoon with

Allen Kennedy," he wrote on a postcard to Charlie Miller. Vernon probably dropped the card in the mail on Monday in Fort Scott, Kansas, but he made a point of dating it March 20, 1932, the same day as his extraordinary meeting with the cardsharp. Kennedy, he wrote, was "a man of mystery." Vernon was careful not to mention the center deal by name, but he concluded, in bold capital letters, "HE REALLY DOES IT PERFECTLY."

"More later," Vernon added. "It's a long story."

10

THE GAMBLER'S ROSE

Everyone returns to Pleasant Hill. After going on the lam to Chicago in the wake of his boxcar caper in the early Twenties, Allen Kennedy had come back. Midnight Underwood had come back from Wisconsin. And Dai Vernon, after returning to Wichita, also decided he had to get back to the little town in Missouri. He wanted to have a look at Kennedy's mesmerizing sleight once more.

"There is one very essential point I must see him about," Vernon confided in a letter to Charlie Miller three weeks after the session with Kennedy. Vernon was already working relentlessly on Kennedy's center deal. But, as always, he was a stickler for practice. He was as careful as a surgeon about getting every detail exactly right, an approach he had first learned through his close study of Erdnase as a boy. Vernon found he was having trouble at a key moment in Kennedy's sleight, when he picked up the deck after the cut to begin dealing. He told Faucett Ross that he estimated it was going to take him a solid year and a half of daily practice to perfect this center deal. That was a lot faster than it had taken Kennedy to conquer the move. But then, Kennedy had had to create the sleight from scratch. Vernon had been lucky enough to learn it from the master himself. Now he wanted to go back for another class.

After he arrived back in Wichita from Pleasant Hill, the Innes Department Store hailed Vernon as a returning hero. They didn't have a clue about why he had been gone, of course, but the store was pleased to feature him as their special Easter weekend attraction. (Innes urged its customers not to miss out on this last chance to get a Vernon silhouette. "Have several cut and use them as Easter remembrances," the store's newspaper ad read. "Your friends will cherish them far above their price.") Once the holiday was over, Vernon left Innes for the year (he would return the following January for the same gig). For a few weeks he did little else but practice with a deck of cards. He had a new obsession to consume him.

After his success with the scissors at Innes, Vernon decided he might as well open a silhouette studio in downtown Wichita. He rented a small storefront, but he ended up doing little business there. It wasn't that his popularity had waned. He covered living expenses, but he didn't pursue the business much further than that. After he met J. M. Stull, the new Kansas state checkers champion, he was content to kill hours with him in the back of the studio playing checkers. When he wasn't huddled with Stull, he was out playing pool with Faucett Ross. Even alone at the studio, Vernon shunned the silhouettes. He would while away the time by practicing walking on his hands or balancing on a chair (Kennedy had stressed that strong grip). Vernon seemed to be skating through the days without a thought for his responsibilities. Finding a cardsharp with an impossible sleight was a worthy pursuit. Now he was trying once again to push away the boredom that daily life presented. "He's a funny guy," was the only way Ross could sum him up, in a letter to a friend.

Jeanne, of all people, gave Vernon an excuse to break the

drift. It came through a challenge she threw at him when he was telling, yet again, of the amazing work of his new friend, the cardsharp from the farming town south of Kansas City. They were actually in Missouri at the time, having gone to visit Ross on one of his trips home to St. Joseph, about 75 miles north of Kansas City.

"You magicians are the craziest people," Jeanne declared flatly as Vernon described Kennedy's creation. "How could anybody deal cards from the center of the pack?" She laughed at him. "You people are idiots. . . . I see these magician friends of yours show me second deals. . . . A blind person could see they don't take the top card. . . . So how is somebody going to deal a card from the center?"

Vernon picked up her gauntlet. "Jeanne, I want to take you down to Pleasant Hill and see this fellow." Naturally, he was dying to visit again anyway. "You won't believe it."

"I'd like to go," Jeanne shot back. "Because I bet he's a fake. I bet I can see it every time."

Vernon built up the suspense a bit, telling Jeanne to get ready for the long drive she'd have to endure before she got to see the unique magic of the great Allen Kennedy. He expected that Kennedy's deal would fool her. But what suddenly concerned him was his son. He realized he had to prepare the precocious seven-year-old before they traveled to see the cardsharp. As with his long sleep episode, Vernon had to bring Ted into his conspiracy. As friendly as Vernon and Kennedy had gotten, their camaraderie was built on the flat lie that Vernon was actually a mechanic, too. He didn't want Ted to blow his cover.

Vernon took him aside, talking to the boy the way he had instructed Miller on the way to Kansas City. "Listen, Ted, don't say your father's a magician." Ted was already old enough to have learned a little magic. Vernon had even taught him a simplified four-ace trick with a gambling theme. With just a cut and a shuffle, the boy could deal out four aces into a poker hand. Vernon had schooled him to stack the aces first, starting with the ace of spades, which he told Ted to remember as "the big black ace."

It was full spring when Vernon returned with his family to see Kennedy again, the season when, in many ways, Pleasant Hill would put on its best face. Overnight, all of Cass County would be painted in broad complementary shades of green, and the breeze would be sweetened with the rich smells of the countryside. Vernon knew where he was going this time. The visit was relaxed, with the air of a family gathering. The wives joined the card men in the conviviality and when Vernon put Jeanne's challenge up to Kennedy, he willingly obliged, demonstrating his masterpiece for her. She was flummoxed. "They're coming from the top!" she protested. She thought it was all a put-on. But Kennedy proved to her that he wasn't dealing off the top of the deck. For the sharp-eyed, doubting Jeanne to be a believer now, too, was extremely satisfying for Vernon.

At one point in the afternoon, Kennedy turned his attention to Ted. Though he had no children of his own, the cardsharp liked them, and in his soft-spoken way was actually good around them. "You've got a nice boy there," he announced to Vernon. "Does he do anything?"

"What do you mean?" Vernon laughed. "He's only a kid." But he handed Ted a pack and instructed his son to "show him how you can stack four aces." Ted then ran through his routine for Kennedy, dealing around five hands. For the dramatic finish, he turned over the cards he had dealt to himself, revealing the four aces.

Kennedy smiled approvingly at Ted's cards. He turned to Vernon and put out his hand as if he wanted to shake. "I want to congratulate you," he declared. "You're certainly bringing that boy up right."

For Jeanne, Kennedy's crack about Ted was as entertaining as the deal itself. She thought it was one of the funniest things she had ever heard in her life. Vernon was thrilled, too. He could see that Jeanne felt it was, indeed, well worth taking the long drive down. Kennedy had far surpassed even the soaring reviews that Vernon had given him, and with a tougher audience than he knew.

After the Vernons left Pleasant Hill, the magician and the cardsharp never saw each other again.

Over the years, magicians would come to refer to something they called "Vernon's Luck." He would lose his close-up case just before a lecture for conjurers and on his way in would meet a magician with a trunk full of cards, cups and balls, linking rings, whatever he needed. He would drive around in circles, lost, looking for someone's house, finally running out of gas, only to roll to a stop in front of the very house he had been searching for all along.

Once, when he and Faucett Ross were together in New York, Vernon lost a fine alligator-skin wallet in a taxi. Vernon had wanted to pay for the cab ride and somehow dropped the billfold, which he had had for years. But he was even more upset about the $20 bill he had inside than the wallet itself. He told Ross he actually had a spare wallet, identical to the one he lost, stored away in his desk at home. When the two magicians got up to Vernon's apartment on Thirty-fourth Street, he fished in a drawer for the backup. "There you are!" he announced as he held it out to Ross to show him how fine the replacement was. When Ross inspected this wallet, absentmindedly opening it, he saw a $20 bill that Vernon had tucked away years before and forgotten about. These small, charming coincidences seemed to happen to Vernon with regularity.

There had certainly been many moments of Vernon's Luck in the search for Kennedy. Ending up in Colorado instead of Reno . . . getting in to see Villasenor in jail just two days before his release . . . finding Old Man Lee at the KC Card Co. . . . spotting the little girl with the ice-cream cone. But the luckiest break of all was the year itself—1932—when he found his way to Allen Kennedy's door. Just a year later, in 1933, the First Street world that Kennedy had helped create for himself with his supreme dexterity, his nerve, and his mischievous larceny, started to change. Everything began to slip slowly away.

Midnight Underwood stood in his bedroom, staring at his haggard face in the dresser mirror. It had been another tormented, sleepless night, a night without solace for either his diseased body or his ravaged mind. The syphilis that had been steadily assaulting him had gone unchecked, and was now warping his perspectives and magnifying his concerns beyond all rational dimensions. Although it was morning, the day had broken rainy and unusually dark. An ice storm was bearing down on Pleasant Hill, farmers had been warned to mind their livestock, and the temperature was dropping drastically by the hour. It was Monday morning, February 6, 1933. Exactly two months earlier, on December 6, Midnight had turned fifty-two.

It had been a ragged two months since his birthday. Besides the relentless onslaught of the "old thing," some of the utility stocks he had placed a bet on had flopped completely. Those losses nagged at him now, an illness-fueled obsession that the old Midnight would have waved away easily. Then, on December 26, the day after Christmas, his father, Thomas, had died in the next bedroom, fading away in the predawn, the hours when Midnight used to be at his most jaunty, his appetites surging their strongest. Those appetites had long since turned on him with a vengeance.

Midnight had left his room at about nine o'clock to talk briefly with his mother. Nancy Underwood, seventy-six, was also unwell. She had practically been an invalid for the last few years. She and Midnight had managed to leave the house in early November to go vote in the big election that brought Teddy

Roosevelt's cousin Franklin to office, but since then they had
been living pretty much like recluses. Midnight had told her that
he hadn't been able to get any sleep at all and asked for an aspirin tablet. Then he had returned to his room.

The aspirin didn't help. It wasn't going to help. Sleep didn't
come. It wasn't going to come. Midnight stood before the mirror, staring at himself and turning over whatever feverish
thoughts his brain would allow. For some reason, he seemed intent on watching what he was about to do, as if he needed to
confirm that he was actually going through with it. He brought
up his right hand, now holding his 38-caliber revolver, and
pressed the barrel of the gun tight against his head, just above
his right ear. Then, he pulled the trigger, sending a bullet ripping
through his brain and out the left side of his head. Midnight fell
to the floor of his bedroom, dead in a flash.

Though the Underwood home on Randolph Street was small,
the aged, infirm Nancy Underwood didn't even hear the shot
that killed her son in the next room. A young boy scurrying by
on the street heard it, but he wasn't sure where the sound had
come from and he just kept on moving. At 2:30 in the afternoon,
as the rain outside began to harden into a thick coating of ice,
Nancy opened the door to Midnight's room. Because he hadn't
come out since the morning, she assumed that her son had finally succeeded in falling asleep. Instead, she found him in what
the obituary writers of the day had dubbed the "dreamless rest."
She called Dr. L. V. Murray, who rushed over through the storm.
Dr. Murray determined that Midnight had already been dead
for a few hours. When county coroner Ernest Runnenburger arrived, he took one look at the body on the bedroom floor and
decided immediately that there was no need for an inquest.

That night, as the ice storm lashed Pleasant Hill, the temperature dropped to 8 below. By Tuesday night, it was 15 below, the

coldest it had been in Pleasant Hill since 1921—the year that Midnight Underwood, lusting after Alice Gant, had crashed through the locked door of Mass Gant's little house off Main Street downtown and opened fire. By Wednesday, the day of Midnight's funeral at the Hon Chapel, the roads were still largely impassable.

Midnight's brother Fielding managed to get to Pleasant Hill from Stoughton in time for the funeral, but he wasn't told the circumstances of his brother's death until after he arrived. Midnight's body was taken to Lone Jack, near where he was born, to the Underwood Cemetery that his family had founded many years before. The gravediggers managed to chop through the frozen earth and six pallbearers carried his coffin. The lead pallbearer was Allen Kennedy, Midnight's star worker down on First Street.

Kennedy helped out at yet another funeral in 1933 that would end up changing the direction of his life. A month earlier, he had served as a pallbearer at the funeral of his friend Woodrow Hipsher, one of the seventeen Pleasant Hill men who thirty-five years earlier, in 1898, had enlisted to fight in the Spanish-American War. For Kennedy, the death of Midnight took something away—those rollicking First Street poker games, his main means of making a living in Pleasant Hill. The death of Wood Hipsher gave him something new—Hipsher's widow, Kate.

Kennedy was not really cut out to be a gambling boss, to oversee a whole operation the way Midnight had done. (Though Midnight had told the census enumerator who had knocked on his door in 1930 that he was just a lowly foundry laborer, he had left an estate worth more than $5,000 at the time of his suicide, a solid fortune in a Depression-era small town.) The cardsharp was better at working the table. Quiet and reserved, he could never play the gregarious operator that Midnight had been for so many years. Besides, Kennedy needed to spend a lot of his time when he was away from the games practicing his sleights, keeping the moves fresh. He worked better if he had partners taking care of the business end of things.

He also, as it turned out, needed a new woman. Not long after Vernon had come calling with Jeanne and Ted, Mary moved out of Kennedy's life. And not too long after that, he took up with Kate Hipsher. She was an interesting choice for a mate. Mary had been six years older than Kennedy, but Kate was a full eleven years older. (She had been only fifteen when she married Wood Hipsher in 1901, when Allen was four years old.) She became a wife to Kennedy now, even though they never married officially. Wood Hipsher had been receiving a steady veteran's pension check for his service in the long-ago war, and after he died, the pension transferred to Kate. If she and Kennedy had married legally, she would have lost it. It probably didn't seem like a wise bet at the time.

Even in a town where common-law relationships were routine, this union of the gambler from the shadows and the older widow with two grown children—Kate was even a grandma—was considered something of a scandal. Both Allen and Kate had relatives all through Pleasant Hill and they apparently decided that it would be smoother, easier for everyone if they moved away. But also because of those ties, they didn't want to leave the area completely. So they decided to relocate in Harrisonville, the county seat town where both Kennedy and Midnight had been hauled to court in 1921. Harrisonville was only eleven miles to the southwest, but it was far enough away to make a new start. And there, they could live openly as husband and wife without worrying too much about it. As the years went by, Kate would come to be something of a mother to Kennedy as well as a wife.

The news that Vernon had actually succeeded in locating a gambler who could deal cards out of the center of the deck spread like a seismic wave through the underground of elite magicians. The first reports came from Vernon himself, in letters he sent around the country. As they read them, his close friends in the Inner Circle must have been stunned indeed to hear their beloved Man Who Fooled Houdini, who normally shunned all exaggeration or hints of bombast, gushing more breathlessly than any magic catalog copy ever could.

"Sam the left hand remains absolutely still and the thumb or fingers never even seem to so much as quiver," he wrote to Horowitz from Wichita a few months after meeting Kennedy. As he wrote, Vernon seemed to be working himself into a fever pitch of description. Horowitz was one of the most accomplished sleight-of-hand men in the entire world, and yet Vernon raved to him now like an excited child. He seemed to struggle, as soon as he set down one sentence, to compose yet another one that could outdo it. In Kennedy's miraculous deal, he wrote his close friend, the cards "can be propelled . . . as if by some unseen force."

An unseen force. Vernon made the gambler sound almost supernatural. Normally magicians, especially sleight-of-hand artists, didn't want even to hint at such a possibility. Theirs was an art, not a cult. But Vernon was unstoppable. Kennedy's creation was simply without flaw, he wrote to his friend. "Further, there is never any danger of any unlooked for snap or noise," he added, "the cards could not be drawn out by an attached hair as cleanly, and I mean this." The deal was safe from detection by observers. It was a pure move. "The left hand does all the work," he stressed again to Horowitz, "yet the movement cannot be seen as it is entirely shielded." Just in case Horowitz wasn't getting it, Vernon fairly shouted in his letter. Kennedy's center deal, he wrote, was the "FINEST THING I KNOW."

The great Dai Vernon, the leading card virtuoso in magic, had never gone on like this before about anyone. He even began freely throwing around a word he normally rejected. "I would give anything if you could only see Kennedy the user of this deal 'in action,' " he wrote to Horowitz in January 1933. "<u>Perfect.</u>" That was the same word that Villasenor had tossed out in the Sedgwick County Jail when he told Vernon about seeing a man in Kansas City who could deal from anywhere in the deck. Vernon had always maintained that perfection was unattainable in art, especially in sleight of hand. But that was before he met Allen Kennedy.

As they heard about the center deal, the magicians were naturally eager to learn how to do it. Secrets were their currency, and Vernon now had the buried doubloon. With his knowledge of the inner workings of this mythic sleight, Vernon was presented with a choice, one he would have to keep making again and again for the next sixty years. Some magicians would get only the story of how he had found the center dealer. Some would also get the details of the technique, the "real work," as card handlers said. The first group would grow to be vast. As the years passed, and Vernon's stories became as celebrated as his tricks, he would tell his tale of searching for Kennedy hundreds of times over. But the second group would remain tiny. Vernon only taught the Kennedy center deal to a select handful of magicians, all of them among the greatest sleight-of-hand artists of the twentieth century.

"This thing is far too good to let out to any magiis," Vernon declared in his June 1932 letter to Horowitz. "Even if they knew all the details I doubt if any of them would ever give it the practice required." He was right. Even for magical purposes, which had a much lower threshold of deception than cheating, the deal was out of reach. Essentially, Vernon had to decide who was worthy of anointing. He guarded the move jealously.

"As soon as Jeanne has her Kodak fixed I'll have her take some pictures," Vernon promised Horowitz. He wasn't putting his friend off. He wanted to send Horowitz a complete manuscript on the deal but thought it would be "utterly impossible to describe" in writing without some photographs of how the hand held the deck. Because he knew he wasn't going to be making it back to New York any time soon to show Horowitz the deal in person, he wanted to send him as good a written description as he could manage. Apparently, Jeanne didn't get the camera repaired in the end, because the long letter Horowitz ended up with contained sketches instead of photos. The drawings, which Vernon did himself, depicted his own hands in the exact positions that Kennedy had taken such care to explain to him.

Just as Vernon hadn't included Faucett Ross in any of his expeditions to Kansas City, he now shut him out completely on the method of the Kennedy center deal, too. He made sure to regale his friend with the details of how he had found Kennedy, meeting the little girl and throwing all his best moves at Kennedy at the table to try to get him to open up. But he didn't want Ross to see him working on it.

It wasn't so easy to hide what he was doing from Ross, and it added a furtive element to Vernon's practice sessions. The Vernons were still living in the apartment next to Ross and the two magicians were still sessioning at all hours. And Ross always let Vernon have the run of his vast collection of manuscripts ("Sam old boy I wish you'd write to me as soon as possible . . . and tell me anything you are interested in," he urged Horowitz. "I am making notes on several items from Ross's collection"). But Vernon apparently succeeded in keeping Kennedy's deal from him. "I have shown Ross a great many things," Vernon assured Horowitz, "but although I see him every day and night or nearly so I have never once let him catch me practicing the centre deal."

But Vernon had no qualms at all about giving up the work on the deal to T. Nelson Downs. Although the venerable Downs had released several influential books (one, *The Art of Magic*, ghostwritten by John Northern Hilliard, had a special impact on the teenage Vernon when it first appeared in 1909), he still had many unique tricks of the trade that he had never shared with the fraternity. Vernon was anxious to pry several of them from

Downs, and since he now had the greatest secret of them all, he figured he was well fixed to bargain with the "King of Koins."

Despite the world renown he had won for his great coin act, Downs still liked to consider himself first and foremost a card man. When he first heard that Vernon was going off to chase a gambler rather than come for a session with him and Sprong, he had scoffed at the center deal as old hat, claiming to a friend that it had already been mastered decades before. But when Vernon finally came to see him in Marshalltown later in 1932 and showed him the Kennedy center deal, Downs's attitude about the sleight changed completely.

"Downs thinks it is the greatest thing he has ever seen or heard of," Vernon wrote Horowitz in February 1933, after Downs had been working on the deal for several months. "I have dozens of letters from him in which he raves about it." Vernon restated his own judgment, too. "Personally I think it is worth a fortune to any crooked gambler," he added, "as it is all he'd need." A few months later, in May 1933, Vernon reported to Horowitz that when he visited Downs again he had found him "completely 'dippy' over the CENTRE DEAL" (Vernon was apparently still in the habit of shouting about the move in his letters). Vernon was amused to find that Downs was practicing the deal "almost continually to the exclusion of his coins and everything else. . . . He says it is positively the greatest thing he has ever known and is really completely 'nuts' about it."

Downs reported to Vernon regularly on his progress. "I'm getting it," he wrote to him at one point. Vernon had noticed when he first started practicing the Kennedy deal that he developed a blister on the middle finger of his left hand, the finger that did the surreptitious work of pushing the center card out of the deck into the waiting right hand. He had advised Downs when he showed him the technique that that might happen to the finger. Not long after their session, Vernon received a telegram from Downs. "Vernon," it read, "I got a blister!"

Ross, a longtime friend and student of Downs, was astounded when the old master revealed to Vernon the gimmick that he used to palm eight coins at once on the back of his hand. It was one of Downs's most famous tricks, and his most closely guarded ruse. It was crucial to his reputation that the gaff remain a secret because Downs's audiences had always assumed that everything he did with coins was the result of dexterity (and most of it was). Downs had never let the secret out, but after much back and forth with Vernon, he finally showed him the ingenious gimmick. It was what magicians call a "holder" to clip the coins together so they won't move or spill. The beauty of Downs's holder was that it was made from a coin, which ensured that it was undetectable. The Kennedy center deal was already paying off for Vernon.

Downs, too, grew fiercely protective of the center deal. Vernon diligently sent him a series of letters on the technique, asking him to forward them to Horowitz, a common practice among magicians in the pre-photocopying era. But Downs withheld most of those letters and, after he did send one, immediately began pleading, almost desperately, with Horowitz by mail to send it back. "My idea is the thing will loose its value," he wrote, using his unorthodox spelling and phrasing, "the moment Tom Dick Harry know there is such a thing such a possibility as taking a card from Center." Downs was apparently forgetting that Horowitz was even more secretive than he.

Vernon had to apologize to his old friend in New York for Downs's stubbornness, and then sent Horowitz a letter directly with more information on the deal. "I am anxious to hear from you after you have attempted the centre deal," Vernon declared in January 1933. "Had wanted you to keep the letters but [Downs] seems very anxious to hang onto them." Vernon was solicitous, urging his old friend to "write me a questionnaire Sam re—the deal any points that are not clear."

As he continued to communicate with Downs, Vernon began

to grow disappointed with the past master. "In spite of his keen interest," Vernon wrote to Horowitz about the old King of Koins in May 1933, "he himself has missed all the finer points of the method which I sent him so I did not bother to try and point them out to him owing to his attitude."

Downs faced some real disadvantages with sleight of hand by that time. In 1932, he was sixty-five, an advanced age to be learning such a difficult move, especially one that required an unusually drastic combination of brute strength and light touch. But he continued to bull ahead nonetheless, and like the vaudeville veteran he was, soon began to devise a card trick using the Kennedy center deal.

"I'm doing that card from the center like nobody's business now," he wrote his ghostwriter John Northern Hilliard, who was gathering material for a mammoth work called *Greater Magic*. The book was eventually published posthumously in 1938, three years after Hilliard's death. (In making notes for this now classic book, Hilliard jotted down that Downs's earlier assertion that the center deal was a common riverboat move from the 1880s was a "false claim.") The trick Downs sent to Hilliard, which never made it into the book, involved having a spectator glimpse a card in the deck, and then name it out loud. The magician would then spell out the name, using one card for each letter. The last letter would be the card named. Downs's method called for that final card to be dealt out of the center of the deck, using Kennedy's sleight. Downs proposed that the routine be performed three times in a row, quickly, without any hesitation whatsoever. "It's the best thing with cards, ever," he wrote to Hilliard.

Charlie Miller was in something of a bind. While he was dying for word from Vernon on how to do the deal, especially after his "dice man" debacle, he was also trying desperately to appear cool and reserved. It would be bad form to pester Vernon. Miller had a difficult stance to reconcile and he responded to it in a characteristically quirky and original way. Just three weeks after locating Kennedy, Vernon had written to his erstwhile Sancho Panza about how he had tracked the legendary gambler down. But he didn't include any details on the method and he didn't say whether he planned to do so. Miller dutifully responded with a long return letter, in which he ran through a range of magical subjects before touching, as he signed off, on the move everyone was so interested in.

"Well, Dai, I guess I had better stop now," Miller wrote in closing. "I guess you noticed that I kept rather quiet about asking you anything about the _____ of <u>Allen Kennedy</u>. I'm very anxious to get it and the 'peep,' but I want you to keep it, too." Miller didn't write the name of the sleight down on paper. That's how deep a secret he felt it was. Yet as soon as he wrote Kennedy's name, Miller's resolve seemed to crumble. "Can you write anything to me about it"? he implored Vernon.

But Vernon had his own conflicting feelings to sort out. "I have sent him no information on the centre deal," Vernon confided to Horowitz about Miller on the first day of June 1932, just over two months after first meeting with Kennedy. "And he is 'killing himself' I feel sure trying to fathom it." Vernon wasn't being cruel, but he admitted he was suddenly gauging just how much he should trust Miller. Vernon apparently realized that he had fallen in love, artistically, with Miller awfully fast and he wondered now whether he was rushing things. He also fretted, without any evidence whatsoever, that Miller may have traded on his new friendship with Vernon to try to gain access to some of the more guarded sleight-of-hand men, including Walter Scott.

"I'm going to put him to a few tests before I show him certain things," Vernon wrote, sounding like an anxious lover. "I've been foolish before on occasions so this time I'll be overly cagey." But he did love this genius kid from El Paso, after all. He freely admitted it, and went on lauding him to the other elites. "Sam do not misunderstand me," Vernon declared. "Miller is a friend of mine now and I like him very much and admire his ability."

Sometime later that year, probably in the fall of 1932, Vernon did teach the work on the Kennedy deal to Miller. It was inevitable, as was Miller's reaction, which was remarkably similar to Downs's despite the forty-three-year difference in their ages. Again, Horowitz was the repository for the news of how Kennedy's deal was spreading through the magic community. "He tells me he has neglected everything else in magic just to practice the Centre Deal," Vernon wrote to Horowitz of Miller at the beginning of January 1933. A month later, Vernon reported on a telegram he had received from Miller, who was moving from El Paso to Los Angeles. "He is completely 'nutty' over the Centre Deal," Vernon informed Horowitz, echoing his earlier judgment of Downs. "I feel certain that he has it down fairly well by now as he certainly practices."

There was still another elite magician out there who would positively lust after the center deal. "By the way if you see Johnny Scarne tell him to write me and send his address," Vernon wrote Horowitz in June 1932 from Wichita. "He'd give his right eye for the 'deal from anywhere.' "

By 1932, the intense, dark-eyed John Scarne was one of the leading card handlers in all of magic. He was twenty-nine, nine years younger than Vernon, but he had already made a name for himself playing exclusive clubrooms and private parties in New York. Like Vernon, Scarne had an intense interest in gambling-related sleights, which had been sparked when he was still a kid named Orlando Scarnecchia hanging around carnivals in New Jersey just across the river from New York. He had cultivated friendships with many of the Broadway sporting figures of the

Twenties, including, so he said, Legs Diamond, Lucky Luciano, even Arnold Rothstein, the man who was suspected of having fixed the World Series in 1919 and who served as a literary inspiration for both Damon Runyon and F. Scott Fitzgerald.

Vernon always thought of Scarne as the skillful teenager called Flukey Johnny who had first appeared on the magic scene with a talent for outlandish proposition bets and sophisticated gambling sleights. Vernon had heard about Scarne before he ever met him. Horowitz had called him to say that there was a young magician going around fooling everyone with a trick in which he always managed to cut for high card. It was a variation of a game that gamblers called "banker and broker," which was often played as a quick, surefire short con. Scarne seemed to be able to hit the high card without fail, Horowitz said, and nobody could tell how he was doing it. He had shown the trick to Horowitz, but he couldn't see it, either.

"I can't figure out what he does," Horowitz told Vernon. "You cut the cards and he always gets the high card." Vernon told Horowitz to bring this Scarne around to Frank Ducrot's magic shop in Manhattan one evening and he would take a look at what he could do. It was the first time they met. Vernon caught on immediately to Scarne's method, but he didn't tip it to Horowitz. Vernon and Scarne became friends.

Scarne eventually developed a bullish, bombastic personal style that was the direct opposite of Vernon's more reserved, gentlemanly demeanor. But despite their differences in personality and approach, the two card masters developed a deep respect for each other. Vernon knew Scarne would appreciate the center deal and was eager to teach it to him when he returned to New York, sometime after 1933. Though Scarne was one of the chosen few who rated both the story and the work on the Kennedy deal, when Vernon sat down with him over the cards, he quickly learned that Scarne was only interested in the method.

Before he got into the fingering, the grip, and so on, Vernon started in with his tale of how he had undertaken a search out in Missouri for the center dealer. Scarne interrupted him sharply. "Cut out all that bull," he told Vernon.

"This isn't bull, Johnny," Vernon protested, "this is a true thing . . ." Before he could get another word in, Scarne interrupted again. "Cut out that crap and show me the deal," he barked. "I don't want to hear these fairy stories." Vernon tried to defend himself once more. "This is absolute truth, Johnny," he tried again, but Scarne was all over him. "Cut it out," he commanded, "cut it out." Vernon went ahead and gave him the real work.

But for all his skepticism about Vernon's search, Scarne played a part in cementing Allen Kennedy's reputation as an unknown celebrity in the eyes of the card-playing public. During World War II, Scarne assisted the armed services by giving lectures to soldiers around the world on how to avoid being cheated at gambling. After the war, many years after Vernon taught him the technique of the center deal, Scarne published his influential book *Scarne on Cards,* a guide to rules and strategy for most of the popular card games of the day. The book also included a much-studied and much-imitated section on the most common techniques for cheating at cards. One of Scarne's stated ambitions had always been to surpass the Hoyle books in popularity. He dreamed of people saying "according to Scarne" instead of "according to Hoyle." Although that never happened, his books always sold well and *Scarne on Cards* has stayed in print for the fifty-six years since it first came out.

In his section on "Card Cheats and Their Methods," Scarne had some glowing words for Kennedy, though he didn't name him (he may not even have remembered the name by that time). "To execute this deal smoothly is perhaps the most difficult of all the moves of the modern card cheater," Scarne wrote. "When a cheater has mastered middle-dealing he is about as dangerous as a man can get with a deck of cards in his hands."

Self-promotion figured in Scarne's description, too. "I happen," he wrote, "after twenty-odd years of practice eight hours a day, to be able to deal middles without the move being detected." Talk about fairy stories. Because *Scarne on Cards* was first published in 1949, would have meant Scarne had been practicing the move since 1929, a full three years before Vernon ever met Kennedy. (In fact, many magicians came to believe that after Vernon taught Scarne the technique, Scarne never actually took the time to master it fully.)

Despite that rather obvious publicity ploy, the photos Scarne included in the book did indeed reveal the hidden reach of Allen Kennedy. The pictures featured Scarne's hands demonstrating various moves, all posed against a dark background that looked suspiciously like a bedspread. The photo captioned "Middle Card Deal" clearly showed Scarne's left hand feeding a card out of the deck into his right hand. The grip he's using to get the center card is the same one that Kennedy had demonstrated for Vernon at his dining-room table in Pleasant Hill seventeen years earlier.

Lost in all the excitement about which card men Vernon was going to grace by revealing the technique of the center deal was that clever Chicago magician, the man who years before had first nurtured the seed of obsession in Vernon's head about a mysterious sharp somewhere in the fertile heartland who had managed to dream up a sleight that even the greatest magicians, with all their fanciful dreams, hadn't even been able to imagine.

Somehow, Vernon apparently never got around to teaching Kennedy's center deal to John Sprong, the man who had started it all.

Allen Kennedy had no inkling of the frenzy he had set off in the upper reaches of the world of magic. He had absolutely no idea that a world-famous vaudeville master was trying to get a card trick employing his deal into one of the classic books of magic, no clue that a photograph of his masterpiece was actually featured in a bestselling book intended to arm card players against cheaters. Kennedy just continued doing what he had always done—playing cards and shooting dice.

In downtown Pleasant Hill, Kennedy had First Street. In downtown Harrisonville, where he began to operate in the mid-1930s, Kennedy had the town square. It was four blocks surrounding a three-story yellow-brick county courthouse with a prominent clock tower that had been built in the late 1890s. The square was like First Street cubed. These two towns had always seen themselves as rivals, dating back to Pleasant Hill's losing out to its larger neighbor in a bid to become the county seat. When it came to gambling, they were pretty much neck and neck.

"Knock, knock—knock, knock, knock," began a January 1922 story out of Harrisonville in the *Cass County Leader*. "All had been quiet in the room save the rattle of chips on the table, or the shuffling of cards as the dealer passed them to the other men." The report detailed a middle-of-the-night holdup at a poker game on the second floor of a building on the northwest corner of the Harrisonville square. It was a garden-variety robbery except that many of the players were prominent politicians who then had to spend the next week denying there had been a holdup because they didn't want to have to admit that they were running a regular game up there. "We have often criticised certain things in Pleasant Hill," the *Republican* stated after word of the holdup leaked out, "but in such a game as that we 'doff our hat' to Harrisonville and are willing to acknowledge that she can give P. H. cards and spades every inning."

It was true. And when Allen Kennedy and Kate Hipsher moved there, downtown Harrisonville was still as lively a gambling center as First Street. They settled right on the square, living at first in the Harrisonville Hotel, which catered to salesmen, farmers, and others in town on county business. Kennedy's commute to work was even shorter than in Pleasant Hill because the hotel itself was home to several regular poker games. These were high-stakes games that drew lawyers and businessmen. Hundreds of dollars would be on the table at any one time and Kennedy had little trouble getting in and working them. The change of venue from one town to another was actually good for him professionally, too, because his reputation as a gambler who seemed to have trouble losing had come to be well-known back in Pleasant Hill.

Allen and Kate did return regularly to their hometown, though, to visit family. Often, Kennedy would leave Kate off at her relatives while he went out into the night in search of a game. Dicksie Rinker, who was twelve in 1935, looked forward to these visits by her Aunt Kate. Her aunt's "friend," Bill, would always linger for a bit, too, and he enjoyed entertaining the kids for a few minutes with some little tricks and touches with his ever-present cards. Dicksie's favorite was a charming little flourish that Bill seemed to favor, too. Kennedy wouldn't talk much or act like a big magician. He would just quietly hold the deck in both hands and then give it a quick, gentle twist, fanning it out until the cards resembled a flower. The children came to look for it whenever Kennedy brought Aunt Kate by. Make the flower, Bill, they would call to him as they gathered around him in the living room. Make the flower. The move was called the Gambler's Rose.

Kennedy's first years in Harrisonville were like the old high times with Midnight in Pleasant Hill. Kennedy and Kate eventually moved out of the Harrisonville Hotel and into a house on a two-acre plot about a mile away. Kate's grandson Harold Capper, who was born in 1931, would come to stay with them for the summers as a boy. Now Kennedy used Harold's sharp kid's eyes to monitor his practice. Harold had his own sport that he much preferred. Whenever Kennedy would relax on the porch swing for a smoke, he would toss a firecracker under the swing and watch the cardsharp jump. But he was willing to be dragooned into watching as Kennedy worked the tools of his trade.

First Kennedy would sit at a dresser dealing in front of the mirror, but then he would sit Harold down at the dining-room table, as he had done with Vernon, and challenge him to try to catch him doing something that didn't look right. The twist was that he would first show Harold the bottom card of the deck before he started the session. Harold never really caught him at anything. But sometimes, more to break the monotony than anything else, he would call out that a deal looked fishy. Kennedy would respond by turning the deck over to show that the bottom card hadn't changed. He was intent always on proving that he wasn't bottom dealing. His cards were coming from somewhere else.

Harold was always amazed that Kennedy could build whatever poker hands he wanted and then deal them to whichever position at the table he felt like. Sometimes he would deal the winner to himself, sometimes to an imaginary partner. Sometimes Kennedy would deal several good hands, with one being just a little better than the rest. He was practicing the old crossfire. Kennedy would spend all afternoon running through these different scenarios.

Then they would move to the living room floor. Kennedy would have Harold watch his dice switches closely as he substituted his "horse dice," his mis-spots, for the true dice, using the same finesse move he had once featured on First Street. He would also practice controlled shots with a dice cup. Harold, who like the kids back in Pleasant Hill would get bored because he couldn't see anything unusual happening, did notice that Kennedy always seemed to prefer red dice.

(In the late Thirties, Kennedy had to find a different supplier than the KC Card Co. for his gaffed dice. Because of political pressure, and its own runaway success, the company decided to relocate to Chicago, where it did a thriving business until well into the Sixties, when Illinois state officials started to crack down. And just as 1933 had marked the turning point for Kennedy in Pleasant Hill, the year turned out to be the beginning of the end of the whole Pendergast-Lazia empire, too, up in Kaw Town. The spectacular Union Station Massacre in June of that year, in which several officers and federal agents were killed, gave the FBI the excuse it wanted to come crashing down on Kansas City. Lazia suddenly had pressures from within and without and a year later, in 1934, he was gunned down in front of his wife outside their apartment house. "If anything happens," he supposedly said as he hovered near death after the shooting, "notify Tom Pendergast, my best friend, and tell him I love him." As for Boss Tom, his insatiable gambling, which had fueled the machine, now helped bring on its downfall, too. Desperate for cash to bet on the ponies, he began to take spectacular payoffs, brazen even for him, and the federal government was able to get him on tax evasion charges. He went to jail in 1939 for a year and came out a broken man.)

By the Forties, Kennedy and Kate Hipsher had moved to an apartment on North Independence just off one of the corners of the Harrisonville square. They had two rooms in the front and a large, long room in the back where Kennedy eventually put card and dice tables. Out on the square, they had everything they could possibly need.

In the war years, it was tough to walk the streets of Harrisonville because they were so crowded. It was like the Cass County Fair every night. Gas rationing—four gallons a week—kept people close to home. Three train lines brought farmers, section hands, even soldiers looking for diversions swarming in. Vendors would hawk popcorn, hotdogs, and tamales along the sidewalk. With the war shortages, customers had a harder time

getting their Three Feathers whiskey (there was a 60-day version at one time), but they could still wash everything down with
beer, which remained plentiful. Grocery stores would stay open
till midnight so people could shop before playing. They would
leave their bags and then rush over to pick them up before closing time. Kennedy usually picked up his groceries at Scavuzzo's
Market. Though they let regulars run monthly accounts, Kennedy always insisted on dealing in cash, pulling his roll out of his
front pocket.

Kennedy was forty-four when the Second World War broke
out. He did his patriotic duty again and registered with the draft
board. But he didn't really have to worry about being shipped
out this time. His biggest chore was deciding which game to play
in. Sometimes he only had to walk a half a block from his apartment to the pool hall to get something going. They had a card
room in the back.

After the war, Kennedy had some fun breaking in a new
young crew of gamblers, guys like G. J. Clary and Charlie Scott.
Clary, whose father had gambled with Kennedy in the Thirties,
first got to know Kennedy well when he too worked at the Harrisonville Hotel. He would often join Kennedy in jaunts around
Cass County looking for farm sales where they could get a little
craps action going. Kennedy still had the old Model A coupe
that he had once used as a taxi in Pleasant Hill. (In Harrisonville, he used different covers. For a while, he pretended to
run a lumber business with a friend in town, which required
them to cut down the occasional tree. Kennedy couldn't get too
close to the cutting, of course, because he had to protect his
hands.) He and Clary, who developed into an excellent dice
shooter himself, would pull up at a farm sale and go to work.
Kennedy would take a piece of canvas that he had cut from the
convertible top of his car to use as a dice blanket, spread it out
on the grass and they would start rolling the bones. In no time a
crowd of men would join them, cash fanned eagerly in their fists.

Charlie Scott was actually a cousin of Kennedy's on his mother's side (Hattie Kennedy's maiden name was Scott), and he also developed into something of a local legend. Supposedly he once won a man's house in a poker game. Unlike the soft-spoken Kennedy, who avoided rough stuff if he possibly could, Scott was a tough hombre who was just as comfortable brawling, if he had to, as gambling. He would then relax with a cold beer after either pastime. In the Fifties, Scott and Kennedy began to run a regular poker game up in the big back room of the second-floor apartment that Kennedy shared with Kate.

Sometimes Kennedy still worked games by himself. Once he was in a game in Harrisonville that was held up by a masked gunman. Thinking that it would keep them from running after him, the robber ordered all the card players to strip naked and give him their clothes. As soon as he was gone, they all headed right out, not after him but to the police. Even though he had worn a mask they knew exactly who he was, a local man with a cleft palate. They could hear the distinctive way he talked through the mask. When the cops hauled him in, he angrily demanded to know how they could have possibly identified him with his mask on.

By the mid-1950s, Allen Kennedy had been testing his hands, and his nerves, at card and dice tables almost every night for over thirty years. Liquor had always been his standby palliative. Whereas in the past it had only occasionally flared into a full-fledged beast, like when it sent him to the Mayo clinic, in Harrisonville it began to exert a stronger pull than the remnants of his artistic ambitions possibly could. Kennedy needed the bottle more and more. Before long, he needed little else.

Kate and Kennedy's apartment was right above Floyd Mc-Cord's liquor store on Independence, but he made a point of trying not to get drunk right in front of the woman who tried as best she could to hold him together. However, abstaining at home didn't help much. Kennedy was around town much of the time anyway, and there was liquor everywhere, especially in the nighttime world he had prowled for so long. His practice sessions began to get shorter and shorter, and the sparkling skills that had so thoroughly dazzled Dai Vernon began to tarnish and grow dull.

Kennedy was never a mean drunk. He was a quiet, deliberate guy and, when the liquor would start to get to him, he would only get quieter, and slower. Capper, who was in his twenties at this time, usually saw Kennedy at family holidays in those days, and he could see how the drinking—and years of smoking harsh roll-your-own Velvet cigarettes—had weathered his craggy looks. To Capper, Kennedy's face started to look like a road map that had been folded too many times.

At Christmastime, Kennedy and Kate would head up to Kansas City, not to KC Card or a miners' gambling joint, but to her daughter Thelma's place to join the family and celebrate the holidays. Sometimes, Kennedy would already be drunk when they arrived, and he would just keep on drinking beer steadily through the day.

Whatever kids were there would still flock around him, swarm him, as he arrived. Children always seemed to love old Bill. Eventually, he would find his way to a chair off to one side. Sometimes he didn't even bother to take off the dark felt hat that had come to be seen as his trademark back on First Street in Pleasant Hill. He would sit with yet another can of beer just within reach on the floor at his feet and with another cigarette burning between his talented fingers. He would grow quieter and quieter, until he appeared to withdraw completely into his own thoughts.

What was Kennedy thinking? Was he remembering his months in Chicago so many years ago? Was he seeing his old boss Midnight Underwood down by the depot? Was he picturing that handsome cardsharp in the fancy suit who had once come all the way from New York to Pleasant Hill because he had heard of Kennedy's impossible deal? Was he wishing he had chased his own ambitious dream, after all, and gone off to play cards on those cash-laden ships?

What did the center dealer see?

11

ONE CARD

Allen Kennedy the cardsharp never needed to live like a cross-roader, the type of cheater who was constantly on the move in search of new places to hustle each day. Enough of the world came to him in his little corner of it, Pleasant Hill and Har-risonville, that he was able to work his unique magic for a long time before he finally retreated into a bottle.

But Dai Vernon the magician did live his life like a cross-roader. He was a rambler, an endless searcher, and after 1932 he continued for years to hunt secrets and the men who cultivated them. "If we heard that an Eskimo had a new way of dealing seconds with snowshoes we'd be off to Alaska," Persi Diaconis, one of Vernon's many protégés down through the decades, re-called of his mentor. In 1959, as a preternaturally skillful fourteen-year-old card handler, Diaconis had taken to the road like a wizard's apprentice, joining the sixty-five-year-old Vernon for an exhilarating, maddening couple of years learning magic and tracking cardsharps.

As Vernon aged, his energy, and his obsessions, only seemed

to increase. Back in New York in the Thirties, he returned, sporadically, to performing, first at nightclubs and then mounting an influential show dubbed the Harlequin Act at such hallowed venues as Radio City Music Hall and the Rainbow Room at Rockefeller Center. He also continued with his silhouette tours. In 1941, when he was forty-seven, he survived a potentially devastating freak accident in Manhattan. In need of work, and remembering his early engineering training, Vernon had taken what was supposed to be a cushy, high-paying position reading blueprints at a construction site on the East River. ("It's time you did some honest work," Jeanne had chided him when he told her of the job possibility.) But he had insisted on helping out with the labor, and while he was carrying a heavy pail of mercury across a wooden plank, it broke and he fell six stories into the East River. He was badly mangled and both his arms were fractured. Doctors, worried about the possibility of gangrene, considered amputating one of them, but he refused to sign the release form giving them permission. "I guess I'll have to turn to mental magic," he thought to himself as he lay in his hospital bed. "I'll never be able to do sleight of hand again." But he was wrong, and after six months in the hospital, he was able to resume his magic. During World War II, he toured the Philippines for the USO, entertaining troops with his card tricks.

In the Fifties, the still-dashing Vernon became a boat-rider of sorts, not as a high-rolling cheater, but as one of the magicians on the Moore-McCormack cruise line to South America. He worked the ships for five years, doing no-sweat stand-up shows that featured old favorites like the card on the ceiling and the rising card from the clockwork deck. It was pleasant, convivial work. He would be gone for 38 days at a time, with stops in all the major Caribbean and South American ports, and then have a week back in New York before the next cruise. The performing didn't stretch him or challenge him artistically in any way, though. The biggest effect the stint had on him was the staunch anticlericalism he developed after one of the ship's chaplains convinced a young woman he had been eyeing to stay far away from him.

When he wasn't working on a ship, Vernon was running with other magicians, his favorite hobby. A new generation of young card men was coming of age in New York, and they were eager to learn from this elder master, who was pushing retirement age. But despite being decades his junior, many of these youngsters had trouble keeping up with him. "You could go with Vernon, you might be gone for two or three days," the sleight-of-hand master Harry Riser remembered of his trips to New York in the Fifties. "He just spent his whole life worrying about card tricks . . . and if you got in the middle of one of these three- or four-day things . . . you could . . . go without food, sleep, you name it . . . until he finally decided to go back to wherever you started from. It could just go on like that."

In 1963, when he was nearing the age of seventy, Vernon went out to Los Angeles to visit a good friend, magician Jay Ose. It was a social trip. Vernon was all but retired from performing now, and he was eager to spend some time with Ose, whose brisk, direct style of card magic Vernon admired. The visit was also Vernon's first chance to see the Magic Castle, a private club that had just opened in Hollywood. The club was a new idea, an exclusive gathering place where the magician members could meet and session at all hours and where guests could come to eat, drink, and see them perform. The idea was that magic would be showcased exclusively. It wouldn't have to play a supporting role or settle for second billing to any of the other performing arts.

The Castle was housed in a striking, eclectically appointed mansion that had been renovated by the Larsens, a family of amateur magicians and devotees of the history of the art who also happened to have the money to back up the somewhat wacky project. Ose had been brought in as the first resident magician and, in short order, had started working on Vernon to come out for a look-see. What he really wanted was for Vernon to visit before the Larsens decided it was all a big mistake and closed the joint down. Most observers of the magic scene gave the Castle about a year. Vernon headed for the West Coast with plans to stay for three weeks. He ended up staying for thirty years.

Vernon's move to Los Angeles ushered in what was probably the most productive, consistently satisfying period of his long, magical life. That it ran from when he was almost seventy until he was almost a hundred only made it more remarkable. It was in this era that he solidified his standing as both the dean of American magic and the absolutely dominant force in twentieth-century close-up sleight of hand. His influence extended not only into the future, through the many talented young magicians he mentored, but even into the past. In the same way that Jorge Luis Borges wrote that Kafka's influence on modern literature was so powerful that he had to be seen as influencing even his predecessors, so Vernon now served as the man who interpreted the greats of the early twentieth century for the modern generation. The conjurers of the past weren't just historical figures to him. He had known them and learned great skills from them. They had been his friends. Now he kept them alive by sharing their work and their techniques, their sleights, and by sharing wonderful, entertaining stories about them. He was the prism through which their bright lights now shone.

Vernon bridged a mind-boggling span of time and history in his art. He had first begun studying magic as a boy in Ottawa at the turn of the century, the end of the Victorian horse-and-buggy age, and here he was in Hollywood in the Sixties, Seventies, Eighties, even into the start of the Nineties, overseeing a new crop of practitioners of deception. Many of them moved to

Los Angeles expressly to be near him. Brilliant young magicians like Larry Jennings, Mike Skinner, Bruce Cervon, Earl Nelson, Ricky Jay, David Roth, John Carney, Steve Freeman, Max Maven, and many others came from all over the country to sit at Vernon's knee and learn from the great master. He became the guru to all of them, and sometimes delighted in wickedly playing them off against one another. And he did all he could to draw a broad artistic line from the old masters—Leipzig, Downs, Malini, Elliott and the others—to these new phenoms.

Despite his advancing age, Vernon remained a probing, flinty teacher, who excelled at identifying weaknesses in even his most advanced students. Once, after watching John Carney, one of his most talented and original protégés, perform an excellent set, he told him he was getting too polished and elegant. Carney's initial reaction was, "That's a bad thing?" But then he realized the master was right, that his style wasn't natural.

Vernon's voice grew rougher with age, taking on a craggy rhythm. He was given to repeating phrases in the middle of a sentence, as if the needle had stuck momentarily—"the coin can't be seen . . . the coin can't be seen . . ."—a tendency actually well suited to magic instruction. (It may indeed have been deliberate.) As he talked about magic, especially cards, long into the night, he seemed to get younger, more energetic. His memory was still phenomenal, kept sharp by all those years of focusing on the most exacting details.

Vernon's moves could still be scalpel sharp, too. "I'm not senile, don't ever think so," he would command, and it was true. Even well into his ninth decade, Vernon continued to stun, even though his hands were no longer as supple or agile as they had once been (he would declare that he had been "fifty times better" before the construction accident, which observers had a tough time imagining). "Excuse me," he would announce openly as he pulled a small vial from his jacket pocket (he almost always wore a jacket and tie), "you don't mind if I put a little something on my hands . . . this is just ordinary hand lotion." Like many aging magicians, Vernon battled the inevitable drying of his skin. "A poor workman blames his tools," he would explain cheerily, "but my hands are so dry now that certain things I used to do with great facility I can't do well now."

But even with the disclaimer, younger magicians continued to be thrilled whenever he would execute the move they were struggling over. Of course, he was especially celebrated for his unrivaled handlings of the Erdnase sleights, his hands almost the living embodiment of the famous drawings by artist Marshall D. Smith. (Vernon had met Smith in 1947 at a Society of American Magicians convention in Chicago, shaking the hand of the man who likely had shaken the hand of Vernon's unknown mentor in 1902.) Vernon would talk of knowing nineteen versions of a card switch, a gambling sleight used by a cheater to replace a card on the table with another one more to his liking, and if he couldn't do every single one perfectly anymore, he could still walk someone younger through them. Young hotshots were constantly amazed when they came to "the Professor" to show off what they thought was some great new move. He would stare at their hands with the old microscopic intensity, lean back, and say something like, "What if you tried it like this . . ."?

Vernon's luck still held, too. The air around him still seemed to be charged with happenstance. His disciples joked that his car would get radio stations that theirs could not pick up. And his well of arcane knowledge seemed bottomless. He would constantly throw out odd facts, like how to walk through a room in the dark without crashing into anything (the secret was keeping the arms extended fully with the hands touching lightly at the thumbs in a flying wedge). He would urge young sleight-of-hand artists that if they wanted to count off cards secretly in the deck with one hand, the best method was to count like a violinist. They would exchange puzzled looks. How does a violinist count? So Vernon would show them, counting off "dilly um dum dum . . . dilly um dum dum . . ."

Improbably, the elderly Dai Vernon became the Magic Castle's star attraction. The Castle, as magicians came to call it, proved to be the perfect place for him. Everyone pronounced his name "Die" there, which came to be considered the West Coast way to say it. (Those who said "Day" dated themselves to his pre-1960s New York era.) He even came to accept the nickname "the Professor," which had been foisted on him years before by a New York friend, lawyer Garrick Spencer. He had hated the moniker, but he conceded now that with his wild white hair and "screwy" ways, it probably fit. The Larsens basically subsidized his thirty-year tenure at the Castle, but it was worth it for them because the Professor's presence gave the club prestige and helped it thrive. He imbued the odd new establishment with just the aura of charming artistic credibility that they needed to draw in the magician members and the paying audiences. With Ose's influence, Vernon even began to perform again, in the Castle's close-up gallery.

The Castle was now his headquarters, his home, his family. It was an unreal sanctuary where he could immerse himself in magic, day and night, without a thought of the consequences. He and Jeanne were finally separated, after years of marital tension brought on in large part by his spendthrift, vagabond ways (they never divorced). Ted and Vernon's other son, Derek, who had been born in Colorado Springs the summer after Vernon met Kennedy in 1932, were all grown up and had long been on their own. With his quick lines and the glint behind his large Swifty Lazar eyeglasses, the Professor could now play the wily, silver-haired rascal with the ladies to the hilt. When Vernon first arrived in Hollywood, he actually lived at the Castle, sleeping on a cot in a secluded section of the mansion. After he moved to a nearby apartment, he would amble over each day and hold court far into the night on a little couch reserved for him in the corner of the club's bar. That's where he met all comers for three decades.

By the Sixties, the Professor's card tricks were firmly enshrined in the magical pantheon. Effects like "Triumph," "Out of Sight, Out of Mind," and "Cutting the Aces" were established classics. Magicians performed them the way musicians would feature the popular standards of Cole Porter or the Gershwins. But now his stories competed with his tricks, for Vernon was not just magic's greatest artist, but its greatest witness, too. He developed his tales, honing them the way he did his sleights and routines. To his rapt listeners, the Professor sounded like a cross between Damon Runyon and Scheherazade.

His stories played best late at night, when he was surrounded by a clutch of worshipful magicians in the Castle bar, or at one of their nighthawk hangouts, like Canter's Deli. The Professor usually had a glass of whiskey or cognac in one hand and a large cigar in the other. The raffish cigarettes had given way to the more utilitarian, and slightly healthier, stogies. Vernon's students came to be as familiar with the names of the great cardsharps he had known as they were with the great magicians of the golden era. Vernon spoke of John Rakanakis, Mexican Joe, Pop Kelly, Dad Stevens, and, of course, Allen Kennedy the way a baseball fanatic would bandy about the names of Ruth, Gehrig, Cobb, DiMaggio, and Williams. He not only raved about their skills, he made it plain that, to him, the cardsharps were the ultimate magicians. He even compared their work to classical music.

"The old boy—I call him boy because of the great enthusiasm he has at his age," Charlie Miller wrote to Faucett Ross in the late Sixties of a "fine" evening he had spent with Vernon. Miller had also gravitated back to Los Angeles (he had lived there in the Thirties) to be part of the Castle constellation. He was sixty by then, still struggling mightily with his weight, and admitted freely to Ross that he was jealous of the seventy-five-year-old Vernon's "fine appearance." Still, he added, "I do NOT envy his living in the past." But the Professor wasn't living in the past with all these stories of the cardsharps. "I am certainly no oracle," Vernon would declare loudly. He was simply trying to make points about secrets, techniques, misdirection—all still relevant to enriching the art of magic. He could be aggressive in pressing the issue, and defensive when it came to the gamblers' techniques. If he thought a magician wasn't following along, he could be withering.

Once, in 1982, when he was eighty-eight, while conducting a session on videotape about the Kennedy deal, a younger magician had a seemingly throwaway question about whether the sleight could be useful for dealing "consecutive centers." Vernon stopped in midsentence and stared at him for a long moment. When he answered, his whole tone had changed, to one of impatient disgust. "No . . . no . . ." he started slowly, "you're talking like a magician now." He seemed to spit the word *magician*, as if it was the worst insult he could think of. It was an odd epithet, indeed, to throw at a budding magician. How was he supposed to be thinking?

"If you said that to a gambler," Vernon declared, raising his voice as if speaking to a wayward child, "he'd say, 'Who the hell wants consecutive centers?'" Back in 1919 in Chicago, when he had met the great Dad Stevens, another mythic cardsharp who went by the nickname "The Mysterious Kid," Stevens had shown how he could get any three of a kind he wanted just by riffle shuffling the cards. He had told Vernon that he had practiced for eighteen years to be able to do it and the move had brought tears to Vernon's eyes. But Vernon recalled now how he had foolishly challenged Stevens by asking him, "Can you do four?"

"Four!" Stevens exploded, the way Vernon was exploding now. "Who wants four!? Ya get killed if you take four of a kind." He swore bitterly at Vernon for his idiocy. "Three! That's all anybody needs, three. . . ." That was a lesson Vernon never forgot. The gamblers knew the value of cards.

"One second [card] may save them a thousand dollars," Vernon lectured on. "One little card may save you five hundred." Magicians who had mastered gambling sleights, especially the false deals, loved to show them off, dealing down through the deck until there was a heap of cards in front of them on the table. But that had nothing to do with the magic of the cardsharps, Vernon said. "They do them at the right time," he stressed. "When there's a lot of money involved."

"One card," he declared, perhaps remembering the first king Allen Kennedy had dealt him, "can break a hand or one card can win a hand." One card. He was really talking about the distillation of his own long, hectic, creative life. That had always been his focus in the end. One card. Pick a card. Think of a card. A card palmed secretly in the hand. A card out of the center of the deck. "One card!" he yelled.

Sometimes, Vernon could sound as if he really despised magic and what it had become. That's how he would talk, anyway. It was another reason he idolized the cardsharps so much. They didn't have to bother with all that nonsense.

He knew that card magic's lousy reputation had endured and he blamed shoddy magicians for how the art seemed to have settled permanently on the low rung of the cultural ladder. Despite his solid standing as a revered elder and sage, mentor to many of the modern stars of close-up magic, Vernon seemed to take an almost perverse delight in bluntly revealing to other magicians what audiences really thought about their beloved tricks and their flashy flourishes. He would imitate people who turned up their noses when the cards came out. "'Oh, for God's sake,' he would cry, mimicking a gathering of people watching a magician, "'he does card tricks, he's one of those guys who annoys you with cards.'"

Vernon would quote the Somerset Maugham short story "Mr. Know-All," which has the narrator describing, with "rage and hatred" in his heart, an exchange with one Max Kelada, his unwelcome cabin-mate on an ocean liner. Kelada was the archetype of the pushy amateur card trickster who won't take no for an answer.

"Do you like card tricks?" Kelada asks, after interrupting the narrator's game of "patience," the British name for solitaire, and grabbing hold of the deck.

"No, I hate card tricks," the narrator responds.

"Well, I'll just show you this one," Kelada answers. "He showed me three," the narrator reports. Card tricks were the noxious weapon of the social boor.

"They get disgusted," Vernon would say of people's reactions to endless card tricks. And most people, he said, found magicians' attempts at presentation "tiresome." When his protégé Ricky Jay, who loved Vernon but came to loathe the scene at the Castle, asked him how he tolerated the shabby elements of their art, Vernon's blunt answer was, "I forced myself not to care."

But he did care, deeply, and he went on preaching. "Card tricks can be very entertaining," he proclaimed with conviction. "If you make them entertaining." Hofzinser had called card tricks the "poetry of conjuring," and Robert-Houdin had urged magicians to incorporate the principles of drama. To Vernon, the key was storytelling. "When you tell them a story of interest, it appeals to them," he would say. The audience would follow along then. In "Cutting the Aces," he told of an intriguing encounter with a one-armed gambler down in Mexico who could always cut to an ace. He called it a "realistic story" and urged his students to feature similar stories. Of course, for Vernon it was a realistic story. "Let me show you what happened to me in Tia

Juana many years ago," he would begin as he picked up the deck to start the trick.

It all began in a Wichita jail. That was also a story he told often. After Vernon returned to New York City from his heartland ramblings, it hadn't taken long for the tale of finding Kennedy and the "deal from anywhere" to make it to the press. Over the years, it was often embellished or exaggerated in some wild and entertaining ways, sometimes by Vernon himself, sometimes by others.

In 1938, when he was performing at the Rainbow Grill atop Rockefeller Center, Vernon gave an interview to Associated Press features writer Jack Stinnett in which he mentioned the center deal. Vernon actually referred to Kennedy by his real name. It was a stunning breach of cheater protocol, because as far as Vernon knew Kennedy was still an active cardsharp. He did obscure some of the details of his identity, though, calling Kennedy a "Mississippi gambler" who had spent "ten years" on the sleight and "had made a fortune with it." But Vernon didn't try to hide how meaningful the deal was to him. "One of the greatest moments of my life came when I first saw Kennedy do his center deal," Vernon declared to Stinnett, gushing as he had six years earlier to Sam Horowitz. "It was beautiful, awe-inspiring—like the discovery of a new world."

Later that year, Vernon mentioned Kennedy's name in the papers again, in an item that was then picked up by magician Theodore Annemann and included in *The Jinx*, Annemann's influential magic magazine. It lightly mixed fact and fantasy. "He is one of the few honest living men who can 'center deal' successfully," the report said of Vernon, adding that he "learned that trick from an old Mississippi River boat gambler named Kennedy." The embellishments were growing now, too, with this article describing how Vernon had combed the Mississippi Valley in search of Kennedy before a "banker" in Joplin told him where to locate him. Vernon had hired a "Rolls Royce" to play the part of a sharp ("Gamblers hate magicians," the dispatch advised) and had found "Old Kennedy" in a "little cabin." "Kennedy had used that center deal to make a fortune—which he later lost. Vernon could use the trick to make a crooked fortune. But he doesn't gamble—doesn't even play bridge." These seemed to be reassuring themes, that Kennedy had zeroed out on his ill-gotten gains while Vernon was too honest even to try for them.

Just two years later, in 1940, Annemann himself got into the act, writing up a fanciful, error-laden report on Vernon's search that he published in *The Jinx*. This time, the hunt supposedly started in Nashville, clearly a play on Asheville, where Sprong had first written to Vernon with the tip. According to Annemann's report, Vernon and Jeanne had been scheduled to leave for Boston, where Vernon was supposed to open a show, when Vernon noticed an item about a "middle dealer in St. Louis" in the newspaper he was reading while having his shoes shined. "Cancelling Boston, Dai and Jean [*sic*] were on the road west in an hour," Annemann wrote. First, they searched at a "gambling house" in St. Louis before moving on to Kansas City, where Vernon got the tip to try "Pleasantville." There, a bank teller told Vernon of a "mysterious sort of fellow" who made "big deposits." He still couldn't find the address until he met up with the girl with the ice-cream cone, her first entry into the lore. In Annemann's write-up, Kennedy was now a "truck driver type of person with an ambition to belong to the genteel and elite fraternity of gamblers."

The most high-flown versions of them all, though, came in the pulp men's "adventure" magazines *Saga* and *Bold* in the Fifties. Bruce Elliott, actually a clever New York magician whose day job was as a writer and editor, composed both pieces in the requisite overheated, two-fisted style. By this time, Kennedy's identity was thoroughly hidden again. Except for Vernon's name, the articles were almost completely fiction, with occasional faint wisps of the real story.

"The man on the left opened the pot with a high bet," read the *Saga* article, which appeared in March 1952, exactly twenty years after Vernon met Kennedy. "The next raised, driving out the third player, but the fourth and fifth stayed, pushing their money into the center of the table. The bet was back to Vernon." It was a great scene, with Vernon losing at a poker game because he had dealt himself, legitimately, a straight flush only to realize that, because it was the last hand of the night, everyone would just assume that he had been cheating. He folded. While chatting after the game, one of the players, a "professional magician" no less, tells Vernon that he had recently heard of a gambler "somewhere in the Middle West" who could deal from the center of the deck. The magician had picked up the tip at a Chicago gambling joint and stressed that "it's just a rumor." Nevertheless, the comment "lit a fire" and "the next afternoon Vernon was on a bus bound for Chicago."

In the *Saga* version of Vernon's search (the *Bold* piece was essentially an abridged rewrite that appeared two years later), Vernon didn't pose as a cardsharp. Instead, continuing the magician-centric tone of the whole article, he posed as a "down-on-his-luck magician" who showed off card tricks as a way to convince grifters to open up to him (perhaps out of pity?). In Chicago, he meets an old-timer who had just done time in St. Louis with a Mexican named Garcia, a man who had heard of the center dealer. In St. Louis, he learns that Garcia was now in a cell in Kansas City. There, Vernon bluffs his way into the jail by presenting himself as a "lecturer on the habits of cardsharps" and then talks his way in to see this Garcia. The Mexican confirms that, yes, he had heard of a gambler "living respectably in a small town nearby" who could deal from the center.

Once he arrives in the town, which goes unnamed, Vernon has no luck finding his man until he hears some locals in a barbershop discussing a man named "Thompson" (very likely a nod to the legendary cardsharp and proposition hustler Titanic Thompson), who seems to have a large, unexplained income and spends a lot of time traveling. Vernon realizes he may have found the famed gambler. His "hands trembled, and beads of perspiration broke out on his forehead."

The meeting between Vernon and Thompson is pure pulp. After walking "back and forth over the countryside for hours, planning what he would say to the man," Vernon finally knocks on his door. At first he is crestfallen when he sees a portly, open-faced "personification of the legendary traveling salesman" at the door. But when Vernon introduces himself as "Hemingway," supposedly a well-known code name in the cheating fraternity, Thompson throws the door wide and invites him in. Vernon is unsure whether this is really the center dealer, but decides that "he would win or lose on his ability as a card magician." He wows the cardsharp—"Thompson's eyes were practically popping out of his head as he watched Vernon go through some of his more intricate magical moves." When the gambler offers up his great move, it's the magician's turn for the ocular gymnastics. "Vernon's eyes bugged out" as he saw the center deal at last. Elliott complemented his tale with a photo of himself mimicking a center deal. He looked as if he were trying to strangle a deck of cards.

As Vernon told the Kennedy story over the years, he didn't embellish so broadly, but he did add a few creative touches. He would regularly tweak the part about the little girl with the ice-cream cone. Sometimes she would be watching a group of children eating cones, longing for one of her own, and Vernon would go into the store to get the treat for her. Vernon would never call John Lazia by his real name, perhaps because he was aware that Lazia's Mafia inheritors were still active in Kansas City well into the Eighties. He always called Lazia "Snakey Davis," which had a nice, roguish ring to it, like a crook in one of the Nick and Nora movies. But he always made it clear that he was talking about the "czar" of crime, the "Al Capone of Kansas City," who could only have been Lazia. In the oddest twist of all, sometimes Vernon would say that when Kennedy first opened the door to him in Pleasant Hill, he had a bandage on his hand. When Vernon asked him what was wrong, Kennedy told him he had cut it on his car while trying to start it. The anecdote was nonsensical—how could Kennedy then have performed the deal?—but Vernon included it occasionally, seemingly for no other reason than to illustrate that once, long ago, people had had to crank their cars to get them moving.

Vernon could sound a little like *Saga* magazine in later years when he described what he had shown to Kennedy to convince him to give up the work on the center deal. Back in 1932, sitting at Kennedy's dining-room table posing as a deep-sea gambler, Vernon had run through all the gambling sleights he knew in a quietly frantic effort to convince Kennedy that he was a worthy member of the fraternity. But sitting at the bar of the Magic Castle, years later, he would turn the scenario around and describe how, just as he reached into his pocket for some cash to offer to Kennedy for the secret, he had a flash of inspiration. He would do the Trick That Fooled Houdini for the cardsharp instead. "Is that a second?" Kennedy was supposed to have asked, referring to the second deal, when Vernon ran through the routine for him. "Well, that's a new form of second," Vernon said he had advised the cheater. It was almost touching the way he added this bit, and the magicians who listened lapped it up like kittens. Here, in their imaginary, never-ending contest of Magician versus Gambler (the name of an entire subgenre of card tricks, no less), the greatest magician of all time had duped the greatest cardsharp of all time with a trick that truly did baffle the most famous name associated with their art.

As the years passed and that world of crank-up cars and speakeasies, roving gamblers and right towns receded into the shadows of history, Vernon's story of the center deal just seemed to go over better and better. It had less and less to do with the immediate world his audience lived in, which only made it more entertaining. When he had first heard of the center deal, he had all but written it off as a fairy tale. Now, when he would tell of finding it, a lot of his audience took it as pure fable. Vernon knew the story was unbelievable. He knew that it sounded, as he put it, "ridiculous." But as his listeners pounded their knees and guffawed at the good parts—about the "dice man," or Ted dealing the aces for Kennedy—he would add a simple conclusion. His voice would rise, certainly in humored appreciation of the effect his words were having on his listeners, but with something else, too, an edge of vexation in his voice. He wanted something understood.

"No . . . no . . . no . . ." he would intone loudly so he could be heard over the high spirits. "Now, this is not funny. . . . This is true."

Allen Kennedy went from being a myth to being a legend, from a mystery to a move. In magic, his deal came to be referred to casually as "the Kennedy," as if he were the sleight now. What he never quite became in magic, amid all the frenzy, was a man. On the day Vernon turned eighty, June 11, 1974, some friends of his set up a camera at the Castle to videotape him reminiscing about his colorful life. They presented him with a special deck of cards that had been designed just for the occasion, and he toyed with them as he talked, using them to illustrate some of his points about sleight of hand. Eventually, he was asked about the search for the center deal. As he referred to Kennedy, he added, in a quick aside, "He must be dead. . . ."

Vernon didn't really know that for sure. He was making an offhand guess. Despite getting Kennedy's address when he left Pleasant Hill forty-two years earlier, he had never stayed in touch and Vernon had no firsthand knowledge of what had become of the cardsharp. But he was, in fact, correct—Kennedy had been dead for a good thirteen years by the time Vernon turned eighty and sat down to tell, once again, what a brilliant artist the center dealer had been.

Kennedy's final slide had been steep and quick. Harrisonville had remained lively, with new highways making it more accessible by car, but the cardsharp had been unable to keep up anymore. He kept on gambling for a while, with mostly disastrous results. Charlie Scott tried to run a regular around-the-clock poker game with him on the Harrisonville square, but when Scott would return to the table to play his shift, he would find that Kennedy had lost all their money. When Kennedy would shoot craps, he could be so drunk that when he leaned over, on his knees, to grab his winnings following a good roll, the other players would reach over and take some of the money scattered at his feet. He would just go on winning and losing the same cash all night. Finally, a story circulated among the Harrisonville gamblers of how Kennedy had badly flubbed the switch he had once been famous for and accidentally rolled three dice in a game. It's a common myth among dice shooters, almost a cliché, and now it replaced the myth of the cardsharp in the Middle West who could do something that had never been done.

Eventually Kennedy took to just hanging around the square, quiet and soused, lost to the world. Kate would try to look after him, care for him, but like a wayward child he would drift away. Scott and Clary would find him sitting outside, slumped over in a stupor, his dark hair hanging down over his blurred eyes. They took to calling him Willie, and people began taking him for the town drunk. Once, when he smashed up his car just outside his elderly mother's house—Hattie had moved to Harrisonville, too, after remarrying—a neighbor rushed out and shouted that he was drunk. "He's not drunk," Hattie quietly defended him, "he's sick."

The drink was, indeed, a sickness for Kennedy and by the

end he would have still another illness to contend with. Back in the Forties, when Capper frequently stayed in Harrisonville with Kennedy and Grandma Kate, he would watch as the two of them actually spent the occasional quiet night at home together. They would play cards, of all things, a variation of gin rummy known as Coon Can, and smoke incessantly, using a pie plate for their cigarette butts because a regular-sized ashtray just wasn't big enough. Capper would look on in amazement as the evening wore on and the pie plate filled up. By 1960, all those roll-your-owns caught up to Kennedy and he developed lung cancer.

When he died in March 1961, Kennedy was brought back to Pleasant Hill. Because Kate and the few relatives he had left there quarreled over the costs of his simple funeral, he was buried next to his parents in the Pleasant Hill Cemetery without a headstone. The obituaries in the local papers identified him only as a "laborer." He was already slipping back into the shadows, that gray part of the world he had once inhabited years before down on First Street. Nobody in town ever heard about his great creation that had once brought a famous magician to his doorstep twenty-nine years earlier. Kennedy had never told them about it.

Charlie Miller lived his life in the shadows, too, but there was one shadow larger than the others. As brilliant as he became at sleight of hand, and many of the top magicians of his time thought he was perhaps the best of them all, he could never get out of the shadow of Dai Vernon.

"Charlie was the most knowledgeable magician I've ever met," the conjurer Johnny Thompson once said. "The shame of it all was that he and Vernon were alive at the same time." Thompson, considered the best all-around magician in the business, supremely talented at everything from cards to stage illusions, was close to both men, but came to regard Miller as almost a second father when Miller came to live with Thompson and his wife, Pam, in Los Angeles.

Vernon had been the first to introduce Miller to gamblers and the whole notion of the supremacy of the cardsharps on their unsuccessful expedition in 1932. The experience seemed to mark Miller deeply, and for the rest of his life he flirted inconclusively with that world of the hustlers. Like Vernon, Miller began to chase gamblers, too. He never got to meet Kennedy, but the search for the center dealer remained the gold standard by which he measured the elusiveness of other cardsharps. "It was as bad as locating Allen Kennedy," he once wrote Faucett Ross about some unidentified cheater he was hunting.

Unlike Vernon, Miller even got involved in some cheating himself. Rumors abounded in magic over the years about whether Miller had ever brought his prodigious skills to bear during a card game, whether he had ever moved "under fire." That talk certainly adds to a card handler's cachet, but Thompson, who probably knew him better than anyone, says it's unlikely. Miller was "really too timid" and "too uptight" about trying to cheat at cards, Thompson says. (That timidity also stifled Miller's magic career, Thompson believed.) That specific type of nerve is extremely rare among magicians, who nevertheless may not think anything of performing delicate sleight of hand before crowds of people. It also helps explain why drugs and drink were so common in the world of the cheaters.

Miller did get involved in some gambling schemes that didn't call for sleight of hand in a game. He worked so-called peek store operations, illegal carnival gambling scams, and he was once charged with receiving illegal gambling equipment when he took delivery of a rigged table for a friend. An amateur magician who also happened to be a lawyer got him off.

Miller's deepest relationship with cheaters, though, was as a tutor. "That was his tie-in," says Thompson, who used to watch the cardsharps cutting across his yard to get to the separate entrance leading to the part of the house where Miller stayed. Miller charged $500 an hour and "kept himself alive for many years that way," Thompson recalls. He even taught several of these cardsharps the Kennedy deal, sending the sleight back into gambling. "He did it better than anyone I've ever seen," Thompson declares.

Although Miller wrote a column on magic for *Genii* magazine for fourteen years (1964–78), he developed a nasty attitude about any magician he felt was exposing the secrets of the cheaters. They were "finks" and "punk magicians" who lacked the "guts" and "backbone" needed to do the dangerous work of the cardsharps. Once, when he was living with magician Jay Marshall and his wife in Chicago, Miller was asked by another magician who was over for dinner if he would demonstrate the second deal. Miller did a clumsy version of the deal, and the man left visibly disappointed. After he was gone, Miller took the deck and dealt off seventeen straight seconds for Marshall, all flawless. He had a complicated relationship with secrets.

When it came to rambling, Miller made Vernon look like a homebody. He was known in magic as "America's Guest," and moved continually around the country for decades staying with different magicians. One time, when he was living with magician Robert Parrish and his wife in Chicago, he suddenly announced that he was going to stop freeloading off other people and get a job. He had made an appointment at the Kimball Piano Company. "My father taught me a skill that very few people know anything about," he told Parrish. "I know how to make ivory piano keys." When he got to the company for his interview, he was told that except for one small manufacturer in Indiana, all the piano keys were now made of plastic. To Parrish, Miller was "born obsolete . . . one hundred years too late" for the beautiful skills he had acquired in his life.

He struggled with his own personality at times, too. His weight was always a challenge. He could get up around three hundred pounds and he had a binger's approach to food—two steaks, two ice-cream cones, and so on. And his attempts to free himself of the prudishness of his childhood led to the development of a particularly disconcerting tic. He had always had a neurotic aversion to swearing and when a doctor told him that he should swear from time to time, that it was healthy, he started to drop the most extreme vulgarisms, entirely out of context, into the middle of conversations. He might be sitting with friends at a restaurant and turn to the person next to him and blurt, "cocksucker."

But out in Los Angeles as part of the Magic Castle community for the last years of his life, Miller thrived. He wasn't as charismatic as Vernon—no one was. But he, too, became a mentor to younger magicians, who came to be awed by his encyclopedic knowledge of magic and his deft touches. He was famous for putting them through their paces when they would practice a sleight, often moving around the room, even lying on the floor, to see if it was deceptive from all angles. With his light, self-deprecating style, and surprising grace, Miller could also win over audiences handily. He would flash just a hint of an impish smile and present those "obsolete" tricks that he loved so well.

Miller could never forget the humiliating "dice man" episode, though, mainly because Vernon and Ross never let him. Besides being one of the highlights in Vernon's best tale, it became a kind of all-purpose joke whenever Ross and Vernon were kidding around. "I'm a dice man!" one of them would cry and they would both start laughing uproariously. Sometimes, when Vernon was telling the Kennedy story and reached that part yet again, Miller quietly left the room. The laughter would ring after him, chasing him as it once had down Twelfth Street in Kansas City.

It had taken only about six years for the story of Vernon's search for Kennedy to get into print, but it took almost fifty years before the "real work," the method itself, was included in a book.

Although Vernon had once been scrupulously closed-mouthed about his magical secrets, in the Fifties he began to publish his techniques and tricks. He had put out a couple of small works over the years, including the legendary "$20 manuscript" of card tricks that he and Faucett Ross wrote in 1932 to help pay the hospital bill when his son Derek was born, but he had always resisted publishing anything comprehensive. He had a change of heart twenty years later, when he came to feel "cluttered up" by what he called "all this foolishness" of too many sleights and effects, so with the help of two dedicated Boswells, Ross and Lewis Ganson of England, he delved into a cornucopia of choice material. The *Dai Vernon Book of Magic* was followed by the influential four-volume *Inner Secrets of Cards* series, as well as tribute volumes on the magic of two of his heroes, Leipzig and Malini.

"I'll now show you three things which must not be published until I say the word," Vernon announced to Ganson on one of his working trips to England in the early Sixties for the final volume of his *Inner Secrets* series. He then performed a rope-cutting routine, a card trick called "Joker Monte," and Allen Kennedy's center deal. It was thirty years after Vernon met Kennedy, and he may have been toying with the idea of releasing the work then, but he never did give Ganson the word.

Center deals had started to trickle into magic books starting in 1940, when *Expert Card Technique,* by magicians Jean Hugard and Frederick Braue, was published. A comprehensive compendium of card sleights, the book was filled with Vernon material both credited and not. (Indeed, the publication caused a temporary problem between Vernon and Miller. Miller had shared some of Vernon's material with the authors, who then put it in the book without Vernon's permission and without crediting him.) "Here is a will-o'-the-wisp that has had the super card experts agog for years," the authors announce in their section on

"The Middle Deal," which presents five different versions of the deal, none of them practical for a card game and none of them the Kennedy deal.

Scarne on Cards, which came out in 1949, offered a warning about the danger of the center dealer, and the picture of the Kennedy grip, but no method. Ten years later, the obsessively inventive card genius Ed Marlo in Chicago released a small book called *Seconds, Centers, and Bottoms* in which he offered his ideas on the subject, including a fantasy dubbed the "Tabled Center Deal." Three years later, magician Frank Garcia put out his Scarnesque guide *How to Detect Crooked Gambling,* in which he tipped his hat to Vernon for having found the nefarious "artist of artists," but he didn't get into the method. Garcia lavished praise on Vernon in the book, saying that he could "do more things with cards than Beethoven could with chords."

It wasn't until 1978 that Vernon finally released to the magic world the method that Allen Kennedy had used to deal out of the center of a deck of cards. It was forty-six years after they had sat together at Kennedy's dining-room table in Pleasant Hill. Vernon let a fellow Canadian, the sleight-of-hand master Ross Bertram, include it in his opus *Magic and Methods of Ross Bertram.* Bertram rounded out the small handful of magical aces to whom Vernon personally taught the sleight. The muscular hands performing the deal in the stop-action photos complementing the text in Bertram's book were Vernon's own.

Even though he finally allowed the release of the raw method, Vernon never released the card tricks he had devised employing Kennedy's deal. In a quick line buried in a letter that he wrote to Horowitz back in February 1933, almost a year after he had learned the move and begun practicing it day and night, Vernon confided that he was already spicing his magic with it. "I use it for certain tricks and fool them all with it," he declared to Horowitz, his close magical confidant. But he never included those tricks in any of his books. He may have written some of them up and given them to Horowitz, in which case they're probably buried deep in a box in some magic collector's basement. The letters may have been lost or destroyed. Vernon may have decided that that was all he would say to Horowitz, that he wasn't even going to share the tricks with him, his closest magical confidant at the time. It is the final, unresolved mystery of the Kennedy center deal.

Other magicians certainly struggled to come up with suitable tricks that would justify the extraordinary skill required to master the deal. They had trouble, which Vernon apparently did not, in weaving it into their art. Mostly, it became a totemic move, a display of prowess for exhibition purposes only.

In the gambling world, it remained an extreme rarity, like those prehistoric fish everyone thinks are extinct until one pops up in a net. Most working cheaters, echoing their brethren from Twelfth Street in 1932, dismissed it out of hand as a dreamily impractical move that would never work. In a profession rich with slang, they never even bothered to come up with a nickname for the center deal.

In 1982, casino surveillance expert Ron Conley was working the catwalk above a ten-draw poker game at the Rainbow Club in Gardena, California, when he spotted a bottom dealer with a phenomenal shift. These were the days when the poker clubs of Gardena still followed the throwback tradition of letting players pass the pack and deal themselves. The Rainbow didn't have video surveillance cameras yet, so they still relied on the catwalks above the tables to police the games. Conley could see this guy setting two aces on the bottom of the deck, offering it for a cut, and then bottom dealing them to himself. But he couldn't for the life of him pick up the guy's shift. When Conley grabbed some binoculars and switched to another angle on the catwalk, he saw that the man wasn't shifting the cut after all. He was dealing from the center.

Normally when a cheater was spotted in the poker rooms, he would be "brushed" from the game quickly. A club employee would walk past his chair and brush his back to signal to him that they were on to him. Usually they left quietly and the club would avoid the bad publicity of a scene over cheating. In this case, Conley, a longtime poker player himself, had a different idea. He called one of the other managers down on the floor to alert him. "You've gotta come up here and see this," Conley told him. "We got a guy dealing centers in the ten-draw game." Instead of brushing the man, the two sat up above for about a half an hour, watching the center dealer. No one at the table picked up on the move, and because they felt he wasn't doing too much "damage" to the game, they wanted to study his work. Given the rareness of the sleight, Conley figured they'd probably never have another chance to see it "under fire." When the night shift came on, the game broke up, and the man left the Rainbow. Conley never saw him or his center deal again.

A full half-century after Kennedy and Vernon met, the cardsharp's great creation was slipping back into the realm of myth.

To the gang at the Magic Castle, it started to look like Vernon just might live forever. When he was in his eighties, he began, jokingly, to invite friends to his hundredth birthday party. He said he wanted to have a lavish party like the ones Hollywood producer Mike Todd used to throw. They would chuckle along with him and say, sure, sure, but by the time he was in his midnineties, they started to mark it down on their calendars.

Just as he had never been derailed by the Depression, or the possibility of losing an arm, or the restrictions of the workaday world, so Vernon refused to acknowledge aging. Even in his nineties, he tried not to slow down. He still sessioned at all hours, and even began to develop a new bottom deal. He still drank, still lit up the big cigars. He was even able, amazingly, to enjoy the intimate company of women occasionally, albeit ones with what he used to call "negotiable affections," who would be summoned for him by his cronies at the Castle.

Vernon's legendary focus, those furious powers of concentration that had fueled the fires of his obsession for magic since he was a small boy on his bicycle in Ottawa, when cards would follow him down the street, seemed to be undiminished by age, too. One night in the late Eighties at the Castle, Jamy Ian Swiss, a magician visiting from New York, sat at the bar and watched Vernon. The Professor was alone at his usual corner. "This Couch Reserved For Professor Dai Vernon When He Is In The Club" read the sign on the wall behind him.

Vernon had a drink set on the table before him and a cigar anchored firmly in his mouth. Swiss, like most of the great sleight-of-hand men of his generation, had been deeply influenced by Vernon. He had studied his books closely, the way Vernon had once studied Erdnase, and had even had a chance to sit with the Professor a few times, going over some coin moves and sleights out of *The Expert at the Card Table*. But that night, Swiss didn't approach him. He just watched quietly, taking in the image of Vernon as he sat, staring intensely at the deck of cards in his hand. "He's working on another card problem," Swiss said to himself while watching Vernon trying to come to yet another artistic agreement with those 52 vexing talismans that had accompanied him everywhere on the long journey of his life. The pose Vernon assumed reminded Swiss of Rodin's famous *Thinker*. Vernon's gaze seemed so strong that Swiss thought the cards might burst into flames at any moment.

Vernon outlived them all—not just his elders, Houdini and Malini and Downs and the rest, but Kennedy, Scarne, Faucett Ross, who died in 1987, and the boy with the "real dope,"

Miller, who died in 1989. Vernon eulogized Miller in his "Vernon Touch" column in *Genii* magazine, telling the story one more time of how they had met almost sixty years earlier in Wichita and had set off for Kansas City to find the center deal together. "It is a sad fact," Vernon began the column, "that living to my age one loses so many close friends."

For a while, Vernon managed to reconcile that threat of death, too. One night at the Castle he was talking with Johnny Thompson when he suddenly asked how Thompson's health was. Thompson said that it was good, that he never got sick, "kind of like you. . . ." Vernon then pulled out three yellow legal-size sheets of paper. They were marked off in columns, and when Thompson looked closer, he saw that in each column there was a list of names of famous magicians. Thompson spotted Houdini, who died in 1926, and Chung Ling Soo, who died in 1918. It looked to Thompson like every great magician from the past hundred years was somewhere on the list. "Those are all my friends," Vernon announced. "They're all dead." After a long, silent moment, Thompson replied hesitantly, "Dai, I don't know what to say . . ." Vernon cut him off. "No, it's all right, Johnny," he declared loudly. "I keep making new friends."

Finally, of course, despite the continuing work on the card problems, despite the steady stream of new friends, Vernon began to surrender reluctantly to age. He started to have physical problems, took a fall, and his hearing fell off drastically. Friends tried to tend to him, but when he was ninety-six, he had to move to his son Ted's house outside of San Diego. It was far from Hollywood, and although he had occasional visitors, it was nothing like the crowds that had once spun like comets around him in the constellation he had created at the Castle.

One friend who came out to visit in 1991 was Herb Zarrow. Zarrow and his wife, Phyllis, had been close with Vernon for many years, dating back to his New York days. Their kids called him "Uncle Dai," giving it the East Coast pronunciation "Day." Zarrow had been a twenty-one-year-old magic hobbyist from Paterson, New Jersey, in 1946 when he went to see Vernon give a lecture at the Hotel McAlpin in Manhattan—the setting more than two decades earlier for Houdini's epic temper tantrum at Sam Margules when he suggested that Vernon give Houdini some tips on palming. Vernon's lecture changed Zarrow's whole approach to the art of magic. He didn't become a professional magician—he was a full-time CPA--but he did become an advanced card handler who created many original tricks and moves. Among these was his masterpiece, the Zarrow Shuffle, which became one of the truly epic sleights of the twentieth century.

The Zarrow was a false riffle shuffle, the poker player's table shuffle, that preserved the order of an entire deck. It was so efficient and practical that it became one of the only sleights ever to make the move from magic into gambling. In the Fifties, Zarrow taught his shuffle to Vernon, who kidded him that he shouldn't have revealed it to anyone, that he could easily get $1,000 a pop for it from cheaters. Eventually, Zarrow, a thoroughly humble, soft-spoken family man, began to get letters at his suburban home from cardsharps testifying to the power of his shuffle. "I'm doing the Z all over the Mediterranean," one wrote.

When Zarrow and his wife arrived at Ted's house, Phyllis decided to wait in the car. They knew that Vernon was diminished now, and she was worried that he might not want her to see him that way. But when Herb arrived at his bedside, Vernon perked up instantly, calling out, "Oh Herbie, how the hell are you . . . ? Where's Phyllis?" Zarrow went and got her and when she approached, Vernon immediately grabbed her arm and began kissing it.

Even though he was almost completely deaf, and confused, Vernon was all smiles. The Zarrows sat on the edge of the bed and at one point Herb brought out a deck. He thought he would show

Vernon a card move he had developed way back in the Forties but had never shared with him before. Despite their long friendship, and his own towering standing in magic by then, Zarrow, himself sixty-six at the time, still felt a little self-conscious, like a presumptuous student before the Professor. This takes chutzpah, he thought, as he worked the cards for Vernon.

When Zarrow had finished, Vernon suddenly reached over and took one card from the deck. Zarrow watched closely as Vernon inspected the card, turning it over and over slowly and then cradling it gently in his hand.

Dai Vernon died the following year, just two years short of his hundredth birthday. He was cremated, and after the box with his ashes was brought to the Magic Castle, it was placed for display on a ledge at the top of a wall filled with photos and other memorabilia from his long life in magic. The ledge was so high up that the box was almost out of sight.

NOTES

As I worked on *The Magician and the Cardsharp*, I started calling
it a piece of "investigative folklore." I took a story that was, after
decades of retelling by Dai Vernon, thought of as so much folklore and I investigated it. The more I dug, the more I discovered
that, lo and behold, just as Vernon had always insisted, the story
was true. What came across at first as a thoroughly entertaining,
somewhat far-fetched, tall tale was, in fact, a detailed field report from his past.

The magician gave me a lot of help. Over time, Vernon
evolved from one of the most secretive and closed of all the card
men into one many of his fellow conjurers thought had become a
hopeless "mouth." Some of them laughed at this evolution. Others were appalled. "Tell this to no one," Vernon had once commanded young Charlie Miller in a 1932 letter, in a reference to
yet another sleight Miller had written to ask him about. A decade
or so later, Miller was pleading with their common friend
Faucett Ross in an undated letter not to share news of a particular development with Vernon. "Dai simply can't keep quiet,"

Miller wrote with exasperated finality. ("I know," Miller had added to Ross, "for I've been that way myself.")

Lucky for me Vernon couldn't keep quiet. Not being a magician myself, I judged him with a reporter's standards. And by those measures, I would have to say that Vernon was as great a storyteller as he was a magician. Not only did he tell his tale of finding Allen Kennedy in Pleasant Hill often and in great detail, he even provided dialogue. As early as a couple of weeks after meeting the center dealer, Vernon was peppering the letters he wrote to other magicians with quotes of what Kennedy and others had said. If I have exchanges in my narrative between Vernon and Kennedy, or Vernon and Villasenor, or Vernon and Old Man Lee, it's because Vernon himself reported both sides of those exchanges. In the case of his questioning Villasenor at the Sedgwick County Jail in Wichita, Vernon would sometimes even relate the gambler's answers in a rough, guttural Mexican accent. (It tended to sound suspiciously similar to Vernon's version of the rough, guttural Eastern European accent of Max Malini or the rough, guttural Greek accent of the mechanic John Rakanakis, but never mind.) In the few instances in the story where I have Vernon thinking something, I have based it on his statements that that's what he was thinking then. I do no mind reading in *The Magician and the Cardsharp*.

Unfortunately, I never had the chance to meet Vernon. He died at age ninety-eight in 1992, long before I got on the "card beat." So I took, as my starting point, the versions of his search for Kennedy that he had told on audio- and videotape, which are noted below where appropriate, as well as in my bibliography. I also threw in the versions he wrote up from time to time in his long-running column in *Genii* magazine called "The Vernon Touch." With some slight variations, these all followed generally the same arc. Taken together, they complement each other and fill out the basic story nicely. A missing detail in one could usually be found in another. I relied on them for the fundamental leads on the trail to finding Kennedy.

But Vernon's versions were only the starting point. I then checked them rigorously against the primary sources of the day, first and foremost the letters he and others wrote both before and after he found the center dealer in 1932. Throughout my narrative, when I quote a letter, I usually provide the date it was written and where. And if there were any differences between the letters and the versions of his search he told as an old man looking back, naturally I favored the letters. Usually, and reassuringly, the letters written in 1932 and 1933 only confirmed what Vernon related years afterward (with some exceptions that I detail in the notes below).

Which brings up another important point about Dai Vernon. The letters were not my only method of checking up on him. I spent months going back over other sources from the Twenties and Thirties—newspapers, municipal records, and so on—and discovered something I consider truly stunning. In an assignment filled with investigative thrills, it was certainly one of the greatest of those thrills. Vernon's memory, for which he was so justly famed, checked out time and time again. I discovered that even the tiniest details he related years, decades, later held up when I compared them to the contemporaneous sources.

One of the biggest details, of course, was Amador Villasenor, who had gone down in magic history only as the "Mexican gambler" in a Wichita jail who had once told Vernon about seeing a man who could deal from the center of a deck of cards. Vernon never used his name. In fact, he had probably only heard it the one time, when he met him that first week of February 1932, and most likely even he didn't remember it. But when I went back through the Wichita papers, abracadabra, there he was—a Mexican gambler being held on a murder charge. Amador Villasenor. The name is revealed for the first time here in *The Magician and the Cardsharp*.

"Mexican gambler" was a whopper of a clue, of course. But even the smaller stuff panned out nicely. Vernon remembered that the KC Card Co. was at Twelfth and McGee, and when I checked the old city directory in Kansas City, sure enough, it was at Twelfth and McGee. Vernon remembered that an Old Man Lee ran the dice department, and there he was, H. B. Lee, also in the city directory, a salesman at the KC Card Co. Ditto "Red" Langworthy, the manager of KC Card, whom Vernon remembered meeting. Certainly Vernon's memory seems, to borrow a word Villasenor used to describe Kennedy's deal, phenomenal. But maybe, when we consider that Vernon was a man who spent ninety odd years remembering things like which phalanx of which finger needed to go where in order to smoothly execute a sleight, it should instead be considered routine.

Checking back through the primary sources also allowed me to keep Vernon honest, to flush his embellishments out of the bushes of his entertaining tale. There were a few, the biggest one being that Vernon had fooled Kennedy, and convinced him to come across with the "real work" on the center deal, by doing the famed "Trick That Fooled Houdini." When I read the letter that Vernon had written Charlie Miller just two weeks after meeting Kennedy, I found out that Kennedy had, in fact, put Vernon through his paces on gambling sleights. Vernon had even demonstrated his version of the closely held second deal of Walter Irving Scott, the so-called "Phantom of the Card Table." Another letter, written by Faucett Ross to magician Eddie McLaughlin, confirmed that Vernon had had to show Kennedy "almost everything he knew" before Kennedy would open up. But the Houdini trick was a wonderful touch, and it certainly scored one for the magicians versus the gamblers.

I was almost ready to write off another great detail in the story, the famous girl with the ice-cream cone, as embellished, too. I wholeheartedly believed Vernon's story that a little girl had been the one, finally, to point him in the direction of Kennedy's house. Indeed, Vernon was using the "little child shall lead them" line in letters to other magicians within weeks of his visit to Pleasant Hill. I knew kids hung around First Street back then because I had found and interviewed some of them. (And in my months in Pleasant Hill doing research, I also got to know the modern-day version of them.) But I also knew from checking over weather reports for March 20, 1932, the day Vernon found Kennedy, that even though it was the first day of spring, it was frigid in Pleasant Hill, still winter. I couldn't see a little girl buying an ice-cream cone on a day like that. Then the incomparable Bob Shortridge, who worked at a drugstore downtown at First and Wyoming for many years (in fact, his family's Lain-Shortridge drugstore might even have been the one where Vernon's meeting with the little girl took place), reassured me that ice-cream cones were, indeed, sold year-round in the Pleasant Hill drugstores in 1932. Kids bought them eagerly for a nickel and devoured them on the sidewalk during all kinds of weather, Shortridge said. The ice-cream cone stayed in the story.

For his part, the cardsharp gave me no help at all. Allen Kennedy essentially put a pick and shovel in my hands and challenged me to try to dig up something on him. Here was a man who lived his life as a card and dice cheater, an artistic criminal. "People like that," advised the sage Shortridge, who as a boy down on First Street in the Twenties and Thirties had kept a fascinated eye on both Kennedy and Midnight Underwood, "they lived in the gray part of the world." Even forty years after his death, Kennedy seemed doggedly determined to stay hidden there, to throw up roadblocks along his trail.

There was no birth record on file. (I eventually got his exact birthday from his funeral records.) There was no official record of his marriage to Mary Kennedy that I was able to locate (even after searching in two states). Apparently, he also almost avoided being listed in the 1930 census, the last one that's been released to the public. It was only because a diligent enumerator, who certainly gets a tip of my hat these many decades later, bothered to return again when the couple was home that Kennedy was listed at all.

Kennedy even managed to be elusive in his grave. We knew from his obituaries in the local papers that he was buried in the historic Pleasant Hill Cemetery. But when my wife, Mira, my Pleasant Hill mentor, Professor Robert Kennedy (no relation to the center dealer), and I spent hours under a thudding Missouri sun canvassing the rows of headstones there looking for him, we came up empty. When we checked the original burial records with the Wallace Funeral Home, which had put him in the ground, we found that he was definitely listed next to his parents. But when we located their graves, there was no marker for Allen Kennedy. Later, we learned that, in fact, no headstone had ever been laid at the spot. The center dealer seemed to be trying to stay hidden even after his death. For years, card men had tagged the center deal as the "will o' the wisp" because it was so hard to pin down. Kennedy became my "will o' the wisp."

Vernon came to the rescue, partially. The magician remembered some illuminating details that the cardsharp had related about himself, beyond just the work on his sleight. Shortly after meeting Kennedy, Vernon reported by letter to Miller that the cardsharp had traveled regularly up to the KC Card Co. Kennedy told Vernon about trying on the hold-out "machines" there, and meeting an old "machine worker." (Old Man Lee also told Vernon about meeting Kennedy and seeing his deal there, of course.) Vernon remembered, because the cardsharp told him about it, that Kennedy had visited the music conservatory in Kansas City to consult them about exercises to strengthen his hands when he was developing the center deal. And Vernon was one of the few people who remembered that Kennedy had once had a wife named Mary, something almost no one in Pleasant

Hill was able to recall anymore (yet another tip of the hat to the census enumerator for confirming that one).

In literal terms, the place where Kennedy grew up and lived much of his adult life is not a gray part of the world at all. The town of Pleasant Hill, which took me in so warmly as I hunted after the cardsharp from the Twenties and Thirties, is in fact a bright, open place where history seems to have grown as thickly as any crop coming up out of the fertile soil. In fact, I took to calling Pleasant Hill, quite seriously, the epicenter of American history, because of its direct involvement in, proximity to, or connection with so many of the epochal events and trends that comprise what we consider to be the story of our country— agriculture, the railroads, the Civil War, racial relations, Prohibition, and so on.

Kennedy's life intersected much of that, both directly and indirectly. The town was certainly the epicenter of his own adventurous, oddly artistic life, even when he moved 11 miles down the road to Harrisonville, the nearby county seat. Just as Vernon had done, I was finally able to locate Kennedy by spending time in Pleasant Hill. It was there that I gathered the raw material for the portrait that I've drawn in this book. I did it over hundreds of happy hours spent hunched over the microfilm reader at the Pleasant Hill Historical Society (just across the street from where Allen Kennedy and Midnight Underwood once played poker), rooting through county archives, court records, and libraries.

And I did it, of course, by talking to the good people of Cass County, who welcomed me into their living rooms, dining rooms, their shops, restaurants, and businesses to talk about the colorful past of Pleasant Hill and Harrisonville. I conducted one interview on a tractor while a man plowed his soybean field. One of my many interviews with Kennedy's former partner from the Fifties, Charlie Scott, himself something of a legend in those parts, was at Scott's crossroads produce stand on North Commercial in Harrisonville. (When I started to get nervous because I seemed to keep missing him there, his sister said there was no need to worry. "Charlie's like a cat on a hot rock," she reassured me.) Jim Wallace, Earl Mitchell, Paul Kapke, and Shortridge recreated the First Street of the late Twenties and early Thirties for me. Luke Scavuzzo set the scene of the Harrisonville square of the Forties and Fifties by walking the square of today with me and pointing out where Kennedy's old haunts had been. I sat with old gamblers, some retired, some still at it, at Dave's Wagon Wheel in Harrisonville as they shared their memories of Kennedy and the old days. They helped me get the cardsharp, finally, in sight.

I learned so much in the last few years chasing after Dai Vernon and Allen Kennedy, not just about them, but about the country, about art, about subcultures, about secrecy. I learned that magic is the most democratic of the arts. It allows its motivated beginners to huddle, in rather short order, with its great virtuosos. And I learned that while magic is bolstered by its preoccupation with technical secrets, it can also be denatured by it. I've tried in this book to be sensitive to concerns about the exposure of magical secrets and I don't think I've been gratuitous in that regard. I've tried throughout to hew to the standard articulated by the magician and writer Jamy Ian Swiss on exposure—that it's ultimately a question not of morality, but of taste. As for the center deal itself, to me it's one of those sleights that is, through its very title, self-exposing. If anyone can figure out a way to do it, or to master Kennedy's impossible technique, more power to them. It's been more than seven decades since Vernon first learned it from Kennedy himself and in the ensuing years only a small group has ever been able to.

Vernon used to talk about the "keys" to a difficult sleight, the crucial points to remember in order to conquer it. For me, there were many keys to unlocking this story. Solving the mystery of Kennedy's missing headstone . . . receiving a copy of Vernon's 1932 letter to Miller, describing the session with Kennedy, from Andy Greget, a magic book dealer and unofficial historian of both magic and gambling . . . finding Amador Villasenor on the front pages of the Wichita papers . . . watching Ron Conley perform gambling moves for a table full of magicians . . . finally seeing what the center dealer himself looked like, in pictures provided by Harold Capper, Kate Hipsher's grandson.

I found still more keys in Kansas City. While doing research there, I kept hearing about a series of undercover pictures of gambling joints that had been taken in 1939 for *Life* magazine by a photographer from the *Kansas City Journal-Post* named Jack Wally. The pictures caught the scene in many of the Twelfth Street gambling clubs, including the famous Baltimore Recreation, toward the tail end of Boss Tom Pendergast's reign. Wally had taken the pictures surreptitiously and *Life* had run them without a credit to protect his identity from, among others, the *Journal* itself, which was a staunch devotee of the Pendergast machine.

As I looked further into the story of these photos in 2003, I discovered that Jack Wally was, in fact, one of the stars of that glorious era of the intrepid newspaper photographers. (He once took photos of a derailed Rock Island train by standing up in the rear cockpit of an open biplane.) Then I discovered that not only did his photos still exist, but so did Jack Wally himself. When I headed out from the city to meet him at his home in Overland Park, just over the Kansas border, he surprised and amazed me by proving to be a quick, energetic man who didn't look much older than his early seventies. In fact, as he buzzed around his downstairs den, where he had laid out the photos on his pool table (another nice touch), demonstrating for me how he had brought columnist John Cameron Swayze into the clubs for misdirection while he snapped the shots with a little camera hidden in a sock, I started to fret that he was too young to have done all that in 1939. Finally, I asked him how old he was. "I'll be ninety next month," he reassured me.

Jack's revealing photos grace this book. They give us an idea of what Vernon and Miller might have seen when they were searching futilely downtown for a lead on the center dealer. That's one key Jack gave me. Another was when he offered a simple, and what to him must have been obvious, explanation for why he had gone through such trouble to get these photos.

Vernon used to talk about the sense of danger he felt when he was in Kansas City asking about a center dealer. He even said he always wondered how he and Miller had gotten out of Peg's dingy little joint alive after the "dice man" incident. I'm sure it's one of the reasons Vernon gave John Lazia an alias for all those years, even after Lazia was long dead. But I was having trouble imagining it, a mob-run city built on gambling where you could get in trouble just for asking about someone who could deal out of the center of a deck of cards.

Jack Wally set me straight. He sounded almost like Vernon as he went on describing for me what he had done to get these astounding photos. He still had the little German camera he had used and he showed me how he had positioned it unobtrusively, with the lens poking through a hole in the sock, and kept his hand down at his side. He explained that he would brace himself a little because of the long exposure, a half a second, required in the low light and how he would hold his breath while the shutter whirred and then snapped shut again. All the while, Swayze, a real celebrity back then, would distract the gamblers. It seemed like a lot of trouble to go through just to get some pictures of some men gambling. Was it really necessary?

"Now, of course, with gambling legal most places, it doesn't mean that much," Wally explained patiently. "But at that time, this was run by the Mafia." Wally assured me that it was danger-ous to interfere in any way. "Hell," he said, without smiling, "they'd a killed my ass if they'd known who did it."

1: Perfect

I was thrilled to discover Amador Villasenor in the Wichita pa-pers, the *Eagle* and the *Beacon*, after reading references to the case made by both Vernon and Faucett Ross in letters they wrote in 1932. Vernon wrote to magician Sam Horowitz on March 7, 1932, two weeks before he met Kennedy, to report on his con-versation at the jail. (My copy is from the collection of magician Etienne Lorenceau via book dealer Andy Greget.) He cata-logued the various sleights the Mexican gambler demon-strated and included an emphatic reference to how Villasenor had judged Kennedy's deal "perfect." Ross wrote to Eddie McLaughlin on July 13, 1932, almost four months after Vernon met Kennedy, and detailed the same meeting without going into such detail about Villasenor's sleights. (My copy is from the American Museum of Magic via magician David Ben.) Other details and the dialogue of the Vernon-Villasenor meeting ("Show these fellows a couple of those things you were doing with the cards . . ." etc.) come from a colorful interview Vernon gave at age eighty-three to British magician Pat Page in England in 1977 (on cassette entitled *From the End of My Cigar*).

The newspaper coverage of Villasenor's case was lengthy and detailed. The stories in July 1929 included lurid accounts of Leija's death outside the poolroom. When Villasenor was brought back to Wichita from Amarillo at the end of December 1931 by Deputy Marshal Fred Kaelson, the papers again gave the case big play. The *Eagle* even provided lengthy quotes from Villasenor's statement to Capt. W. O. Lyle on how he had killed Leija in self-defense after having been held up by him earlier.

The cops went on the record in the paper immediately that they bought Villasenor's story. (Lyle even told Villasenor that the police had kept his dog for him while he was on the lam.) The newspaper provided a full description of Villasenor, down to the halting way he spoke English. General details about the size of the jail and the population of prisoners were included in items in the *Eagle* on October 20, 1929, and January 9, 1932.

My thumbnail account here of how the Vernons worked their way across the country and ended up in Colorado Springs comes from Vernon's detailed reminiscences found in *He Fooled Houdini: Dai Vernon A Magical Life*, which is the fourth volume of the wonderful *Vernon Chronicles* series put together under the direction of magician Bruce Cervon, one of Vernon's protégés from the Magic Castle. *He Fooled Houdini* was culled from a week's worth of taped interview sessions with Vernon conducted in 1965 by *Los Angeles Times* columnist, and magician, Richard Buffum at Buffum's home in Montecito, California. Magic scholars owe a great debt to the late Buffum, as well as to Cervon, Keith Burns, Stephen Minch, and the rest of the team that put together the *Chronicles* series. *He Fooled Houdini*, which is told in Vernon's own voice, really stands as the closest thing there is to his autobiography. I relied on it throughout my work on *The Magician and the Cardsharp*. To get an idea of just how helpful it was, even the reference to the raw, rainy weather (which was confirmed by checking the Wichita papers) on the night Vernon went over to the Sedgwick County Jail comes from there, too.

My brisk survey of stage magic during the period that Vernon came of age comes primarily from the delightful book *Hiding the Elephant*, written by magician and historian Jim Steinmeyer and published in 2003. The reference to T. Nelson Downs accepting stamps is from a letter Downs wrote to Eddie McGuire on Feb. 7, 1932. (My copy of the letter is from the collection of magician Gary Plants.) Downs's letters, like the magician who wrote them, are highly entertaining. They are composed with his unique penmanship, with its linked letters and quirky under-lines, and reflect his cranky, engaging voice.

2: Cards on the Tracks

For the history of Vernon's magical apprenticeship in Ottawa, I relied not only on *He Fooled Houdini*, but the other great reposi-tory of Vernon reminiscences, the comprehensive set of videos called *Revelations*. These tapes, recorded from September 2–6, 1982, in St. John's, Newfoundland, provide almost seventeen hours of a spry, sharp Vernon at age eighty-eight telling about his life in magic and sessioning with magicians Steve Freeman, Michael Ammar, and Gary Ouellet. The videos, which are now available from L&L Publishing on DVD, are requirements for any serious student of his magic because they feature Vernon himself giving the "real work" on a vast cornucopia of sleights (including the Kennedy Center Deal). They are also a pure gold mine for someone who never had the pleasure of meeting the Professor.

For the sections on the cold-deck switch, the gambler at the north woods lodge, the man with the perfect pass at the Carnegie Library, J. Warren Keane's amazing psychological trick, and Vernon's truncated military experience and his subse-quent move to New York, I relied on *He Fooled Houdini*. (I found additional basic information on the history of both Ashbury and the Royal Military College on their respective Web sites.) For Vernon's childhood experiences hanging around Ottawa's race-track, I relied primarily on volume fifteen of the *Revelations* videos.

I then dovetailed *He Fooled* and the *Revelations* videos for sto-ries and quotes about his strict, Victorian mother and for the evolution of his name from David Frederick Wingfield Verner to Dai Vernon. Magician Max Maven, yet another one of Vernon's brilliant protégés from the Magic Castle, also uses Vernon's "eee-ther or eye-ther" line about the pronunciation of his name in *The Spirit of Magic*, a fine Canadian documentary about Vernon from 2000 and still another fundamental source. (The spellbinding opening sequence of the film, an old home movie of Vernon performing his beautiful Slow Motion Card Vanish, is crucial for understanding the aura of the New York Card Expert in his prime.)

A note on slang: I got the term "rattlers"—trains—for the cold-decking episode from *Language of the Underworld* by the groundbreaking linguist David Maurer. Both that monumental work and *The Big Con*, his delightful social history of the con artists of the early part of the twentieth century, are simply invaluable, not only for capturing the argot of these various criminal subcultures but also for an understanding of the world Vernon kept visiting in search of new sleights for his magic. Along with my *Random House Webster's Unabridged Dictionary*, I relied on Maurer's books many times each day as I wrote *The Magician and the Cardsharp*. The story is laced with his work.

To place Erdnase in historical perspective, I referred to the fine introduction by Prof. Persi Diaconis (yes, another Vernon protégé) included in Vernon's annotated version of *The Expert at the Card Table*, which is also entitled *Revelations*. Among many other fascinating points, Diaconis discusses Vernon's history and relationship with the book, and how Erdnase's terminology and sleights were revolutionary and enduring. Much of my brief treatment on the mystery surrounding the book and its author is derived from the tireless work of magician-translator-writer-book dealer Richard Hatch, the preeminent Erdnase hunter.

Vernon loudly and happily acknowledged his lifelong obsession with the cut, which I trace as a source for his obsession with the center deal. After eighty years of trying, he even shrugged with a smile on his face during a discussion of Erdnase on the *Revelations* videos (volume one) and acknowledged that his unknown mentor had been correct all along, that there is no shift that "can be executed by a movement appearing as coincident card-table routine." But Vernon still didn't rule it out. "He doesn't say it's impossible to do a perfect shift," Vernon observed cheerily. "But he says, 'The shift has *yet to be invented* . . .,' which is a verrrrrryy nice way of putting it. It's verrrrrrry different from saying it's impossible." There had been other goals of human endeavor once thought impossible, too, hadn't there? "It's the same thing," Vernon said. "' A trip to the moon has yet to be accomplished.' If they'd said that a long time ago they'd be right, wouldn't they?"

The archaic names for the various players at the poker table, as well as the rules for cutting and dealing, were found in a 1937 edition of *Foster's Complete Hoyle*.

The material on Vernon's relationship with Nate Leipzig is taken from Vernon's *Tribute to Nate Leipzig*, which was written by Lewis Ganson, probably the most prolific of Vernon's Boswells. The reprint edition from L&L Publishing includes a lengthy biographical article on Leipzig by David Goodsell, which originally ran in the *M-U-M* magic magazine (volume 86, no. 10, February 1997), in which I found the Leipzig quote about applying the techniques of acting to sleight-of-hand magic. The material on Malini is from Vernon's tribute book to him, *Malini and His Magic*, also largely written by Ganson, as well as from *He Fooled Houdini* and magician Ricky Jay's essential history, *Learned Pigs & Fireproof Women*. Vernon relates the anecdote about Malini pretending to admire a target's physique in volume fifteen of the *Revelations* video series.

3: Pleasant Hill

The sourcing for much of this chapter is worked right into the narrative, mostly from the local Pleasant Hill newspapers of the day, which I quote liberally here. What is not is taken largely from an extraordinary resource called *Echoes of Home* by the late Norma Rouse Middleton. *Echoes of Home* is a voluminous compendium that was originally self-published in 1988 that covers the history of the town until 1929. (Apparently Middleton, a lifelong Pleasant Hill resident, planned additional volumes, but she died in 1997 before she could complete them.) It's not a written work in the traditional sense. She essentially culled, lovingly and painstakingly, all manner of source material—newspaper accounts, municipal records, business listings, family scrapbooks, transcripts of interviews with local residents and so on—and put them into this mammoth, astoundingly detailed chronological guide to the history of the town (now available through the Pleasant Hill Historical Society).

Echoes was endlessly useful for me. It was like getting the combination to the bank president's safe. I especially appreciated that Middleton was careful not to soft-soap her history of the town, as her inclusion of the coverage of Pleasant Hill's flirtation with the Ku Klux Klan attests. If the Buffum transcripts and the *Revelations* videos are the primary texts for Vernon researchers, this is the fundamental guide for anyone interested in life in Pleasant Hill, and by extension Allen Kennedy, at the beginning of the twentieth century.

As I read through years of old newspapers at the Pleasant Hill Historical Society museum, it struck me that threats to the hands were ever-present back in the years following the First World War. It seemed to me that this would have been a particular challenge for an aspiring cardsharp. Practically every week there were items in the papers about somebody losing his fingers through a work accident. It became clear that it would have been impossible for a person to both farm and handle cards and dice at the level Kennedy eventually attained.

I have based my general conclusions on the astoundingly fertile conditions of the land around Pleasant Hill on the weeks I spent there in the spring of 2003.

The section on Kennedy's parents' history on the Bill Allen Farm is taken primarily from their obituaries. The records noting Allen Kennedy's removal from school were in the archives of the Historical Society. Much of the anecdotal history of the farm itself comes from conversations I had with the late Bill Gray, a Pleasant Hill resident who also grew up in the area of the Allen farm. I found a copy of the probate court petition that Hattie Kennedy filed after her husband died in 1922 in the archives of the Cass County Historical Society in Harrisonville.

My surveys on the history of poker and craps come from *Sucker's Progress*, the popular history of turn-of-the-century gambling by *Gangs of New York* author Herbert Asbury, as well as *Scarne on Dice* and *Scarne on Cards* by the indefatigable John Scarne. (Good old dependable Maurer provided the glossary on the slang of dice mechanics for Scarne's book on craps.) Scarne's dice book was also useful for outlining some of the more common methods of cheating at back-alley craps, the type most commonly played in Pleasant Hill back then. *The Encyclopedia of Gambling* by Carl Sifakis was another useful reference on both rules of play and cheating at various games. The reference to "Missouri Marbles" is from the entertaining *How to Detect Crooked Gambling* by Frank Garcia (a Scarne protégé).

The development of the railroads and their importance to the growth of Pleasant Hill is detailed in *Echoes of Home*, as well as *Cruel Wheels: Death and Injury by Train*, a Pleasant Hill Historical Society publication written by Robert Kennedy.

I found the details of the Kennedy and Courtney boxcar case in newspaper accounts from 1920 and 1921. Ona Courtney's case was also logged in the old county circuit court records book. Kennedy's was not because he pleaded guilty immediately and took the $90 fine. The papers all made a point of stressing that his ailing father had guaranteed payment of the money.

4: With It

Vernon almost always prefaced his accounts of his search for Kennedy by saying that he had first heard rumors of a center deal from the "clever" Chicago magician John Sprong. Not much is known about Sprong in the magic community. What is known—that he was born in Holland, and worked in Chicago in the Twenties as a mailman, doorman, and watchman—is the result of the diligent and sharp-eyed research of California magician Mike Perovich, who knew Vernon during his Magic Castle period. Perovich was kind enough to share the results of his labors with me. This version of Vernon's exchange with Sprong comes from yet another important resource, a videotaped interview that Vernon did with his friend Tony DeLap at the Magic Castle in Hollywood on June 11, 1974, Vernon's eightieth birthday. On volume fifteen of the *Revelations* videos, Vernon relates how Sprong questioned Drake on Erdnase's identity. In his book *Ultimate Secrets of Card Magic*, Vernon included an original shift (what else?) called "Sprong's Pass" that the devotee of pure sleight of hand had devised.

The material on Vernon's experiences at magic shops when he first arrived in New York, as well as his introduction to Coney Island, silhouette cutting, Jeanne, Frances Rockefeller King, and performing is from the interviews with Richard Buffum that went into *He Fooled Houdini*. The withering "paper dolls" quote was recounted by a smiling Vernon on volume four of the *Revelations* videos.

Additional material about Coney Island in this chapter is from *Coney Island: The People's Playground* by Michael Immerso, as well as *The Encyclopedia of New York City*, edited by Kenneth Jackson. Additional material about King is from a lengthy profile of her that was published in *The New York Evening Post* on September 27, 1932. Vernon's quote about how many magicians didn't get her "knife and fork" quip is from a particularly biting, and entertaining, interview he gave to Michael Albright, the editor of *The Conjurer* magazine in the March 1976 issue of that lively and short-lived magazine. Vernon's complaints about the "Hoivey and Goity" speech patterns in New York are from both *He Fooled* and volume fifteen of the *Revelations* video series. The quote from his mother on how he sounded "so beastly American" is from volume sixteen of the videos.

Magician and tireless Vernon biographer David Ben was the one to determine that Vernon fooled Houdini at the Great Northern Hotel in Chicago in 1922. The dialogue is from volume nine of the *Revelations* videos. (Vernon delivers the blunt judgment that Houdini "didn't know his ass from a hole in the ground about cards—nothing" in the Pat Page interview from 1977.) The "Rio Rita" incident and the episode with Houdini exploding at Sam Margules at the Hotel McAlpin were recounted to me in a memorable interview with the late, great Jackie Flosso on May 22, 2000. I conducted the interview at his magic shop on Thirty-fourth Street in Manhattan, not too far from where the McAlpin had once been. Flosso provided the colorful Houdini-Margules dialogue. He had heard it from his father, the legendary Al Flosso, who was at the table that night and watched, mortified, while Houdini worked himself into a lather.

Vernon himself often took the trouble to tell, and then refute, the anecdote about how he had blithely continued on with a card trick after getting the news about Ted's birth on the telephone. In *He Fooled Houdini* he attributes it to comic magician Judson Cole, and also makes the telling point of adding that Jeanne Vernon herself always believed that the incident was true.

Descriptions and instructions for doing some of Vernon's most famous card tricks are featured in his many books, including *The Dai Vernon Book of Magic, Stars of Magic*, and the four-volume *Inner Secrets* series. In *More Inner Secrets of Card Magic*, Lewis Ganson provides a delightful disclaimer to open his chapter on "The Trick That Cannot Be Explained," the essence of Vernon's jazz approach, to excuse what Ganson calls "the method which cannot be complete." (Jim Steinmeyer unknowingly bolstered my whole thinking about Vernon and the jazz ethos in his review of a memoir by CIA master of disguise Antonio Mendez, which appeared in the *Journal of the American Intelligence Professional*, vol. 46, no. 1, 2002. Jamy Ian Swiss directed me to the Steinmeyer review at, of all places, the Web site of the CIA.)

For a thoroughly enlightening and entertaining overview of Vernon's innovations in card magic in the Twenties, as well as the creative efforts of other members of the Inner Circle, see "Trouping Around in Magic with Max Holden" in volume three of *The Vernon Chronicles*. This is an expanded version of an excellent piece William Miesel first wrote in 1986 for *The Linking Ring* magic magazine, which was then supplemented for this 1989 book with additional material provided by Max Maven and Vernon himself.

It's interesting to note that while the confounding "Five Card Mental Force" first saw print in the famed "$20 manuscript" in 1932 and then in the influential *Expert Card Technique* in 1940, Vernon makes it abundantly clear in volume seven of the *Revelations* video session that he didn't really perform the trick the way it had been described in print. He stressed instead the importance of framing the chancy trick as a flat-out gambling challenge.

Vernon favored the "Hanky Poo" patter for his engaging three-card monte routine, which he performs on volume fourteen of *Revelations*. I have taken this snippet of patter from his *Further Inner Secrets of Card Magic*, which also details his Erdnase-based monte handling. The material on Vernon's meeting with Shock is from *He Fooled Houdini*. Vernon presents the ruse as "Elastic Touch" in *Inner Secrets of Card Magic*.

5: Midnight

Although he was the "public face," so to speak, of their gambling enterprise, in some ways Midnight Underwood was even harder to pin down than the cardsharp Allen Kennedy. Underwood died almost three decades before Kennedy, and so there were not many people left in Pleasant Hill who remembered him.

There were an important few who did, though, and their memories were crucial in shaping my portrait of Kennedy's boss. It was Midnight's nephew Max Underwood who stunned me—when I knew little about his uncle beyond his name and that he used to gamble with Kennedy—with the news that Midnight had killed himself because he was suffering from syphilis (interview in Pleasant Hill on February 4, 2003). That revelation, to use a word associated with Vernon, pointed me in all sorts of new directions. It cannot be stressed too firmly here that the life Max Underwood chose to lead was as far from Midnight's as the Alaskan tundra is from the Florida Keys and was, in fact, in keeping with the upstanding traditions that typified the rest of the Underwood family. Max's life was characterized by diligence, devotion, hard work, and heroism. He was awarded the Bronze Star for his service in World War II and was still an active cattle farmer in his eighties as the twentieth century drew to a close. It was the uncle who was the anomaly.

I got other important details, such as the speculation on Midnight's nickname, from the late Earl Mitchell (interview on August 16, 2000) and the late Paul Kapke (interview on February 8, 2003). Bob Shortridge provided key details, such as how Midnight dressed (interview on February 8, 2003). Shortridge also told me a hilarious story of watching as Midnight scarfed a steak dinner at Hayes Restaurant in front of a cowering milquetoast—an image that in a flash gave me the theme of Midnight's relentless appetites. I have the pointed conversation between Arch Hipsher and Midnight regarding the beautiful Ginseng courtesy of the late Jim Wallace, who happened to be standing right there with them when she walked by (interview February 20, 2003).

But even this venerable group of Pleasant Hill elders didn't remember what *The Pleasant Hill Times* had dubbed, back in 1921, "The Underwood Case." That was just a little too far back for them to recall (even Jim Wallace, the oldest of the bunch—he made it to ninety—would only have been eight in 1921). It was during my regular reading of decades of the *Times* on microfilm, looking for any old shreds on my gamblers, that I happened, on a cold Saturday evening in February 2003, upon the explosive case. Then, the coverage in the Harrisonville papers proved even more useful, as they seemed to take particular delight in detailing anything that put Pleasant Hill in a bad light. (The crucial nugget that Alice Gant had traveled with Midnight to Wisconsin, for instance, comes from *The Cass County Leader*.) The stories about the case also spurred me to look into the interesting history of Mass Gant.

After reading up on the Underwood-Gant case in the various newspapers, I was then able to locate the county circuit court records of the case still on file in the old logbooks in Harrisonville. To me the episode illuminates not only the world the gamblers operated in, but also shows how far Midnight was willing to go to flout the established laws to satisfy his appetites. He, more than any of the gamblers, just seemed to live by his own set of laws.

The history of the scale foundry and the manufacturing boom in the early twentieth century in Pleasant Hill is from *Echoes of Home* as well as the *Times* and the other local papers. I know that Midnight was back from Wisconsin by the end of World War One because I found him on the same local call-up lists that Allen Kennedy found himself on, which were published regularly in the *Times*. These lists were compiled after the potential soldiers registered with the local board.

My observations on race come from reading hundreds of newspapers. The anti-miscegenation law got prominent play. The history of Ku Klux Klan activity in Cass County and the text of the ominous flier come from press summaries in *Echoes of Home*, as well as newspaper clippings. The summary of Order No. 11 is from material provided by both the Pleasant Hill and Cass County historical societies (a WPA mural that depicts a local family returning to their burned farm after the order is in the

Pleasant Hill post office). Sam Gipson, clearly an unsung civil rights hero, was a prominent presence not only in the newspapers, but also in the same street fair records in which Midnight Underwood kept cropping up, which are in the archives of the Pleasant Hill Historical Society.

I discovered that Midnight Underwood had, in fact, bought the building where they gambled by going through the old municipal real-estate records, which are also on microfilm at the Pleasant Hill Historical Society. (I then found the *Times* referring to it as the "Underwood Building" to correspond with the change in ownership.) I can attest to the advantages of the location because I was up in the rooms. They were subsequently converted into an apartment, which was being renovated when I was in Pleasant Hill in 2003. I stood at the window and looked right down at the depot.

Both Robert Kennedy and I were told tales of "Midnight's kids" by several different Pleasant Hill residents.

6: Single-o

I know about the kids who used to hang around down on First Street watching the comings and goings of the gamblers because I interviewed several of them. They were all in their eighties by the time I got to them, and they remembered some unforgettable things.

Shortridge related his story about Roy Burton's skill with the dice, which put Shortridge off craps to this day, in an interview in Pleasant Hill at Paul Kapke's home on February 8, 2003, and again in a phone interview on January 4, 2005.

The late Jim Wallace actually worked as an all-around errand boy, delivering "white mule" and messages for the bootleggers and gamblers—including Midnight Underwood and Allen Kennedy—which he revealed in a lengthy, engaging interview at his home in Pleasant Hill on February 20, 2003. The description of Midnight's gambling rooms comes from him.

To gauge Underwood and Kennedy's standing in the community, I managed to ferret out various ancient municipal records, now in the archives of the Pleasant Hill Historical Society. These included real estate, tax office, licensing, and street oiling records. I also found them both listed in an old accounts logbook from Benson Bros. Lumber Co., which was also on First Street. The logbook is in the archives of the Pleasant Hill Historical Society. The 1930 census records showed that Kennedy lived with his wife, Mary, and his mother on South Campbell. The train schedules for the period were printed in the *Pleasant Hill Times.*

Just as Woody Guthrie made plain in his famous song, Pretty Boy Floyd was, indeed, a hero to many folks back in the Twenties and early Thirties. After Floyd was shot dead in Ohio in October 1934, the *Pleasant Hill Times* even reported (November 2, 1934) on the westbound Missouri Pacific No. 15 carrying his body through town in "just a plain pine box."

The late Earl Mitchell provided the intriguing detail that Allen Kennedy looked something like the movie star Richard Dix, as well as the anecdote about Kennedy going out a window during a raid up in Kansas City, which became quite a story around town (interview at his Pleasant Hill home on July 16, 2000).

The family legend that Kennedy actually had some kind of "pocket" in his hand to hold his crooked dice comes from Pam Beggs of Portland, Oregon, whose husband, Allen Lee Beggs, was named after his great-uncle (e-mail May 17, 2003). The overview on cheating at a dice table is from *Scarne on Dice.*

My description of some of the more common tactics in "brace games" comes from some of the standard compendiums on the classic techniques of card cheating, including *The Expert at the Card Table, Scarne on Cards, Scarne's Guide to Modern Poker, Foster's Complete Hoyle, Sucker's Progress* by Herbert Asbury, *How to Detect Crooked Gambling,* by Frank Garcia, *Dealing with Cheats,* by A. D. Livingston, *The Encyclopedia of Gambling* by Carl Sifakis, and *Gambling Scams* by card handler extraordinaire Darwin Ortiz. I also got much useful information from many conversations with card men both active and retired.

The theory that Kennedy began as a bottom dealer is mine, based on conventional wisdom on how the center deal was dreamed up in the first place—that it's the bottom deal moved up into the middle of the deck. In *The Card Wizard*, magician Bill Turner writes of a bottom dealer he knew in the Army. When Turner mentioned that he had heard of bottom dealing being detected by ear, "he sat up all night, practicing until he had eliminated that difference in sound. . . ." Rakanakis's bold and resourceful ploy to cover "grabbing air" is related by Dai Vernon on volume twelve of the *Revelations* videos. I once heard a retired card thief use the term as a noun, as in "I dealt an air . . ."

Kate Hipsher's grandson Harold Capper related details on Kennedy's ability to "run up" poker hands (interview at his Kansas City home on February 9, 2003). In Vernon's April 7, 1932, letter to Charlie Miller (Lorenceau collection), he discusses Kennedy's skills at peeking at cards. In that same letter, Vernon reported that Kennedy told him it took him five years to master the deal. Since this was 1932 and he had clearly been using it for some time, I've dated the beginning of Kennedy's work on the deal to the early Twenties.

Both Richard Hatch and Jason England provided me with copies of the relevant passage from *The Secret Out*. The keen-eyed Mike Perovich brought the Benzon article to my attention and I was able to secure a copy from the Cincinnati Library. There is another fleeting written reference to the deal dating almost four hundred years before Vernon met Kennedy. Bill Kalush, another skilled card man who specializes in research into the history of sleight of hand, has uncovered a French treatise on gambling and cheating from 1550 by one Olivier Gouyn who wrote that a cheater, "in dealing cards, instead of taking them from the top, he will take some from the bottom or from the middle. . . ." It's safe to say that Kennedy, who never even made it into the Army for the Great War, much less to the battlefields of France, never saw that reference.

Vernon dubbed the recalcitrant thumb "The Fish Hook" in his section on palming in *Select Secrets* and added that it was actually a term used by gamblers. Kennedy gave detailed instructions on the hand-strengthening exercises he learned at the conservatory to Vernon, which Vernon relates on the crucial volume twelve of the *Revelations* videos. It's in that taped session that Vernon provides "the work" on the Kennedy center deal (he's assisted in the demonstration by the great card man Steve Freeman).

"Kaw Town" and other city slang names come from Maurer. I consulted many histories of Kansas City for this work. The description of Potee's famous club and his suicide come from the lively history of gambling in the West called *Knights of the Green Cloth* by Robert DeArment. The descriptions of the Twelfth Street scene and the Chesterfield Club are from the classic *Tom's Town* by William Reddig and *Pendergast!* by Lawrence Larsen and Nancy Hulston. The detail about the women shaving their pubic hair to look like the suits is from *Goin' to Kansas City*, a truly spectacular oral history of the jazz scene in Kansas City in the Twenties and Thirties by the ethnomusicologist Nathan Pearson Jr. *Goin' to Kansas City* not only paints an alluring portrait of Kansas City in the musicians' own words, but offers the compelling alternative thesis that Pendergast, with all those clubs and "bawdy houses," was, in fact, an unwitting patron of a new movement in jazz.

The architectural history of KC Card's home on McGee was provided to me by the crack Kansas City historian William Worley, who also took a day (February 16, 2003) out of his busy schedule to walk me through downtown Kaw Town and conjure up the ghosts of its colorful past. Scarne refers to the phenomenon of the "catalog men" in *Scarne on Dice*.

Kennedy told Vernon about fiddling with the holdout "machines" at KC Card, and then Vernon dutifully reported it to Miller in his letter of April 7, 1932 (Lorenceau collection). The Kepplinger story has been told many times in the literature. This version is from *Dealing with Cheats* by A. D. Livingston.

On volume four of the *Revelations* videos, Vernon provides an entertaining sequence, complete with coin vanish, of practicing in front of his young sons. "A kid," he advises the magicians sessioning with him, "they're sharp-eyed, you know, and they'll really tell ya. . . ." Kennedy apparently thought the same. The late Paul Kapke, in an interview at his Pleasant Hill home on February 8, 2003, told me the history of May Kennedy coming to live with his family. Ralph McDonald (interview on July 15, 2000, at the Pleasant Hill Historical Society) told of watching Kennedy practice his deal there.

If Midnight Underwood committed suicide in early 1933 because of an advanced case of syphilis, it most likely would have already been raging by the late Twenties. The slang term "old thing" is from Maurer.

The details about the raid on the booze-soaked birthday party are from both the *Pleasant Hill Times* and the *Republican*. During one of his many stints at the microfilm reader, Bob Kennedy discovered the stories in the *Times* about Kennedy traveling to the Mayo Clinic in 1930. Mayo administrator Nicole Babcock (interview July 16, 2003) provided me with documents outlining the fees for exams during that period.

We know that Kennedy showed off his deal to Old Man Lee at KC Card because it was Lee who finally gave Kennedy's name to Vernon, which Vernon relates on both the DeLap tape and in his June 1970 column in *Genii* magazine. The Villasenor story, including details of the miners gambling in the rough joint and his getting friendly with Kennedy, is from Vernon's account on the

Pat Page tape. I date the Villasenor-Kennedy meeting prior to 1929, when Villasenor took it on the lam from Wichita and disappeared into the Mexican community down in Amarillo, Texas.

7: The Best I've Met in Years

It's impossible to determine the exact day Vernon met with Villasenor at the Sedgwick County Jail in Wichita, but based on various clues I think I've narrowed it down to the beginning of the first week of February 1932. According to press reports of the day, Villasenor was held from Sunday, December 27, 1931, until Tuesday, February 9, 1932. According to Ross's letter to Eddie McLaughlin (July 13, 1932, American Museum of Magic), the Vernons arrived in Wichita on January 15, 1932. The *Beacon* reported on Sunday, January 31, 1932, that Vernon was to start cutting silhouettes at Innes the next day, Monday, February 1. In *He Fooled Houdini*, Vernon mentions that Ross came to Innes to tell him about the Mexican gambler, which would mean there was a nine-day overlap when he was at the department store and Villasenor was still in the jail.

In the "romancing" letter that T. Nelson Downs wrote to Eddie McGuire on February 7, 1932 (collection of Gary Plants), Downs mentions that he's just heard in a note from Ross that Vernon is planning to search for the center deal. Ross, an obsessive correspondent who also had some trouble keeping secrets, probably wrote Downs immediately with the news during that first week of February. The Wichita weather reports match another Vernon memory, that it was cold and rainy during those few days of the week.

The dialogue between Vernon and Villasenor is from Vernon's Pat Page interview, except the "perfect" quote, which is from a letter Vernon wrote to Sam Horowitz (Etienne Lorenceau collection) on March 7, 1932, reporting what the gambler had told him.

In 1980, Lewis Ganson, one of the great Vernon Boswells, brought out a book about another, *Magic with Faucett Ross*.

Much of the Ross biographical material is from that book, including the dialogue about Vernon's long sleep, the whiskey bottle in the minister's pocket, and Ross's practical advice to Miller.

In Ross's letter to Eddie McLaughlin on July 13, 1932, he details his all-night sessions with Vernon and Vernon's unwillingness to cut someone's silhouette if he didn't like the person's looks. He also mentions that Vernon liked magician Loring Campbell but loathed magician Carter Harrison, in whose apartment house both Vernon and Ross were living. Both the *Eagle* and the *Beacon* gave Vernon extensive coverage as a silhouette artist, and both carried ads for Innes featuring his work.

The portrait of Wichita as a center for wheat, oil, and aviation, as well as the reference to the original plot being won in a poker game is from newspaper coverage of the day. The "Old Maid" reference to monte is from *Sucker's Progress* by Herbert Asbury. In detailing Villasenor's work in his March 7, 1932, letter to Horowitz, Vernon mentions that Villasenor cheated at monte.

In his *Genii* column of May 1989 eulogizing Miller, who had just died, Vernon recounts the charming tale of Miller doing his own tricks for him when they first met. Vernon raved about Miller to Horowitz in letters of March 2 and March 7, 1932, as well as in many subsequent letters back east (Etienne Lorenceau collection). He reported on the Sprong mix-up and fretted that Miller might have jeopardized his standing with McGuire in a letter to Horowitz on June 1, 1932.

Miller's letter to Ross (David Sandy collection) mentioning the Scott second deal is undated, but based on references may have been from December 1931. Miller's comment that he would go with Vernon to Kansas City is reported by Vernon on the Pat Page tape.

8: Dice Man
Vernon recalled his instructions to Miller, and the laughter his outlandish query provoked, on the Pat Page tape. The ad for the

Atlantic crossing by the *Leviathan* ran in the *Eagle* on December 12, 1929.

The material on the intersection between gambling and jazz in Kansas City is from the wonderful *Goin' to Kansas City* by Nathan Pearson Jr. The book, which grew out of a traveling exhibition Pearson mounted with Howard Litwak, is chock full of details (the story about marijuana being handed through the window at the Reno Club is related in the book by the legendary producer John Hammond). Other Kansas City material is from *Tom's Town* (e.g., the "bloc" vs. "block" anecdote), *Pendergast!* ("He'll guide you"), and Professor Worley, who is known for his vivid impression of Boss Tom.

The term "Italian football" comes from our old friend Maurer. The Baltimore Recreation heist was reported in the *Kansas City Times* on March 14, 1932.

The biographical sketch of John Lazia is from *Tom's Town* and *Pendergast!*. When telling the Kennedy story, Vernon always called Lazia "Snakey Davis" but made it clear he meant the "czar," the "head of the Mafia," the "Al Capone of Kansas City." In fact, all these phrases describe Lazia in 1932. There is no record of a "Snakey Davis" who held such an exalted position in the criminal hierarchy. Vernon, who traveled to nearby St. Joseph well into the 1980s to visit Faucett Ross, surely knew that Lazia's successors still ran the Mafia in Kansas City.

I just assumed the armed tough in a wheelchair was a particularly peculiar Vernon embellishment, until I interviewed Edward Minshall (May 19, 2003, at the Windsor, Missouri, Historical Society). He told me all about the legendary Peg. Minshall, who worked odd jobs for the Pendergast machine during that era before going into the trucking business, knew Peg from around town and detailed some of his street exploits for me. (He also remembered KC Card Co. manager "Red" Langworthy.) No wonder young Charlie Miller was so nervous.

9: And a Little Child Shall Lead Them

Much of the material on Vernon's search after Charlie Miller dropped out is from Vernon's comprehensive report to Miller (letter of April 7, 1932, Lorenceau collection). Vernon makes a point of writing that he "took up my faro box"—a telling detail—and attempted to charm the various characters at KC Card. Vernon obviously believed it was a powerful talisman and his love for the box and its history is detailed in *He Fooled Houdini*. The details on the game of faro are from *Sucker's Progress* by Asbury.

Vernon identifies Old Man Lee as the source of Kennedy's name in both the DeLap interview and his "Vernon Touch" column in the June 1970 *Genii*. In the letter to Miller he calls him only the "old man" and adds he was "very reluctant about talking" but that he got him "warmed up a little." Vernon then provides his dialogue with Lee and details Lee's various suggestions about wiring and then calling Kennedy.

The letter to Sam Horowitz (Lorenceau collection) is from March 7, 1932, and the Downs letter to Eddie McGuire (Plants collection) is from February 7, 1932.

The Lindbergh kidnapping coverage is from both the *Eagle* and the *Beacon* in Wichita. The police department chaos was reported—delicately—in the *Kansas City Times*. A profile of Lazia in the *Kansas City Star* (March 18, 1984) repeated the legend about the mob boss answering the phone at police headquarters.

The idea of Vernon using the improvisatory approach of "The Trick That Cannot Be Explained" is mine. The Cliff Green episode is one of his most famous stories. It appears in *He Fooled Houdini* as well as the *Revelations* video series. Lewis Ganson in *The Dai Vernon Book of Magic* dates it to 1912. The episode with the pit boss is included in an excellent profile of Vernon by Ricky Jay in the February/March 1991 issue of *Buzz* magazine. Vernon demonstrates "The Fingerprint Trick" on volume two of the *Revelations* sessions.

The Alexander case was, in fact, never solved. It was, naturally, all over the papers in Cass County, as well as in the Kansas City sheets.

We know that Vernon met Kennedy on Sunday, March 20, 1932, because Vernon sent a postcard to Miller with that date on it saying that he had just spent the afternoon with Kennedy. He probably mailed it from Fort Scott, Kansas, on his way back to Wichita the next day. Years later, Miller's friend Frank Csuri transcribed much of Miller's correspondence and compiled it into a compendium that came to be known in magic as the "Csuri Files" (thank goodness magicians are as obsessive as they are). Legendary card man Herb Zarrow, the creator of the Zarrow Shuffle, shared the text of the postcard with me from his copy of these "Csuri Files." I place Vernon in Pleasant Hill first on the day before, Saturday, March 19, because in most of his standard versions of the tale he mentions trying banks and filling stations in town. Bob Shortridge told me that the Pleasant Hill banks were open on Saturdays but definitely closed on Sundays in 1932. I got the names of the banks and gas stations Vernon would have visited from old Pleasant Hill phone directories (Pleasant Hill Historical Society).

The confusion over the name "Bill" is detailed—again with dialogue!—in Vernon's letter to Miller. (When I first began my research, I was actually confused myself by the nickname. I only knew the name Allen Kennedy and when I first heard Vernon telling the tale from 1977 on the Pat Page tape, he began, "This fella, his name was Bill Kennedy . . ." Bill? When I first visited Pleasant Hill in 2000, I found out that's how everyone there referred to Kennedy.) Vernon also writes in his letter to Miller that he felt as if his troubles had just started in Pleasant Hill.

This version of the little girl with the ice-cream cone is from volume seventeen of the *Revelations* videos, as is the dialogue about the ships at Kennedy's door and in his living room. Vernon first used the "little child shall lead them" line in his April 7 letter to Miller and he never stopped using it for the next sixty years.

The anecdotes about Muhammad Ali and the king of Sweden are in a great profile of Vernon by Elizabeth Wilson that's included in volume one of *The Vernon Chronicles*. The "new world" quote is from the interview Vernon gave to AP writer Jack Stinnett (August 3, 1938, Oshkosh *Northwestern*).

The description of the session—including how Vernon had to audition, the drawback of the deal, and Kennedy's other sleights—are from Vernon's letter to Miller. Vernon later described Kennedy's "kick-up peek" in a letter to Horowitz dated May 3, 1933 (Lorenceau collection). Vernon called the peek "the best work in this line." The session dialogue ("watching like the devil . . .") is from the Pat Page tape. It's interesting that in most versions, Vernon says that Kennedy dealt kings, which is about as high as a gambler will go in demonstrating. Only magicians do the four-ace trick.

10: The Gambler's Rose
When Vernon wrote Charlie Miller on April 7, 1932 (Lorenceau collection), to report on his session with Kennedy, he was already saying he wanted to get back to Pleasant Hill.

Vernon's aimless period in Wichita, including the time spent at his silhouette shop walking on his hands, is described in Ross's letter to Eddie McLaughlin of July 13, 1932 (American Museum of Magic). The Innes Easter ad featuring Vernon ran in the *Eagle* on March 25, 1932.

The follow-up visit to Kennedy with Jeanne and Ted, one of Vernon's best bits, is described (with the dialogue) on volume seventeen of the *Revelations* videos and on the Pat Page tape. Kennedy gave Vernon his address—the scrap of paper is now in David Ben's archives of Vernon material—but they never kept in touch.

Vernon's Luck, including the story of finding $20 in the backup wallet, is described in *Magic with Faucett Ross*. The anecdote about Vernon running out of gas in front of the house he was looking for was told to me by his son Derek Verner in an interview at his Tuckahoe, New York, home, June 6, 2000.

The article in the *Pleasant Hill Times* on February 10, 1933, about Midnight Underwood's suicide was incredibly thorough. It included the details that he had asked his mother for an aspirin and that he had stood in front of the mirror before he shot himself. It was quite a difference from their earlier coverage of the Mass Gant shooting. The one big missing detail, that he was suffering from syphilis, was an open secret in town and was confirmed for me by Max Underwood. The record cold weather is from other newspaper coverage. The detail about a boy hearing the shot while passing the Underwood house is from an interview with Bill Garrison of Pleasant Hill (January 4, 2005). Garrison was the boy.

The details about Midnight's estate are from old court records found at the archives of the Cass County Historical Society in Harrisonville, Missouri.

Wood Hipsher's history is from his obituary. The material on Kate Hipsher and Allen Kennedy comes from interviews with her grandson Harold Capper (at his Kansas City home on July 18, 2000, and February 9, 2003). Her niece Dicksie (Rinker) Gray also provided many details about her Aunt Kate during several interviews by phone in 2000 and then in several conversations in Pleasant Hill, joined by her husband, Bill Gray, in 2003. Her memories of Kennedy flourishing the cards are from a phone interview on October 11, 2000. She had told me that Kennedy used to make a "rose" with the cards so I sent her some photocopies from Goodlette Dodson's comprehensive compendium *Exhibition Card Fans* (courtesy Darwin Ortiz). She identified the flourish called "The Rosette" there, which is also known as "The Gambler's Rose."

Vernon's letter to Horowitz about the "unseen force" was written on June 1, 1932. Vernon also mentioned in that letter that he didn't let Ross catch him doing the deal. His "Perfect" comment, which echoed what he wrote to Horowitz about Villasenor before he even met Kennedy, was in a letter to Horowitz dated January 3, 1933. Vernon reported to Horowitz about teaching Downs the deal on February 13, 1933, and again on May 3, 1933 (all Vernon-Horowitz letters from Lorenceau collection). Vernon always wrote "centre"—the British spelling— when referring to the deal in his letters.

Vernon quotes Downs on getting a blister on volume twelve of the *Revelations* videos. Downs's note to Horowitz about "Tom Dick Harry" was from January 1933 (Gary Plants collection).

Downs's comments to Hilliard are from Hilliard's fragmentary notes published in *More Greater Magic*. Miller's amazing letter to Vernon, in which he wouldn't even write the words "center deal" down on paper, was undated (Lorenceau collection). But it had to have been written between June 1, 1932, when Vernon complained to Horowitz that he was going to put Miller to "a few tests" before showing him the deal, and February 1933, when Vernon reported to Horowitz that Miller was already happily practicing it.

Scarne's background is from his entertaining autobiography *The Odds Against Me*. On the Pat Page tape, Vernon reminisces about "Flukey Johnny" and the first time he met Scarne. On volume seventeen of the *Revelations* video, he tells of teaching Scarne the deal. Derek Verner spoke in the 2000 interview of his father's respect for Scarne. See "Figure 17. Middle Card Deal" in *Scarne on Cards* (hardcover editions) for the photo of Scarne's hands approximating the Kennedy handling. (Note: the photos in the Scarne book were taken by George Karger, who also did the pictures for the influential *Stars of Magic*, which included so much classic Vernon material.)

The death of John Lazia and Pendergast's downfall are chronicled in *Tom's Town* and *Pendergast!*.

For my sketch of downtown Harrisonville in the Forties and

Fifties, I walked the square on February 20, 2003, with Luke Scavuzzo, who knew Kennedy—and knew enough not to gamble with him. G. J. Clary and Charlie Scott recalled their old gambling buddy in several interviews in Harrisonville in 2000 and 2003, as well as subsequent phone interviews.

11: One Card

Persi Diaconis uses the "snowshoes" line in both the introduction to Vernon's annotation of Erdnase, called, like the video series, *Revelations*, as well as in an interview on the documentary *Dai Vernon: The Spirit of Magic*.

The summary of the Forties, including Vernon's horrific fall into the East River, and the Fifties is from the Buffum interview in *He Fooled Houdini*. In an interview at the Magic Castle on April 7, 2003, Vernon protégé Max Maven told me of how the shipboard chaplain had sparked Vernon's anti-clericalism (Maven also gave me a tour of Vernon's old headquarters). In a late-night phone interview (July 27–28, 2000) Harry Riser told me of his days running with Vernon.

The Borges essay is called "Kafka and His Precursors" and is included in *Selected Non-Fictions*. John Carney talked about the Professor's criticism during an interview at the Comedy and Magic Club in Hermosa Beach, California, on April 8, 2003. Vernon's declaration about not being senile is from volume three of the *Revelations* video series. On the video interview with Tony DeLap on his eightieth birthday, Vernon applies hand lotion before turning some beautiful moves.

Vernon protégé Bruce Cervon tells of how it seemed like Vernon's radio got stations others' didn't, and he and Michael Ammar share his technique for walking through a room in the dark during the Discovery Channel documentary from 2000 entitled *Grand Illusions: Dai Vernon*. Carney told of Vernon's technique for counting like a violinist, as does Vernon himself on volume ten of the *Revelations* videos.

Johnny Thompson has long held that it was Jay Ose who inspired Vernon to start performing again during the early Magic Castle years. Ricky Jay's illuminating profile of Vernon (*Buzz* magazine, February/March 1991 issue) mentions hanging out in the wee hours at Canter's Deli.

Charlie Miller's poignant letter to Faucett Ross (many of Miller's letters are poignant) mentioning Vernon living in the past is undated, but had to be from 1969–70 because Miller mentions being sixty and he was born in 1909 (letter in the archives of Ross protégé David Sandy).

Vernon's "one card" tirade is from volume twelve of the *Revelations* video sessions. His thoughts on the nature of good card tricks is from volume one. The comment about forcing himself not to care is from a lengthy profile of Ricky Jay in the April 5, 1993, issue of *The New Yorker*. The patter for "Cutting the Aces" comes directly from *Stars of Magic*.

The AP story about Vernon ran in the Oshkosh (Wisconsin) *Northwestern* (August 3, 1938). Annemann's versions of the search are in *The Jinx* #49 (October 1938) and #105 (August 1940). In Kansas City, I searched widely and in vain for a "Snakey Davis," the alias Vernon gave to John Lazia.

Vernon suddenly mentions that Kennedy had a bandaged hand on volume seventeen of *Revelations*. Vernon quotes Kennedy asking "Is that a second?" on the Pat Page tape. He insists the Kennedy story is true, over a thundering din of laughter, on the Page tape as well. The aside about how Kennedy must be dead can be heard on the DeLap video.

I heard the story of Kennedy "spilling" dice, as the mechanics say, from just about every gambler I interviewed in Harrisonville. It's an old, generic gambling story, but they had all heard of it happening specifically to Kennedy. Whether or not it really did, just their telling it is a testament to how far he had slid. In an interview in Harrisonville on July 17, 2000, G. J. Clary told me the stories of Kennedy having the money at his feet stolen while he was shooting dice, as well as crashing his car outside his mother's house. Harold Capper detailed Kennedy's, and Kate Hipsher's, smoking in an interview at his Kansas City home on February 9, 2003.

In the obituaries about Allen Kennedy, there is no mention of his ever gambling, much less having been one of the greatest sleight-of-hand artists of all time. Capper detailed the argument about the headstone in an interview at his home in Kansas City on July 18, 2000.

During a lengthy interview with Johnny Thompson on August 8, 2000, he talked about Miller's vast knowledge of magic, his ties to the gambling world, and how quietly embarrassed he was by the constant retelling of the "dice man" story. Miller's comments to Ross about exposers were included in an undated letter to Faucett Ross sometime during the Forties (Sandy collection).

Jay Marshall originally told me about Miller faking a bad second deal during an interview on July 25, 2000. He has mentioned it several times subsequently, as has Thompson. The tale of Miller trying to get a position at the Kimball Piano Co. is from a charming little book called *Words About Wizards* by Robert Parrish (many thanks to budding historian Jake Friedman for that one).

John Carney, who spent time with Miller in his Magic Castle days, provided other details about his struggles with food and his unlikely swearing in the April 2003 interview in Hermosa Beach. Others mentioned it, as well.

Lewis Ganson writes about Vernon's reluctance to give up the "work" on the center deal in *Ultimate Secrets of Card Magic*. Vernon related to Buffum how Miller had tipped some of his material in *Expert Card Technique*, and the story is included in *He Fooled Houdini*.

Amid the long list of center deal variations offered by the incredible Ed Marlo (now collected in *Revolutionary Card Technique*) is one, the "Step Center Deal," that comes awfully close to the Kennedy technique. However he came to it, it's amazing that Marlo figured it out. (Note: Marlo's "Weakling's Center Deal" acknowledges, ipso facto, how much hand strength is required in the standard versions.)

In the introduction to his classic work on boxing, *The Sweet Science*, A. J. Liebling states that "I trace my rapport with the historic past through the laying-on of hands." He writes that boxer Jack O'Brien hit him "for pedagogical example" and that O'Brien had been hit by Bob Fitzsimmons, who had been "hit by Corbett, Corbett by John L. Sullivan, he by Paddy Ryan, with the bare knuckles, and Ryan by Joe Goss, his predecessor, who as a young man had felt the fist of the great Jem Mace." I realized as I interviewed the great card men around the world that sleights are passed along in a similar, if much more nonviolent, fashion. When I interviewed Steve Forte—the "king"—he told me that the first person to demonstrate a center deal for him was Allan Ackerman. Ackerman, a Marlo protégé who had come of age in Chicago, had actually been given a quick demonstration of the center, no work, by Charlie Miller. Miller, of course, had learned it from Vernon, who had learned it from Kennedy. The technique and the handling evolved, but the lineage is direct and stellar: Kennedy to Vernon to Miller to Ackerman to Forte.

Vernon's letter to Horowitz mentioning his tricks using the center deal is dated February 13, 1933 (Lorenceau collection). He never released any of them publicly. In *Expanded Lecture Notes*, Vernon seems to be advocating the Kennedy technique for another venerable magician's sleight in "Hints on the Side Steal." That might be a direct and practical application of Kennedy's deal for magical purposes. (It's amazing how Kennedy's deal can be deceptive even in a still photograph. One popular book on Erdnase features a picture of Vernon's hands doing the Kennedy and identifies it as a second deal.)

In a phone interview (July 25, 2000) from his Nevada home, a retired mechanic who had once worked for Meyer Lansky expressed the conventional wisdom of the gambling world that the center deal was impractical for most cheaters. "You're letting yourself open too much of getting nailed," he said. "It's in the way." In an initial interview on October 10, 2000 (and many subsequent conversations since), Ron Conley told me about how in 1982 he had seen the center deal "under fire" at the Rainbow Club in Gardena, California.

In the Magic Castle interview (April 7, 2003) Max Maven told me about how Vernon still enjoyed intimacy with women and worked on a new bottom deal well into his nineties. Jamy Ian Swiss's riveting story of watching Vernon alone at the Magic Castle bar is from an elegiac essay included in his wonderful book *Shattering Illusions*. Thompson tells of his conversation with Vernon about all the friends who had died on the Discovery Channel documentary *Grand Illusions: Dai Vernon*. In interviews on August 4, 2000, and February 10, 2005, Herb Zarrow told me about his last visit with Vernon.

BIBLIOGRAPHY

Asbury, Herbert. *Sucker's Progress*. Montclair, N.J.: Patterson Smith, 1969 (reprint).

Ben, David. *Advantage Play*. Toronto: Key Porter Books, 2001.

Benet's Reader's Encyclopedia. New York: Harper & Row, 1987.

Bertram, Ross. *Magic and Methods of Ross Bertram*. Pomeroy, Ohio: Jacobs Productions, 1978.

Borges, Jorge Luis. *Selected Non-Fictions*. Ed. Eliot Weinberger. New York: Viking/Penguin, 1999.

Breslin, Jimmy. *Damon Runyon*. New York: Ticknor & Fields, 1991.

Britland, David and Gazzo. *Phantoms of the Card Table*. London: High Stakes, 2003.

Cervon, Bruce and Keith Burns, eds. *The Vernon Chronicles Volume Four, He Fooled Houdini: Dai Vernon A Magical Life*. Tahoma, Calif.: L & L Publishing, 1992.

Chafetz, Henry. *Play the Devil*. New York: Clarkson N. Potter, 1960.

Clark, Thomas L. *The Dictionary of Gambling and Gaming*. Cold Spring, N.Y.: Lexik House Publishers, 1987.

Cook, James W. *The Arts of Deception*. Cambridge, Mass.: Harvard University Press, 2001.

Devol, George. *Forty Years a Gambler on the Mississippi*. Bedford, Mass.: Applewood Books, 1996 (reprint).

Dodson, Goodlette. *Exhibition Card Fans*. Norwood, Ohio: Haines House of Cards, 1963.

Dorsett, Lyle W. *The Pendergast Machine*. New York: Oxford University Press, 1968.

Douglas, Ann. *Terrible Honesty*. New York: The Noonday Press, 1995.

Downs, T. Nelson. *The Art of Magic*. New York: Dover Publications, 1980.

Ellis, Edward Robb. *A Nation in Torment: The Great American Depression 1929–1939*. New York: Coward-McCann, 1970.

Fabian, Ann. *Card Sharps and Bucket Shops: Gambling in Nineteenth-Century America*. New York: Routledge, 1999.

Findlay, John M. *People of Chance*. New York: Oxford University Press, 1986.

Foster, R. F. *Foster's Complete Hoyle*. New York: Frederick A. Stokes Company, 1937.

Ganson, Lewis. *Dai Vernon's Tribute to Nate Leipzig*. Tahoma, Calif.: L & L Publishing, 2000.

———. *Magic with Faucett Ross*. Devon, England: The Supreme Magic Company, 1980.

———. *The Dai Vernon Book of Magic*. Devon, England: The Supreme Magic Company, no date.

———. *Dai Vernon's Inner Secrets of Card Magic*. Devon, England: The Supreme Magic Company, no date.

———. *Dai Vernon's More Inner Secrets of Card Magic*. Devon, England: The Supreme Magic Company, no date.

———. *Dai Vernon's Further Inner Secrets of Card Magic*. Devon, England: The Supreme Magic Company, no date.

————. *Dai Vernon's Ultimate Secrets of Card Magic.* Devon, England: The Supreme Magic Company, no date.

Garcia, Frank. *How to Detect Crooked Gambling.* New York: Arco Publishing Company, 1977.

Giobbi, Roberto. *Card College, Volume 1.* Seattle: Hermetic Press, 1995.

Goldston, Robert. *The Great Depression.* New York: Fawcett, 1968.

Green, Martin. *New York 1913.* New York: Collier Books, 1988.

Gunther, John. *Inside U.S.A.* New York: Harper & Brothers, 1947.

Hatch, Richard, Charlie Randall, and Martin Gardner. *The Gardner-Smith Correspondence.* Humble, Tex.: H & R Magic Books, 1999.

Hilliard, John Northern. *More Greater Magic.* Estate of Helen W. Jones, 1994.

Hobbs, Stephen. *Gene Maze and the Art of Bottom Dealing.* Silver Spring, Md.: Kaufman and Greenberg, 1994.

Hugard, Jean and Fred Braue. *Expert Card Technique.* London: Faber and Faber, 1950.

Hyde, Stephen and Geno Zanetti, eds. *Players.* New York: Thunder's Mouth Press, 2002.

Immerso, Michael. *Coney Island: The People's Playground.* New Brunswick, N.J.: Rutgers University Press, 2002.

Jackson, Kenneth T. *The Encyclopedia of New York City.* New Haven, Conn.: Yale University Press, 1995.

Jacoby, Oswald and Albert Morehead, eds. *The Fireside Book of Cards.* New York: Simon and Schuster, 1957.

Jay, Ricky. *Learned Pigs & Fireproof Women.* New York: Warner Books, 1986.

————. *Cards as Weapons.* New York: Warner Books, 1977.

Kennedy, Robert E. *Cruel Wheels: Death and Injury by Train.* Pleasant Hill, Mo.: Pleasant Hill Historical Society, 2003.

Larsen, Lawrence H. and Nancy J. Hulston. *Pendergast!* Columbia, Mo.: University of Missouri Press, 1997.

Lears, Jackson. *Something for Nothing*. New York: Viking, 2003.

Leech, Al. *Don't Look Now!* Chicago: Magic Inc., 1948.

Liebling, A. J. *The Sweet Science*. New York: The Viking Press, 1956.

Livingston, A. D. *Dealing with Cheats*. Philadelphia: J. B. Lippincott Company, 1973.

Marcus, Greil. *Invisible Republic*. New York: Henry Holt, 1997.

Marlo, Ed. *Revolutionary Card Technique*. Chicago: Magic Inc., 2003.

Marx, Herbert L., Jr., ed. *Gambling in America*. New York: The H. W. Wilson Company, 1952.

Maurer, David W. *The Big Con: The Story of the Confidence Man*. New York: Anchor Books, 1999.

———. *Language of the Underworld*. Lexington, Ky.: The University Press of Kentucky, 1981.

McCullough, David. *Truman*. New York: Simon & Schuster, 1992.

Milligan, Maurice M. *Missouri Waltz*. New York: Charles Scribner's Sons, 1948.

Minch, Stephen. *The Vernon Chronicles, Volume One: The Lost Inner Secrets*. Tahoma, Calif.: L & L Publishing, 1987.

———. *The Vernon Chronicles, Volume Two: More Lost Inner Secrets*. Tahoma, Calif.: L & L Publishing, 1988.

———. *The Vernon Chronicles, Volume Three: Further Lost Inner Secrets*. Tahoma, Calif.: L & L Publishing, 1989.

Nash, Jay Robert. *Hustlers and Con Men*. New York: M. Evans and Company, 1976.

Nelms, Henning. *Magic and Showmanship*. Mineola, N.Y.: Dover, 1969.

Ortiz, Darwin. *Gambling Scams*. New York: Dodd, Mead & Company, 1984.

———. *Annotated Erdnase*. Pasadena, Calif.: A Magical Publication, 1991.

Parrish, Robert. *Words About Wizards*. Glenwood, Ill.: David Meyer Magic Books, 1994.

Pearson, Nathan W., Jr. *Goin' to Kansas City*. Urbana, Ill.: University of Illinois Press, 1987.

Pietrusza, David. *Rothstein*. New York: Carroll & Graf, 2003.

Prus, Robert C. and C. R. D. Sharper. *Road Hustler*. Lexington, Mass.: Lexington Books, 1977.

Pushkin, Alexander. *The Queen of Spades*. New York: Signet Classics, 1961.

Radner, Sidney H. *How to Spot Card Sharps and Their Methods*. New York: Key Publishing Company, 1957.

Reddig, William M. *Tom's Town: Kansas City and the Pendergast Legend*. Philadelphia: J. B. Lippincott, 1947.

Robert-Houdin, Jean-Eugene. *Memoirs of Robert-Houdin: King of the Conjurers*. New York: Dover Publications, 1964.

Ross, Faucett W., ed. *Early Vernon*. Chicago: Magic Inc., 1962.

Runyon, Damon. *More Guys and Dolls*. Garden City, N.Y.: Garden City Books, 1951.

Sante, Luc. *Low Life*. New York: Farrar Straus Giroux, 1991.

Scarne, John. *The Odds Against Me*. New York: Simon and Schuster, 1966.

————. *Scarne's Guide to Modern Poker*. New York: Fireside, 1980.

————. *Scarne on Cards*. New York: Crown Publishers, 1949.

————. *Scarne on Dice*. New York: Crown Publishers, 1980.

Schirmer, Sherry Lamb and Richard D. McKinzie. *At the River's Bend: An Illustrated History of Kansas City*. Woodland Hills, Calif.: Windsor Publications, 1982.

Sifakis, Carl. *Encyclopedia of Gambling*. New York: Facts on File, 1990.

Sprague, Marshall. *Newport in the Rockies*. Athens, Ohio: Swallow Press, 1987.

Starke, George, ed. *Stars of Magic*. Brooklyn, N.Y.: D. Robbins & Co., 1975.

Steinmeyer, Jim. *Hiding the Elephant*. New York: Carroll & Graf Publishers, 2003.

Stiles, T. J. *Jesse James*. New York: Alfred A. Knopf, 2002.

Stowers, Carlton. *The Unsinkable Titanic Thompson*. Palmer Magic, 1982.

Sutherland, Edwin H. *The Professional Thief, by a Professional Thief*. Chicago: University of Chicago Press, 1937.

Swiss, Jamy Ian. *Shattering Illusions*. Seattle: Hermetic Press, 2002.

Terkel, Studs. *Hard Times*. New York: Avon, 1970.

Turner, Bill. *The Card Wizard*. Philadelphia: David McKay Company, 1949.

Vernon, Dai. *Expanded Lecture Notes*. Chicago: Magic Inc., 1964.

————. *Select Secrets*. New York: Max Holden, 1949.

Vernon, Dai, with Faucett Ross. *Revelations*. Pasadena, Calif.: A Magical Publication, 1984.

Vernon, Dai, and Lewis Ganson. *Malini and His Magic*. Devon, England: The Supreme Magic Co., 1976.

Waldman, Carl, and Joe Layden with Jamy Ian Swiss. *The Art of Magic*. Los Angeles: General Publishing Group, 1997.

Wallis, Michael. *Pretty Boy*. New York: St. Martin's Press, 1992.

Wanderone, Rudolph, with Tom Fox. *The Bank Shot and Other Great Robberies*. Cleveland: The World Publishing Company, 1966.

Waters, T. A. *The Encyclopedia of Magic and Magicians*. New York: Facts on File Publications, 1988.

Whaley, Bart, with Martin Gardner and Jeff Busby. *The Man Who Was Erdnase*. Oakland, Calif.: Jeff Busby Magic Inc., 1991.

Winks, Robin W., ed. *The Historian as Detective*. New York: Harper Torchbooks, 1969.

Newspapers and Periodicals
Cass County Leader
Cass County News
Cass County Republican

Genii: The Conjurors' Magazine
Kansas City Star
Kansas City Times
Magic
Pleasant Hill Times
Wichita Beacon
Wichita Eagle

Videos

Dai Vernon: An Interview 1974. Parts 1 and 2. Rising Card Productions, 1993.

Dai Vernon's Secrets of Magic. L & L Publishing, 1994.

Dai Vernon: The Spirit of Magic. Great North Productions, 1999.

Grand Illusions: Dai Vernon. Discovery Channel, 2000.

The Last of the Blue Devils. The Last of the Blue Devils Film Co., 1979.

Vernon Revelations. Volumes 1-17. L & L Publishing, 1999.

Note: The following videos proved valuable as visual references:

Darwin Ortiz on Card Cheating. PR 1.5 Partnership, 1999.

Johnny Thompson Commercial Classics of Magic. Volumes 1–4. L & L Publishing, 1999.

Steve Forte's Gambling Protection Series. Volumes 1-4. International Gaming Specialists, 1994.

Audiotape

From the End of My Cigar. Pat Page interview with Dai Vernon. Parts 1 and 2. 1977 (Note: Part 2 was released in 1997)

ACKNOWLEDGMENTS

Magicians call it the opener, the first trick on their program. It's supposed to dazzle and grab the audience's attention. My opening acknowledgment is easy and is no trick at all. I simply have to start by thanking Professor Robert Kennedy for making this book possible. While Bob's official title is curator of the Pleasant Hill Historical Society, a task he pursues with endless enthusiasm and creativity, to me he would more accurately be described as the curator, the mentor even, of *The Magician and the Cardsharp*.

Bob and his wife, Beverly, welcomed me into their home, their town, and their world as I pursued these elusive men from so long ago. I came to feel that the Kennedys' devotion to this project matched my own, and they set an impressive standard for me through their love of their community and its history, their passion for learning, their resourcefulness, their good humor, and their generosity. Those who know me the best know that it has long been my dream to write a book. Without the contributions of this remarkable couple, I would never have been able to realize that dream. I went to Pleasant Hill looking for Allen Kennedy and was lucky enough to find Bob Kennedy.

More than anything else, it's the wonderful people of Pleasant Hill who make it such a special place. Without their memories, their thoughtfulness, their hospitality, and their help, I never would have been able to find the cardsharp seventy years after the magician had arrived in town. I must thank Bob Shortridge, Dicksie (Rinker) Gray, Max Underwood, Bob and Billie Jean Kimbrell, Martha Wallace, Marcia Wallace-McConville, Ralph McDonald, Nelson Gipson, Bud Alexander, Bill Garrison, and Dorothy Wilson. When I first arrived in 2000, the first friendly faces I saw in town belonged to Pat and Roy Keck. They set the trend. When I returned in 2003, the gang at the Railway Café kept me well nourished for my long days of digging.

I also want to remember, with deep affection and profound gratitude, those Pleasant Hill residents who died while I was still working on the story to which they contributed so much: Paul Kapke, Jim Wallace, Earl Mitchell, and Bill Gray. Their memories, always recounted with great clarity and wit, provided the foundation for the chapters on their fascinating town.

In Harrisonville, Charlie Scott and G. J. Clary provided the colorful details about their old gambling crony Bill Kennedy and his years there, and Luke Scavuzzo painstakingly—and lovingly—painted a portrait of his town's past. Charlie's brother Bill also helped to supplement my knowledge of the Scott side of Kennedy's family. Bob Ketchum provided a few vital details, as well.

Though no longer a resident of Cass County, Harold Capper offered the holy grail of my quest—the photos of Allen Kennedy. He also gave generously of his time to share his detailed memories of watching the cardsharp hone his card and dice moves at the dining-room table and on the living-room floor.

Carol Bohl of the Cass County Historical Society assisted me by directing my excavations of the rich archives there.

Both in the warm sitting room of the Wallace home and in the charming quarters of the Windsor Historical Society, Ed Minshall gave an unvarnished account of Kansas City under Boss Tom Pendergast in the Thirties, which was vital to my envisioning that long-ago world. Then, the ever-inventive William Worley (my personal answer man) walked me through those very streets of Tom's Town, narrating all the while.

I am also indebted to David Boutros at the Western Historical Manuscript Collection for steering me toward both *Goin' to Kansas City* and the legendary Jack Wally. Jack, of course, exceeds any billing one could possibly dream up.

In the magic community, the sluggers let this little leaguer mingle freely among them. Vernon biographer David Ben acted more like an alchemist than the master conjurer he is when he took a situation ripe for competition and turned it instead into one framed by generosity, guidance, and friendship. Richard Hatch constantly took time away from the Erdnase trail to answer my many queries. Magician and writer Jamy Ian Swiss was an unfailing source of moral support, friendship, and advice, besides filling the helpful, and always amazing, role of walking, talking encyclopedia of sleight of hand.

David Sandy, a protégé of Faucett Ross in St. Joseph, Missouri, welcomed me into his home there and gave me unfettered access to the vast archives of his mentor. Max Maven contributed original and perceptive insights into the Professor's extraordinary Magic Castle period, as did John Carney. Herb Zarrow's detailed memories of Vernon spanned almost fifty years and ended with a wonderful coda.

Johnny Thompson offered a complex, telling portrait of his dear friend and mentor Charlie Miller. Harry Riser also helped me to appreciate Miller's epic standing in the art.

Several magicians and researchers (most of them are, of course, both) offered important resources, without which I would have been unable to complete the book. They are: Richard Kaufman, the wizard behind *Genii* who, among many other things, contributed the wonderful Woodfield photos, Andy Greget, Etienne Lorenceau, Mike Perovich, Gary Plants, Bill Kalush, Ron Wohl, Charlie Randall, Jason England, Jake Friedman, Mike Caveney, Darwin Ortiz, and Gene Matsuura.

Though not members of the magic community, Mary Bergman of the Brookline Library and Deb Bagby of the Wichita *Eagle* certainly worked their research magic for me and unlocked an unexpected vault.

I am also indebted to Roberto Giobbi, Martin Gardner, Gene Maze, Noah Levine, David Roth, Patrick Watson, Daniel Zuckerbrot, Jim Klodzen, Ray Goulet, Robert Olson, Stanley Palm, Allan Ackerman, David Alexander, and Martin Joyal.

Derek and Ted Verner were kind enough to share their memories of their father's unparalleled approach to magic.

I am especially thankful that I got to spend some time with Jackie Flosso and Jay Marshall and to hear their many stories and reminiscences before they died.

The talented and generous Ron Conley, who helped to educate me by sharing his vast knowledge of the gambling world, also let me see, up close, just how Vernon must have reacted when he finally got a look at Kennedy's amazing work. Ron is a fine card handler and a fine man. Of course, I would never have even talked to him in the first place if it weren't for Steve "The King" Forte, another unfailingly generous man who set me straight many times. I thank the many others I consulted in the gambling community, and will allow them to remain nameless. "We betray no confidences."

At Henry Holt, my editor George Hodgman brought this story into sharp focus and helped me to shape the manuscript. George knows how to be a blacksmith, a diamond cutter, a lens polisher. Editorial assistant Supurna Banerjee made many helpful editorial suggestions, as well as keeping the production operations moving forward smoothly. Paula Russell Szafranski worked her design magic laying out the photos. Production editor Chris O'Connell oversaw the demanding galley proofing with unerring diligence and precision.

My agent Fred Morris helped me to expand my original magazine article into a book proposal, and then turned around and handled the business side with deftness and tenacity. He also provided crucial support in the home stretch.

I must, once again, thank *American Heritage* editor Richard Snow, the first one to grasp the potential in a story about the mad artistry of Dai Vernon and Allen Kennedy.

My gratitude to my friends is boundless. Life as a writer would be unimaginable without their love and their laughter. David Kaufman and Ken Geist welcomed me to the writing ranks and provided a port even when there were no storms. Ruti and Ori Baron-Gil offered another port. Helen Langone not only gave me the two tools I relied on most each day at my desk—my thumb drive and my Random House Unabridged—she also helped me, through hours of probing conversation, to crystallize my approach to what was, at times, an elusive story. As he has for almost forty years now, Jon Elsen provided constant friendship and guidance (and even that most meaningful of gifts—work). Alan Mirabella, who has managed to be both a mentor and a comrade-in-arms, and Beth Arky were unstinting in their support.

Loraine Obler and Margaret Fearey constantly demonstrate the value of a life based on a rich combination of learning and generosity (and Margaret certainly demonstrated the value of her handy Nikon digital camera). I will always be grateful to Marty Albert, who not only got this story instantly but was then instrumental in allowing us to live the way we needed so that I could see it through. Dan Kempler followed up his gift of instant friendship with the gifts of wisdom and humor. Anya and Max Lianski showed us that love and good cheer are just down the hall.

I must also acknowledge the support and cherished friendship of Peggy and John Jacobson, Erika Levy, Merav Benezer, Hadass Armon, Alon Levkowitz and Yanait Barkan, Carlo Semenza, Yaron Steinbuch, Robert Brum, Ben Marcus and Anita Bernhardt, Flavia and Fulvio Locanto, Elizabeth Galletta and Charlie Scioscia, Filippo Careddu, Scott Wenger, Joy Budewig, Chris Zombory, and Kathy Kessler and Mike Feldstein.

We remember with deep love the profound support and friendship of Michal Bassevitch.

My family has always been the bulwark.

Ruth and Yitzhak Goral embraced me and made me feel welcome from the very first, as did Efi Barkai-Goral, her husband, Nadav, and their magical boys, Itamar and Lior. Helene Blum's immediate love and support will never be forgotten.

My uncle Fred Johnson has had a profound influence on me as both a writer and a man. Guy Johnson is not only my cousin, but a good neighbor and a solid friend.

My brother, Krister, has long been my anchor, steady and true when the winds of changes shift. Mindy Johnson's love and encouragement have been unflagging, too, and Ingrid and William always made me feel like a famous author.

My debt to my parents, Bill and Carol Johnson, is, of course, immeasurable and beyond any repayment. They may not realize it, but my first training came from them—my father the seasoned storyteller, my mother the diligent reporter. What better start could a budding writer ask for? I hope the wait has been worth it.

The last effect—magicians call it the closer—is supposed to be the biggest on the program, the one that stays with the audience after the show. My closer is easy, too. My final thanks go to my beloved Mira. Though the dedication at the opening of the book sums it up, I will add here that everything wonderful in my life is possible because of her.

INDEX

ABOUT THE AUTHOR

Karl Johnson is a former newspaper reporter and editor. *The Magician and the Cardsharp* grew out of an article published in *American Heritage* magazine. He lives in New York City.